CONTACT

A TEXTBOOK IN APPLIED COMMUNICATIONS

Second Edition

C. JERIEL HOWARD

RICHARD FRANCIS TRACZ

CORAMAE THOMAS

PRENTICE-HALL, INC., ENGLEWOOD CLIFFS, N.J.

Library of Congress Cataloging in Publication Data

HOWARD, C. JERIEL.
   Contact: a textbook in applied communications.

   1. English language—Business English. I. Tracz,
     Richard Francis, joint author. II. Thomas, Coramae,
     joint author. III. Title.
PE1115.T47 1974   808'.066'6   73-17345
ISBN 0-13-169573-8

© 1974, 1970 by Prentice-Hall, Inc., *Englewood Cliffs, New Jersey*

All rights reserved. No part of this book may be reproduced in any form or by any means without permission in writing from the publisher.

Printed in the United States of America.

10 9 8 7 6 5

Prentice-Hall International, Inc., *London*
Prentice-Hall of Australia, Pty. Ltd., *Sydney*
Prentice-Hall of Canada, Ltd., *Toronto*
Prentice-Hall of India Private Limited, *New Delhi*
Prentice-Hall of Japan, Inc., *Tokyo*

CONTACT
A TEXTBOOK
IN
APPLIED COMMUNICATIONS

Contents

Preface, vii

ONE / The Importance of Communication, 1

TWO / Communications Etiquette: Telephone, Personal Relationships, 10

THREE / Business Letters, 25

FOUR / Letters of Adjustment, Refusal, and Collection, 44

FIVE / The Job Application Letter, 63

SIX / The Employment Interview, 89

SEVEN / Preparation of Memos and Short Reports, 98

EIGHT / Serving on the Problem-Solving Committee, 113

NINE / Solving Problems Logically, 126

TEN / Avoiding Common Fallacies, 137

ELEVEN / Data Collection, 147

TWELVE / Gathering Information at Professional Meetings, 153

THIRTEEN / Using the Library, 160

FOURTEEN / Effective Reading and Note Taking, 171

FIFTEEN / Organizing, 183

SIXTEEN / Oral Reporting, 188

SEVENTEEN / Writing a Formal Report, 204

English Handbook, 247

Index, 275

Preface

The first edition of *Contact* had its genesis when Professor Coramae Thomas and I were assigned to teach a course in communications skills for vocational-technical students and could find no suitable text. One of the impressive contributions of the book is that its presence prompted numerous schools to develop courses specifically designed to serve the vocational-technical students, courses that had been needed for some time but for which no adequate text existed.

Since the publication of *Contact* four years ago, changes have taken place in all aspects of education, but particularly in the growing vocational-technical specializations. This second edition attempts to serve the needs of that changing curriculum. It includes more discussion of the theory and purpose of communication and presents listening skills as a major part of the communicative process. Assignments give more room for oral performances, and the various types of writing assignments have been arranged into a more logical sequence. Emphasis has been placed upon making the communication tasks less formal while retaining their accurate, functional nature. Thus the formal chapter on outlining gave way to a brief but pointed chapter on organizing, and the chapter on logic now focuses more on how man arrives at a decision than on the syllogistic process per se. Finally, a brief "English Handbook" has been added to this edition. While not designed to answer every question a student might have, it does contain helpful guides that will aid him in avoiding some common errors.

Throughout the work on this second edition, I have missed the deft hand of Coramae Thomas, who was killed in a tragic automobile accident. I can only hope that the changes made are those with which she might have agreed. In her absence, I have been especially thankful for the extensive collaboration of Professor Richard Francis Tracz. A mutual friend to us both, he made numerous valuable suggestions while we worked on the first edition, and his keen sense for organizational detail has left a definite imprint on this new edition.

During the last four years, I have received numerous helpful suggestions that subsequently aided in producing this new edition. I wish especially to thank those teacher-reviewers who have used the book for several years and now have made constructive, formal suggestions for this edition. Finally, I wish to thank Professor Dave Radloff and his student Carol Erickson, both of Western Wisconsin Technical Institute, for their gracious assistance in providing the sample formal report that is included in Chapter Seventeen.

C. JERIEL HOWARD

CONTACT
A TEXTBOOK
IN
APPLIED COMMUNICATIONS

ONE / *The Importance of Communication*

WHAT ARE COMMUNICATION SKILLS?

A communication takes place any time one individual transfers a thought of his own to another person. We may perform this action thousands of times a day, even when we may not be consciously aware of it.

Very sophisticated theories of communication exist, but we can understand them best when we see them all as being composed of three major parts: the sender, the receiver, and the message. The sender may be a writer, speaker, a fellow student in a bull session, or someone studying in the library. The receiver may be a reader, a member of a formal or an informal audience, or someone casually watching the student studying in the library. If the receiver understands the essential message of the sender, communication has occurred. That message may be a formal fact, an idea, an interesting bit of gossip, or the mere fact that the student in the library is bored with his studying. The process is as simple as that shown in Figure 1.

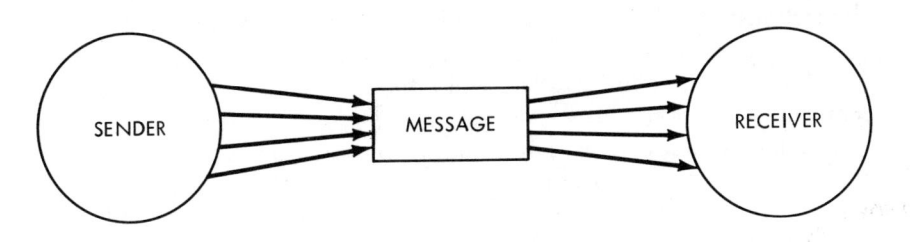

SENDER → MESSAGE → RECEIVER

Figure 1

We are communicating, then, throughout our waking hours and, if body language is considered, even while we are asleep. Communication may be nonverbal (body language) or verbal (reading, writing, listening), but without its presence in one form or another, life simply could not exist.

WHAT IS NONVERBAL COMMUNICATION?

Much interest has been expressed lately in nonverbal communication, and numerous books have appeared that treat this subject in much detail. Nonverbal communication occurs when we transmit an idea to someone without using written or spoken language.

The most recognizable example of nonverbal communication is the game of charades, which almost everyone has played. Here ideas, often song or book titles, are communicated by hand signals or other body gestures. Aside from those in the game, we have worked out other signals and gestures that communicate as much as those in charades. At one level, the way we dress, the style of our hair, our posture, and the way we walk tell volumes about us.

The many excellent studies on body language detail exactly how we reveal our attitudes through using our body. We gesture, cross our legs, and fidget with our fingers. Constantly we are encoding attitudes or ideas that a perceptive receiver can decode to complete the communications cycle.

If we are constantly communicating nonverbally, it is obviously important that we understand the message we are encoding so that the image we are projecting will be what we wish it to be.

WHAT VERBAL SKILLS ARE IMPORTANT?

In an on-the-job situation, your ability to use verbal skills effectively will determine much of your success. One researcher in the field of communications found that anyone with a communication-skills handicap (writing, speaking, reading, listening) will earn approximately 25 per cent less than a fellow worker with the same knowledge but greater communicative skill.

When you report as a full-time employee, you will find that you are constantly communicating—with a customer, a supervisor, a fellow employee. These communications may be written, but they will very often be oral. Numerous studies of on-the-job situations have been conducted, and the results generally list the proportional usage of verbal skills as follows:

Listening	45%
Talking	30%
Reading/writing	25%

WHY IS LISTENING SO IMPORTANT?

If most employees spend nearly half their time listening, then it is obviously important that they know how to listen well. But this is one skill terribly neglected.

The human mind can think at several times the speed that the voice articulates words. This explains why you can daydream entire sentences or paragraphs while a speaker voices only four or five words. Even though good listening is not necessarily easy, it is a skill that can be learned.

HOW CAN YOU LEARN TO LISTEN EFFECTIVELY?

Learning effective listening skills is a slow process that requires careful practice and, even more important, clear recognition of need. Too many people think listening is something done automatically.

Being aware of some of the major listening problems will help you tune in to your own listening activities more, and tuning in may help you become a better listener. But you must also want to improve and practice. Here are some suggestions for you to consider:

1. *Prepare yourself to listen.* This includes both mental and physical preparation. Clear your mind of unrelated matters and focus on what you know about the subject being discussed and what you might expect to hear. You cannot listen comfortably if you are not physically comfortable. As much as possible, put yourself in a comfortable physical setting.

2. *Do not confuse delivery with idea.* Sometimes you are so interested or distracted by a speaker's delivery that you forget you should focus on his ideas. Clever speakers use this weakness of listeners and confuse them with flamboyant clothes, emotional deliveries, or other theatrics.

3. *Do not prepare your response while the speaker is speaking.* Too often you listen to a speaker, get an idea of your own and begin formulating it, then forget everything when you finally elbow into the conversation. Absorb what the speaker is saying; then let your idea develop later.

4. *Do not listen only for facts.* Listening only for the major parts of a speech or conversation may cause you to miss learning how the idea is developed or illustrated, and sometimes this is the important part. Listen for the speaker's details.

5. *Do not sell out to emotion.* Often a speaker uses either an emotional incident or emotionally packed words to detract from his real issue and to sway you. Learn to separate logic from emotion and do not be swayed into a daydream by an emotional comment.

6. *Do not be distracted by outside influences.* Tune in to the speaker and what he has to say. With heavy concentration you can learn to listen to a speaker even when other sounds are present. Train your mind to filter out those other sounds and to focus on the one most important at the moment.

HOW DO YOU LEARN OTHER VERBAL SKILLS?

You learn to listen by (1) realizing the importance that listening skills have to your future and (2) practicing listening skills in a concentrated, concerted manner. Similarly, you learn speaking and writing skills by first recognizing your need for them and then by practicing them intensively. While you use this text you will spend time developing your ability to express yourself accurately and easily in situations similar to those you might expect in your future work.

HOW WILL THIS BOOK HELP YOU LEARN VERBAL SKILL?

In a later chapter you will be asked to write a letter of application to a real or imaginary company similar to one in which you might hope to be employed. As you continue through the book, you also will be asked to prepare interoffice memos; letters to customers, patients, or clients; speeches; demonstrations; and formal and informal reports. You will prepare to attend a meeting of a major organization for members of your chosen profession, take notes on the meeting, and give an oral report to members of a group of your colleagues. In every instance you should fulfill your assignment as though you had been hired by the organization to which you wrote the application letter and as though you were an active, progressive member of the profession which you have chosen.

Because in the future you will keep correspondence and information in a well-organized file, your instructor may help you establish such a habit by asking you to turn in and keep your assignments in individual folders. For instance, in the chapter on gathering information from live sources, your assignments are to find out the identity of a principal speaker at a meeting of your professional organization, acquire background knowledge on his subject, and then take notes on his speech. If you were already actively engaged in your chosen profession, you would file all of this information together. Consequently, you may be asked to prepare such a file folder now. You may want to keep this folder to go into the file of information which you will gather throughout your professional life.

All your assignments should be done as you would do them if they were part of your job. If you can type your assignments, do so. Instructors, like employers, are more favorably impressed by material they can read readily. If you don't type, use blue or black ink and write legibly. All assignments should be done on one side of standard 8½ × 11-inch loose-leaf notebook or typing paper.

Because most of the writing done in your future work will be done somewhat under pressure, you may, for practice, be asked to prepare some of the assignments in class. You must learn to begin writing the letter, the memo, or the report at once without procrastinating, and to write it rapidly, clearly, and accurately without mental anguish or frequent corrections and rewritings. If the student across the aisle from you writes six pages free of error in an hour while you stare at a blank sheet of paper for thirty minutes and then haltingly grind out a page and a half in the remaining half hour, picture the two of you employed in the same office. Either he will do several times as much work as you in a day, or you will put in hours of unpaid overtime.

WHAT YOU CAN DO OUTSIDE OF CLASS TO IMPROVE YOUR COMMUNICATION SKILLS

Some of the most valuable information you will ever acquire will be gained when you least expect it, just as some of your best ideas will come when you aren't looking for them. A television documentary, a speech heard on the radio, a chance meeting in the lounge car on the train —any happening may give you a fact or opinion that you can use later. Consequently, you should have a pen and a supply of 3 × 5 file cards handy. Jot down what you have just learned as soon as possible, being careful to record the facts accurately and to document the information as to source, place, and date. Later you can drop the card into the appropriate folder in your file.

As you read your favorite magazines, your professional journals, and even the advertisements and brochures that come to your desk, clip and file the items and articles that interest you. The busier you are, the more such a practice is necessary. When you have a secretary, you can merely mark the articles you want her to file, perhaps noting the heading you want her to use. When an article is clipped to be filed, it should be labeled with the name of the periodical, the volume number, and the date. If you or your company binds the professional journal and keeps it on hand, you will not need to file the individual article. You can file a card with the name of the article, the author, the journal, the volume number, and the date. Such cards will, of course, be filed by subject.

WHY SHOULD YOU BEGIN A FILE NOW?

It is not too early for you to begin your own professional file. If you have chosen your future work, you may already be subscribing to a professional journal or two from which you should be saving articles. In your school work you will do research that may be valuable to you later. File your notes and bibliography as well as your completed reports and papers. You may take field trips or attend meetings or lectures on which you will take notes that you will need later. Your college teachers are authorities in their fields whom you may be underestimating. After you begin your career, you may wish you had recorded your class lecture notes by subject so that you could file some or all of them. As you take your class notes, be certain to date them and note the speaker, place, and occasion.

HOW CAN YOU BEGIN A FILE?

If you begin now to keep a file and if you develop the habit of recording or collecting any information which is related to your interests and of organizing it according to a usable system, you will enter your vocation with a sizable amount of professional information at your fingertips. Moreover, you will have formed habits which successful workers find extremely valuable. In any field the expert is the man who knows where to find quickly the information which he needs for his task. The successful businessman or technician is the one who is always alert for opportunities to increase his knowledge and his skill. He knows a useful piece of information when he sees it, and he knows how to preserve it until he needs it.

Your early system need not be elaborate. You can file material now under large headings which can be broken down later into subheadings. The important thing is that you establish some order to your collection of information so that you can use it now and so that you will be encouraged to continue collecting information. If you cannot afford a filing cabinet now or if you do not have room for one, an inexpensive cardboard file box such as is available at office supply houses or various mail order houses will probably hold all you will accumulate before you begin your career. If you wish to file separately the notes you have taken on 3 × 5 cards, an ordinary shoe box will hold them.

ASSIGNMENTS

I. Become aware of body language and its importance to the communicative process by performing the following:
   1. Watch a student walking across campus and then describe his mood. Compare your descriptive comment with that made by another student watching the same subject.
   2. Observe two students sitting and talking together somewhere on campus. How do their sitting positions tell you which one feels superior to the other?
   3. List ways that a favorite friend of yours shows boredom or happiness just with body language.
   4. Look around your classroom. What attitudes are projected by dress? by posture?
   5. Explain when you have attempted to influence a group simply by employing body language. Were you successful? What process did you use? Was the reaction to you in body language or was it verbal?

II. Become aware of the importance of listening skills by performing these activities:
   1. Listen to a speech (or lecture) with a friend who has agreed to take carefull notes while you just listen. Afterwards, see how much you can recall.
   2. Join a dormitory or student-center bull session but do not actively participate. When you have left, see if you can reconstruct the main items of discussion. Also, did anyone in the group get in the way of the group's progress because he never really listened?
   3. Play a sentence-building game. One person begins the game with a noun; the next person adds a verb. Then subsequent persons add parts to the sentence (modifiers, clauses) to expand it. The additions must make sense, and each person must repeat the sentence as it exists when it gets to him. How long a sentence can your group build?

III. You may not know the various kinds of communication skills that are needed in your vocational area, but this course will be more meaningful to you if you know what type of communication will be involved in your work. Contact a person who is currently active in the job area that you have selected and visit with him. (Do not go to your vocational instructor for this interview.) There are many different kinds of information you might want to gather, but the interview sheet at the end of these assignments will help you in organizing your interview. You will probably not want to ask the questions exactly as they are worded here. Put the person being interviewed at his ease and use your own words to get him to talk freely and frankly about his job.

IV. You probably already have some ideas about what parts of your work you will enjoy most and what parts will be least interesting to you. Make written lists on the following topics related to the communications skills needed in your future job.

1. List all the communication tasks connected with your job that you think you will enjoy performing.
2. List all the communication tasks connected with your job that you think you will dislike.
3. List areas in which you think you need help if you are to communicate efficiently in your occupation.

V. Begin developing a file to keep the material which you gather from this and other courses. An accordion file would probably be the most useful right now. It is quite inexpensive, and later you can easily transfer the material to a larger filing system.

Begin sorting your material into logical sections within your file. The following divisions might give you some ideas for setting up your own system:

Business Letters
Job Openings
Job Qualifications
Job Requirements
New Trends in _____ (your area)
Professional Organizations and Meetings
Professional Records

VI. One of the purposes of this course is to help you to get to know people actually working in the vocation that you plan to enter. You will also become familiar with the organizations and publications that are important in your chosen area. Begin to learn about these by finding answers to the following questions:

1. What is the name of a national organization that serves your vocational area?

Interview Sheet   9

2. What is the name of a local organization that serves your vocational area?
3. Who is president of the local organization?
4. When does the local organization meet? Would it be permissible for you to attend a meeting?
5. What is the name of a periodical that is directly related to your field of interest?
6. How often is the periodical published? Does your college library have a copy?

INTERVIEW SHEET

Student interview conducted by _Linda Sapp_ (your name)
Person interviewed _Mr. Brother_
Occupation of person interviewed _Art Instructor_
Employer _Art Instructor_ Years of experience _3 years – 5 years_
How important are speaking and writing skills to this particular job? _Same as any business – nothing extraordinary_
How much time each week do you spend in writing or talking to customers or other workers? _Writing – 0 hours Students – 30 hours_
How many letters do you write each month? _1 per month or less_
How many letters do you receive each month? _Personal: 1 month or less – 5 per yr Form letters – 1 per month_
How many memos and bulletins do you write each month? _1 per month_
How often do you use the telephone in your work? _Not very much – not much outside communication 2 per month_
How much time do you spend giving oral instructions or reports to other workers and supervisors? _0 hours_
How much time do you spend with customers? _30 hours per week_
How often do you give speeches to groups of employees or to other groups? _Less than 1 per yr_
Do communication misunderstandings sometimes interfere with the efficiency of your department? _No prob._
How important is written and oral communication as a part of good customer relations? _Advantage_
Do these misunderstandings sometimes affect customer relations in your work? _Very seldom_

TWO | Communications Etiquette: Telephone, Personal Relationships

WHY IS PROPER ETIQUETTE IMPORTANT?

Every segment of society, large or small, has its set of generally accepted procedures; and if you want to be successful within a particular part, you must learn to abide by whatever those procedures might be. Although certain standards of business etiquette may change slightly from one type of job to another, there are certain general standards—all related to common courtesy—that prevail throughout the business world.

No one likes to be mistreated, and verbal mistreatment is as readily detected as physical abuse. The successful small company as well as the important major corporation has built its program upon a solid foundation of good will, and at the base of that good will is most often proper communications etiquette.

WHY ARE TELEPHONE MANNERS SO IMPORTANT?

Very often the first impression an outsider has of you or your employer comes from the image he creates in his mind after or during a telephone conversation. You can vividly recall feeling yourself cut short while talking to a representative of some local firm, and it is to be hoped that you can also remember talking to someone who made you feel as though you and your problem were the only concern he had for the day. The secretary who answers the telephone with hostility in her voice has already shaped the direction of the conversation. The receptionist who promises to have her employer call you but forgets to forward the message has perhaps lost business for him and has certainly caused his firm's reputation to be lowered in your opinion.

WHAT CONSTITUTES GOOD TELEPHONE MANNERS?

The key to good telephone manners is thoughtfulness for others. If you are thoughtful, you will speak loudly enough to be heard and distinctly enough to be understood. You will keep your voice friendly and your manner pleasant. You will be as helpful as you can. You will never keep the other person waiting any longer than is necessary. You will avoid any suggestion of hurry, impatience, or annoyance, regardless of how rude or annoyed the other person is. You will show the person on the other end of the line the same consideration you would show if he stood before you.

DO TELEPHONE MANNERS AFFECT YOUR RELATIONSHIP WITH YOUR FELLOW WORKERS?

What has been said about use of the telephone applies as much to calls from department to department, office to office, and employee to employee, as to calls received from customers and other members of the public. Secretaries, switchboard operators, receptionists, and clerks respond to "thank you" and "please" with even more appreciation than executive board members, administrators, and customers. Executive board members, administrators, and customers expect tact and courtesy when you answer the phone. Secretaries, switchboard operators, receptionists, and clerks may be so surprised by your pleasantness that their short telephone contact with you may make their whole day better. Remember: courtesy, tact, and friendliness are catching.

HOW DO YOU ANSWER THE TELEPHONE?

The best way to answer the telephone is to identify yourself and your company or department immediately:

Brown, Black, and Georgensen Associates, Mr. Black speaking.
Mr. Jacob's Office, Miss March.
Data Processing, Miss Sexton.
This is Arnold Schwartz.

The calling party answers by identifying himself:

> This is Ray Jackson of the Eagle Plumbing Company. Is Al Rich there? I wish to speak with him.

Now that both parties know to whom they are speaking, they are ready to accomplish their business.

"Hello" is seldom used as a business salutation. It accomplishes nothing and wastes time. Notice how inefficient the following conversation is:

> Hello.
> Hello. Who is this?
> Who do you want?
> Is this Brown, Black, and Georgensen Associates?
> Yes.
> May I speak to Mr. Brown?
> This is Mr. Brown.
> This is Jackson talking.
> Who?
> Ray Jackson.
> Who?
> Ray Jackson of the Eagle Plumbing Company.
> Oh, yes, Mr. Jackson. What may I do for you?

HOW DO YOU TAKE TELEPHONE CALLS FOR SOMEONE ELSE?

If the caller wishes to speak to someone else, he may not identify himself. He may say only, "May I speak to Mr. Jacobs, please." You can better help the person calling and the person being called if you know the identity of the caller. You should ask, "May I tell him who is calling?" or "Who may I say is calling?" Never say, "Who is this?" It sounds abrupt and rude.

Sometimes your employer or the person for whom you answered the phone is out of the office; sometimes he does not wish to be disturbed, and sometimes he will accept calls only from certain people. You should respond by saying, "Mr. Jacobs isn't available right now," or "Mr. Jacobs is out of the office just now." You should then add, "May I tell him who called?" or "May I help you?"

Never reverse the order of these two. Never say, "Who may I say is calling?" and then, "I'm sorry Mr. Jacobs is not available right now."

Answering in this way suggests to the caller that Mr. Jacobs became unavailable after you found out who wanted to talk to him.

If Mr. Jacobs is talking on another telephone or is otherwise briefly occupied, you should say, "Mr. Jacobs is talking on another telephone," or "Mr. Jacobs is busy right now." Then you should say "If you will leave your number, I'll have him call you." If Mr. Jacobs will probably be able to come to the phone soon, you might say, "Will you wait?" If the caller has to wait more than a minute or two, you should return to the phone to say, "Mr. Jacobs is still busy. May I take a message?"

If the person you answered the phone for isn't in, you may offer to take a message, or you may be able to get the caller the information he needs. If you have to leave the telephone to get the information, ask him whether he minds waiting: "Do you mind waiting a few minutes, Mr. Jones, while I look that up?" When you return to the phone, say, "I'm sorry to have kept you waiting, Mr. Jones," or "Thank you for waiting, Mr. Jones."

If you cannot help him yourself, you may be able to call someone who can. Be sure to cover the receiver so that the caller cannot hear what is said. (Use the "hold" button on your telephone if it has one.) Do not be too quick to transfer a call. If you must transfer a call, be sure to get the right person or department. Explain the reason for the transfer to the caller, tell him where the call is to be transferred, and wait for him to agree. To transfer a call, signal the operator by moving the plunger up and down slowly. When the operator answers, say, "Please transfer this call to Mr. Wade." Wait for the operator to reply to your request before you hang up.

HOW DO YOU PLACE A CALL FOR SOMEONE ELSE?

Sometimes you may be asked to place a call for someone else. When you do, you should say, "Mr. Alpine of the Healthkit Company is calling Mr. Harcourt."

Mr. Harcourt's secretary will then reply that she will ring Mr. Harcourt or that he is out or in conference and that she will have him call Mr. Alpine.

If she rings him and he answers, you should say, "Mr. Alpine of the Healthkit Company is calling you, Mr. Harcourt. Here he is."

Be certain that Mr. Alpine will be available to talk as soon as Mr. Harcourt is reached. If you keep him waiting, you make him feel that you don't think his time is as valuable as Mr. Alipine's. Such an implication is discourteous and will create ill will for your company.

WHEN DO YOU TAKE NOTES OF A TELEPHONE MESSAGE?

Everyone has had the experience of leaving a message for someone who never returns the call, and almost everyone has had the experience of having his message erroneously delivered so that it was really worthless or even disastrous. A part of telephone etiquette demands that important information be handled accurately and precisely.

It is a good practice to keep a pencil and note pad beside your telephone at all times. In this way you can jot down information as your caller is speaking without having to say, "Excuse me while I get some paper." Many successful secretaries, key salesmen, and others for whom the telephone is important reach for their jot pad and their telephone at the same time.

If the call is for someone else, correctly note the caller's name. If you have a question about the name, remember that it is perfectly correct to ask him to spell it. Take down any information he wishes to leave for the third party, including a return telephone number if he gives it. A final important bit of information is the time the call was made. Jot it down at the completion of your conversation.

Many persons who are using the telephone for business of their own find taking notes during the conversation helpful. In this manner, they will have before them any important bits of information such as names, dates, prices, sizes, etc. Also, these individuals often say that taking notes during the conversation keeps them on their toes and directs their attention to the caller and his problem rather than to what might be going on in the office around them.

HOW DO YOU END A TELEPHONE CALL?

You should close each telephone conversation on a friendly note. Using the other person's name in your closing sentence will leave the impression that you are alert and interested in the other person's problems. You might close the conversation with a sentence such as one of the following:

I shall be happy to tell him that you called, Mrs. Perkins.
I'll call you as soon as I have the information, Mrs. Ford.
Thank you for calling, Mr. Lott.

Wait for the caller to say "goodbye." You don't want him to think you are in a hurry to get away from him.

WHAT ETIQUETTE DO YOU USE WITH YOUR FELLOW WORKERS?

Getting along with the customers is not the only accomplishment an employee must master. If you are really going to be happy in your work and if you are going to be considered a success by your associates and supervisors, then you must consciously work to get along with them. The era of the one-individual office is passing, and more than 96 per cent of all workers today are in situations involving from 10 to 75 or more persons with whom they must communicate.

HOW DO YOU START OUT ON THE RIGHT FOOT WITH YOUR FELLOW WORKERS?

Ancient Greek warriors wore only one sandal, the left one. The right foot went bare because it was the friendly foot. The left foot, the hostile, shod foot, was used in close foot-to-foot combat. If the Greek warrior extended his left foot, the man in front of him braced himself for a swift kick to the groin. If the warrior extended his right foot, the man knew he came in peace even if there were no white flag tied on his right foot. A Greek warrior always took care to cross the threshold of a house with his right foot, since entering a house on the left foot was, like drawing first in the Old West, a signal to return fire.[1] Two results of this ancient custom remain in the modern world: soldiers begin their march to war on the left foot, and we speak of making a good impression as "putting the best foot forward" and of beginning a friendship, relationship, or job correctly as "starting out on the right foot."

Fortunately, starting off your relationship with your fellow workers will not involve having to remember which foot to stand on. It will, however, involve putting the right hand forward.[2] When you report for work, you will be introduced to the people with whom you will work. Naturally, you will want these people to like you. They probably will if you are a reasonably likable person. Your new colleagues realize, as you do, that much of the success and personal satisfaction found in a job comes from pleasant relationships with other workers. They want to like you if they can, but they are in no hurry to do so. They have seen their

---

[1] Robert Graves, *The Greek Myths* (New York: George Braziller, Inc., 1957), I, 223.

[2] In ancient times a man extended his right hand for a handshake as a friendly gesture so that the man who took his hand could see he was not armed.

share of climbers, gunning for immediate promotion to their jobs; grumblers, who, finding fault with everything from the location of the pencil sharpener to the color of the carbon paper, would rather gripe than type; plotters, who spend all their working hours playing company politics; socializers, who think the office is the happy hunting ground; and procrastinators, who never do anything today they can manage to put off until tomorrow. Your new colleagues are therefore willing to withhold their friendship until they are sure you do not belong to any of these unpleasant breeds. They will begin to make that decision when they are introduced to you, so you will want to know how proper introductions are made.

HOW DO YOU INTRODUCE PEOPLE CORRECTLY?

You will meet the people at your company in three ways: (1) You will be introduced to them by your work supervisor as he shows you around the department and helps you to become oriented to your job. (2) People you have met in your work will invite you to join them at lunch or coffee breaks when they will introduce you to people from other departments. (3) You will introduce yourself to those whom you have not already met as you encounter them in your work.

The form of an introduction is simple. The person making the introduction says, "Ralph Arnold, may I present Donald Hall." Obviously, Donald Hall is being presented to Ralph Arnold. There are several other forms of introduction that are in common use:

> Ralph Arnold, allow me to introduce Donald Hall.
> Ralph Arnold, this is Donald Hall.
> Ralph Arnold, Donald Hall.

In all these forms Donald Hall is being presented to Ralph Arnold. If Ralph Arnold is being presented to Donald Hall, the form is reversed:

> Donald Hall, may I present Ralph Arnold.
> Donald Hall, allow me to introduce Ralph Arnold.
> Donald Hall, this is Ralph Arnold.
> Donald Hall, Ralph Arnold.

Double introductions are both awkward and unnecessary. Never say, "Ralph Arnold, this is Donald Hall. Donald Hall, this is Ralph Arnold."

The only problem in making introductions is deciding who should be presented to whom. This problem is not too difficult if you remember that the person that should receive the most *respect* or *honor* is the person addressed first, the one who has the other person introduced to him.

INTRODUCE A MAN TO A WOMAN

Mary Allison, this is Frank Lawrence.

INTRODUCE THE YOUNGER PERSON TO THE OLDER PERSON

Mr. Pierpoint, may I present Junior Rasco.

In introducing one employee to another, you would introduce the newcomer to the old-timer.

INTRODUCE THE LESS IMPORTANT PERSON TO THE MORE IMPORTANT PERSON

Coach Winem, allow me to introduce my brother Bobby.

INTRODUCE THE GUEST TO THE HOST OR HOSTESS

Mrs. Graceholm, this is Alice Gregg.

A person in his own office or at the site of his position of authority would be considered a host as though he were in his own home.

Mr. Topco, J. B. Wright.

INTRODUCE EVERYONE TO YOUR MOTHER OR WIFE

Mother, this is Hector D. Sector.
Sally, my supervisor, Mr. Overmee. My wife.

INTRODUCE THE INDIVIDUAL TO THE GROUP

This is Nora Newcomb.

If the group is small, you can then name the members of the group. If the group is quite large, you can allow the members of the group to introduce themselves to Nora as they meet her later. If it is very important that Nora meet each member of the group, you probably should take her about the room and make individual introductions.

As you make introductions, you may want to identify the individuals to each other so that they will know whom they have met:

Mrs. Allen, this is our new switchboard operator, Nora Newcomb. Mrs. Allen is the manager of the transportation department.

Obviously, some of these rules may conflict with each other. If they do, you will have to use your own judgment. Generally you might give preference according to the most marked difference. If the two are really not very far apart in position but one is much older than the other, you could introduce the younger man to the older man. You will probably introduce the man to the woman, regardless of their status.

HOW DO YOU RESPOND TO AN INTRODUCTION?

When you have been introduced, you may say, "How do you do" or "I am glad to know you." "Pleased to meet you" is not usually considered correct. Repeating the person's name is a good practice. If you say, "How do you do, Nora Newcomb. We are glad to have you here," you will make Nora feel that you have really noticed her and you will be more likely to remember her name. Speak clearly and firmly. When you say, "I am glad to meet you, Stella Starter. I hope you will like working here," sound as if you mean it.

The person who received the introduction or to whom the other person was presented usually speaks first, but you need not stand there silently if he doesn't acknowledge the introduction. As you leave, he may say, "I am glad to have met you." If he does, you should answer, "Thank you. I am glad to have met you."

In some parts of the country people shake hands when they are introduced more frequently than they do in others. The question of who should offer his hand first is decided in the same way as the question of who is presented to whom:

The woman offers her hand to the man.
The older person offers his hand to the younger man.
The more important person offers his hand to the less important.
The host or hostess offers his hand to the guest.

But if someone offers you his hand after an introduction, shake it, regardless of whether he should have offered it or not. If he extends his hand in friendliness, you would be rude to ignore it.

Make your handshake say something positive about you. Clasp the other person's hand firmly but not tightly, with a slight downward movement as you look into his face and smile. There are several handshakes that nobody wants to receive:

The Bone Crusher: This one is also known as the Knuckle Smasher.
The Cold Herring: The limp hand extended in this one is just as exciting to hold as a dead fish. The hand is cold because the person has poor circulation—he doesn't get around much.
The Pump Handle: This greeter is so happy to meet you that he doesn't want to let you go. You wouldn't mind his holding your hand perhaps, but that steady, up-and-down movement is tiring.

HOW DO YOU INTRODUCE YOURSELF?

In the course of your work you will encounter people to whom you have not been introduced. Always introduce yourself. Suppose you have been sent to the shipping department to check on some invoices. You would introduce yourself like this:

> I am Harriet Monroe from the billing department, and I need to check on some invoices.

When someone identifies himself to you in this way, you need not acknowledge the introduction unless you have some special reason for doing so. The other person probably knows who you are, since he called you or approached you on an errand.

If you share a table with a stranger in the company cafeteria, get stuck in the elevator with someone, or find yourself in some other informal contact with another employee, do not hesitate to introduce yourself and identify the area in which you work:

> I am Art Freed. I work in data processing.

The other person will probably reply with similar information:

> How do you do. I'm glad to know you. I'm Phil Lewis. I work in the mail room.

You may then make some pleasant and impersonal remark about the weather or the elevator service. Be friendly, but not pushy. If the other person wants to continue the conversation, he may do so. But if he murmurs, "Glad to know you, I'm Glen," and stares beyond you, don't insist on exchanging confidences. You have made the first move, let him make the second. If he does not want to talk, he has a right to silence.

WHAT IS THE KEY TO GETTING ALONG ON A DAY-TO-DAY BASIS?

You will have made an impression with your fellow employees during the brief period of introductions, and perhaps that impression will last for some time. However, you must continue to practice inter-personal communications etiquette daily if you are to maintain a stable and happy relationship with your peers.

Nothing is more important to such a relationship than *sincerity*. The individual who appears to like everybody and to be concerned about everyone's welfare but is actually self-centered is readily detected and categorized in any working group. The most important word in the English language is *you*, and the most helpful communications attitude is sincere interest in other people and their problems and ideas.

Learn to listen as well as to talk. Be as concerned about the problems of others as you are about your own. Make a point to learn about Harold's plans for his future; know Barbara's husband's name; recall Eugene's children and where they are going to college. When you talk with these persons, reflect your interest in them and their plans. Look at them directly as they speak. Pay attention to what they are saying and do not let your mind and your eyes roam around the room or office.

Above all, don't be a grump. Almost every business office has its chronic grouch—the man who never enjoys anything and enjoys telling everyone how miserable he and the entire world are. Avoid this individual because his venom is poisonous. Your work world probably occupies from one-third to one-half of your day, and that time is too valuable to spend it in chronic complaint.

WHAT DIFFERENCE DO WORDS MAKE?

Getting along with your colleagues and the public frequently depends upon saying the right word at the right time to the right person. Although two words may be defined the same way in the dictionary, they may produce entirely different responses when they are used. You will please your colleague when you praise him for his determination; refer to his stubbornness or bullheadedness, and you may turn him into an enemy. "It's not what you say but how you say it that matters" is good advice, but the "how" involves choice of words as well as tone of voice. Only the right words will get the right response.

HOW DO YOU LEARN TO CHOOSE THE RIGHT WORDS?

In situations that occur frequently, you may have time to experiment, to try several ways of phrasing a certain request, question, or response. If you are observant, you will discover that a certain word choice or placement of words will produce one reaction and that different words or word arrangements will produce another reaction.

Lois learned to make such experiments in her work as a receptionist in a girl's college dormitory. She had some difficulty in handling some of the telephone calls that came to the residence from the boyfriends of the girls. The girls wanted to know who had called while they were out, and the boys were reluctant to leave their names. "Who is this?" sounded abrupt and rude. "Do you care to leave a message?" and "Is there any message?" were too easily answered with a crisp "No," and the caller's name was not really the answer to either question. "May I tell her you called?" had the right tone, and it usually brought an affirmative answer. In fact, this question would no doubt have been the best one except for one thing: some callers answered, "Yes," and hung up without giving their names. Finally she fixed upon the phrase, "Who may I tell her called?" Because the phrase could not be answered with a simple "No," and because it suggested that leaving a name was customary among callers, it usually brought the desired result.

Agnes, who was a saleswoman at a fashionable dress shop that catered to wealthy but frequently overweight women, had a similar problem. The good will of her customer was more important to her than an immediate sale because she wanted the customer to return and to ask for Agnes to wait on her. If the customer made a purchase, Agnes wanted her to be satisfied with its fit; if not, she wanted her to leave neither unhappy with the clerk nor dissatisfied with the line of merchandise carried by the store. Many times the dress the customer chose to try on was too small. Agnes experimented to find a way to give that information tactfully. "That dress is too small for you," implied criticism of the dress, the customer's choice of it, or the customer's figure. "It seems a bit tight," had similar implications. "I noticed yesterday that this model seems to run a little small. Let me get one that will be nearer to your usual size," was the phrase she finally worked out. It suggested no criticism of the dress, the customer's choice of it, nor of the customer's figure. It implied that some other woman had experienced the same difficulty; it removed any uncomfortable suggestion that the customer might have gained a little weight, and it carried the assurance that a dress that fit could be found.

Frank was a supervisor in a machine shop. About once a month it was necessary for him to ask some of the men in the shop to work overtime. Since such requests usually had to be made without warning, he could not expect the men to respond very eagerly. He found they would work more willingly if he used the right words for his request, however. "The boss says we gotta work tonight," was a poor choice for two reasons. It shifted the responsibility for the request to the boss, suggesting that Frank did not think it was necessary, and it carried a suggestion of compulsion, which never evokes cooperation. "Can you work tonight?" was too easily answered with a "No" and implied more choice than Frank could afford to offer. "I need you to work tonight" was better, but it failed to arouse a spirit of cooperation. Frank found he got the best results by explaining briefly why overtime was necessary and then asking the question, "Can I count on you to help?"

The situation which requires your attention will not always be such a matter of routine, but it will require careful handling just the same. When such is the case, put yourself in the place of the other person. Try to imagine how he feels and the effect your choice of words will have upon him. Learn to observe yourself and your reaction to the words other people use in speaking to you. Be honest with yourself until you find why one phrase annoys you and another makes you want to cooperate, why one angers you and another soothes you. Read advertisements and observe the expert at work. See if you can see why one advertisement is successful and why another fails. See if you can tell what kind of people will respond.

Once you become observant in this way, you will notice that some words and phrases can be depended upon to raise the blood pressure. Avoid words that imply that the other person is in error and soft-pedal your own infallibility. When expressing an opinion, admit that it is only an opinion and that it might possibly be wrong. "I may be wrong, but it seems to me that . . ." suggests that you recognize that there may be more than one way of seeing the matter, gives the other person the opportunity to admit that he too is expressing an opinion which may be wrong, and gives you an opportunity to save face if by some strange quirk of circumstances you are wrong.

Another touchy spot occurs sometimes when you are trying to explain something to a person who is hard of understanding. Don't, whatever you do, let him feel that you think any of the blame for the difficulty in communication lies with him. Oh, if he is an Einstein, he might take no offense if you say, "I don't think you understand what I mean." But if he is just an ordinary genius, he will feel at least the shadow of an insult. "Do you understand?" or "Do you see what I mean?" are just as bad. If you watch your listener carefully, you should be able to tell if he understands. If you must refer to the communication problem, assume that your listener's brain cells are ticking on eight cylinders but that you are rather poor at explaining. It might be possible that you are, you know. Say, "Let me see if I can explain that a better way," or "Did I explain that clearly?"

Although the ability to choose your words from the standpoint of the reaction of the other person will be particularly helpful in your work, it will also be valuable in all your personal relationships. Awareness of the value of tactful word choice whenever you speak, write, listen, or read is an ingredient for success in all that you do.

ASSIGNMENTS

I. Using a stage telephone or pretending to, demonstrate the correct way to answer in each of the following situations:
  1. Your telephone at home.
  2. Telephone in the school library where you work as an assistant.
  3. Telephone in your room at home; your mother answered the ring downstairs and told you it was from Bill.
  4. Telephone to you at school; the call from your father has been relayed through the dean's office.
  5. Telephone at TeTox Services, Inc., a business which you operate.
  6. Telephone for Mr. Carter at TeTox Services, Inc.; you are his personal secretary.

II. Introductions sound simple, but only practice helps you learn to make them smoothly and comfortably. Make the following introductions in your class:
  1. A student and your teacher.
  2. Two students and your teacher.
  3. Two boys and a girl.
  4. Two girls and a boy.
  5. Two girls and two boys.

  For the following introductions you and your classmates might assume the various roles:
  6. Your teacher and your mother.
  7. Your father and the dean of the school.
  8. Your mother and father and your girlfriend or boyfriend.
  9. Your brother or sister and your girlfriend or boyfriend.
  10. Your summer employer and your college advisor.
  11. Your aunt and uncle and a close friend.
  12. A visiting cousin and your minister or rabbi.

III. Each of the following situations demands a brief response. Remember that you are dealing with business people; make your response to each problem direct. Approach each subject with an awareness of how the other party will feel and attempt to phrase your comment in a way that will receive a positive response. Even though some of these situations might ordinarily demand oral communication, you are to write out and bring to class a written response to each. You may want to work with another student to produce a dramatization of one of these assignments. Plan carefully. Try to project the real feelings of the persons involved.

1. You are a legal secretary whose boss has forgotten an important appointment. Remind him as gently as possible that he has to meet a client on the other side of town in thirty minutes.
2. You are assistant manager of a clothing store. You have been asked by one of the clerks to explain to a customer that you cannot exchange a bathing suit, which she says is too small, because it has obviously been worn.
3. You are an insurance claims adjuster who must explain to a client that his fire-damaged car was really worth only $350 before the fire and not his alleged $750.
4. You are a police officer in charge of school safety. You must explain to the city council that a stop sign is essential at the intersection of Elm and Piedmont. You want to hint that three recent accidents there have been the result of the council's failure to install the sign.
5. You are a medical secretary whose employer has poor penmanship. You must ask him to clarify for you a certain illegible statement on one of the charts.
6. You are manager of a hardware store and it is your responsibility to call a customer and remind him that his thirty-day account is two weeks past due.
7. You are fire marshal of a small city. In making annual inspections you discover that the mayor's secretary has a storage closet that is a great fire hazard. You must explain to her that the closet must be cleaned immediately.
8. You are personnel manager of a company that has recently begun using a time clock. You must write a one-paragraph memo explaining to all employees that they will be fired if they are caught checking in or out on the time clock for anyone else.
9. You operate data processing equipment for an employer who is noted for being very money-conscious. You must explain to him that it is important for you to attend an annual convention of data processors so that you might keep informed about current ideas and equipment.
10. You are an executive secretary for a very busy employer. He is trying to stall a representative from a certain company until he can gather further data on the company's reputation. The representative is now in the office, and you must persuade him to wait until later to see your employer.

THREE / Business Letters

WHY IS THE BUSINESS LETTER SO IMPORTANT?

In spite of the large number of forms designed for simple reporting tasks, a large number of business communications still require the formal business letter. Probably you will write one when you first apply for a job (Chapter Five), and chances are that you will both receive and send letters as a part of your regular job assignment. Even if you do not, you will at some point in your life write a letter requesting an adjustment in merchandise, asking for more information about a product, or informing your congressman of your exact opinion on a particular subject. Learning the correct form and organization for a business letter, then, is a first step toward developing mature communications skills.

WHY SHOULD YOU PLAN A BUSINESS LETTER?

Your best letters in the past have probably been written in your head. You get a letter from Ed, and you compose a long mental letter in reply telling him all about your new job, your new girlfriend, and your old problems. You spin out a letter eight or ten pages long. When you have finished, you have that nice, satisfied feeling that you always have when you have corresponded with someone you like. There is just one problem: the letter is all in your head, and you can't mail brain waves.

But you have thought through what you wanted to tell Ed, and that thinking process will have helped you organize your thoughts for when you do sit down and write the actual letter.

Well, in the future you will write your best business letters in your head also. You will plan them mentally first, then you will go one step farther. You will write or dictate the letter you have planned. Letters which receive such a head start will actually be written more rapidly, more clearly, and more completely.

Before you write your letter, plan it. If your letter is to be a short one, you can make a brief mental outline of the points you wish to make. If your letter is longer or more involved, perhaps you should write out a word outline. After you have jotted down the points which you wish to make in your letter, you will probably need to rearrange them. Place the most important things first. After you have given some ideas a second thought, you may decide they are not really essential. Scratch them out. Cluttering up your letter with minor, nonessential points distracts the reader from what is really important.

Planning your letter in this way will save you time, both now and later. It will save you time now because the actual writing or dictating of your letter will take less time if you have already planned the points you want to make. It will save you time later because lack of planning may cause you to forget a point or two that you wish to make. Such an omission will probably mean that you will have to write another letter later.

Planning your letter before you write or dictate it will help you to write a better letter. Not only will you be able to handle your points in the best order, but you will also be able to handle them more completely and to express yourself more effectively. Because you have listed the points you want to make, you do not have to worry about forgetting something you want to say. You can concentrate on one thing at a time. When you have covered one point completely, you can move on to the next point, confident that you will not suddenly insert something you should have said earlier and thus destroy the unity of your writing. When you have finished your letter, you will know that you have covered each point clearly and completely.

Some letters will be so long, so involved, or so important that you may want to write or dictate a rough draft first. Then you can revise your letter, cutting out less important words and ideas, marking out words and phrases that do not say anything, making substitutions for hackneyed expressions, and re-forming sentences in the most forceful way. At first it may seem to you that such preliminary work is a waste of time. But in the end it will save you time. It will save your typist time. And because it will enable you to write a clearer, more complete letter, it will save your reader time.

HOW DO YOU WRITE A LETTER FROM AN OUTLINE?

A typical word outline might be something like this:

Thanks
Reason can't fill request
Suggestion where he can find it
Promise to help later

From this outline you might write the following letter:

THANKS	Thank you for turning to us when you needed information on how to train your dog.
REASON CAN'T FILL REQUEST	We are very sorry that we cannot send you the booklet *How to Make Your Dog an Obedient Pal.* The booklet has been very popular, and we have exhausted our first supply.
SUGGESTION WHERE HE CAN FIND IT	The local pet stores that carry Happy Puppy Dog Biscuits were all furnished large supplies of the booklet. You can probably pick up a copy at Peppers Pup Package store in Dalpark.
PROMISE TO HELP LATER	We will place you on our mailing list for a copy, which we will mail when we receive the second printing.

WHEN IS THE BEST TIME TO WRITE LETTERS?

When you receive a letter that requires an answer, whether you plan to answer immediately or not, you mentally form some kind of answer. If your next move is to transfer that planning to paper and then to write your answer, you will save yourself much time. If you put off answering the morning's mail, you will have to read it twice: once when you receive it and once when you answer it. You will also plan your answer twice. If you can answer the letter without additional information, do so at once. If additional information is needed, underscore the main points in the letter as you read it. Make a note of the information you need. Get the facts as soon as possible, while the matter is still fresh in your mind. Be sure to have all the facts before you answer the letter.

You will also save time if you concentrate on your correspondence at one time, rather than scattering it throughout the day. You have probably noticed that once you start writing letters, you can just as easily write several before you stop. Your letters are also more effective because you are handling similar situations at the same time. Letter writing is one chore that invites procrastination. You can reduce the temptation to put off the task if you have a definite time when you handle most of your letters.

WHAT ARE THE PARTS OF A BUSINESS LETTER?

Over the years the various conventions of usage have described what information needs to be given in the formal parts of a business letter and have suggested where these parts need to be placed so they will be most helpful. Various forms for punctuation and indentation are used, and you will need to use the form preferred by your office. However, the changes are not major ones and can easily be accommodated once you have learned the form given below, which is the most commonly used of all business letter forms.

Using the outline that you have just developed, your finished business letter to Mrs. Dorian would look like Figure 2 and would contain the parts noted in the left margin.

If you were writing to Mrs. Dorian from a company that did not have its own letterhead, you would use a different form to indicate your return address. The top part of your letter would look like Figure 3.

HOW DO YOU WRITE THE SALUTATION OF A BUSINESS LETTER?

You will be expected to greet your correspondent with one of several conventional phrases. The approved salutations are given below in order of decreasing formality:

FOR MEN	FOR WOMEN
Sir:	Madam:
My dear Sir:	My dear Madam:
Dear Sir:	Dear Madam:
My dear Mr. Sloan:	My dear Miss Thompson:
Dear Mr. Sloan:	(or Mrs. or Ms.)
Dear Sloan:	Dear Miss Thompson:
Dear Joe:	(or Mrs. or Ms.)
	Dear Fay:

How Do You Write the Salutation of a Business Letter? 29

Return Address	**HAPPY PUPPY BISCUITS, INC.** 8736 Prudence, Dallas, Texas 75222 745-4447
Date	October 14, 1974
Inside address	Mrs. Gilbert Dorian P.O. Box 516 Dalpark, Texas 76111
Salutation	Dear Mrs. Dorian:
Body of letter	Thank you for turning to us when you needed information on how to train your dog. We are always pleased when our customers think of us for their pet supplies and needs. We are very sorry that we cannot send you the booklet How to Make Your Dog an Obedient Pal. This booklet has been very popular, and we have exhausted our first supply. The local pet stores that carry Happy Puppy Biscuits were all furnished large supplies of the booklet. You can probably pick up a copy at Peppers Pup Package Store in Dalpark. We will place you on our mailing list for a copy which we will mail when we receive the second printing.
Complimentary close	Sincerely yours, *John B Griffith*
Signature	John B. Griffith Customer Relations Manager

Figure 2

```
                                              8736 Prudence
                                              Dallas, Texas 75222
                                              October 14, 1974

Mrs. Gilbert Dorian
P. O. Box 516
Dalpark, Texas 75111

Dear Mrs. Dorian:
```

Figure 3

Dear Sir and *Dear Madam* are always singular. *Gentlemen* is used for addressing a company, a committee, a numbered post office box, and an organization made up of men or of men and women. *Dear Sir and Madam* is used in writing to a firm consisting of a man and a woman. *Ladies and Gentlemen* is used in writing to a social group made up of men and women. *Mesdames* is the standard plural for *Madam* and is used for addressing a company, committee, or other group made up entirely of women. *Ladies* is becoming popular as an alternative salutation.

You can decide which salutation you should use by asking yourself how well you know your correspondent. If you have never met the person, you may use *Sir* or *Madam;* but these forms are going out of style. Modern communication leans toward directness. *Dear Mr. Sloan* is probably used a hundred times more often than any of the other more formal forms of address.

Did you notice how the salutations were capitalized and punctuated? The first word of the salutation is always capitalized. *Dear* is not capitalized unless it is the first word. The following are always capitalized in the salutation:

Sir   Madam   Mr.   Miss   Mrs.   Ms.   all titles   all names

Although a comma is used after the salutation in personal correspondence, only the colon (:) is acceptable after a business salutation:

Dear Mr. Colon:

In your salutation you will, of course, use any title which applies to your correspondent. Only a few titles should be abbreviated: Mr., Mrs., and Dr. The plurals for these words are abbreviated: Messrs., Mmes., and Drs. Miss is not an abbreviation and should have no period after it. Some other titles, such as Prof. (Professor), Capt. (Captain), Sgt. (Sergeant), may be abbreviated in the inside address when they appear with the correspondent's full name or surname and initials. In the salutation and body of the letter, when they are written with only the last name, they should be written in full:

Prof. Randolph Bell   Capt. Alfred Strate
Professor Bell: *Captain Strate:*

Addressing governmental and other prominent officials and church dignitaries presents certain definite problems. Suitable titles and salutations are frequently unfamiliar because they are not used very often. It is important, however, that you address such people properly. In the back of any good desk dictionary are some of the most frequently used forms of address. *Merriam-Webster's Seventh New Collegiate Dictionary* contains a rather complete listing of titles and salutations.

HOW DO YOU CLOSE YOUR BUSINESS LETTER?

The complimentary close should match the salutation in formality. The most commonly used closes for business letters are arranged below in the order of decreasing formality:

SEVERELY FORMAL	Respectfully yours, Yours respectfully,
FORMAL BUT WIDELY USED	Very truly yours, Yours very truly,
SEMIFORMAL	Very sincerely yours, Yours very sincerely,
ORDINARY BUSINESS LETTERS	Sincerely,
DAILY BUSINESS CONTACTS	Cordially yours,
CLOSE BUSINESS FRIENDSHIPS	Yours cordially,
INFORMAL BUSINESS RELATIONS	Cordially,
CLOSE PERSONAL FRIENDSHIP WITH OR WITHOUT BUSINESS	Faithfully yours,
CLOSE CONFIDENTIAL RELATIONS INVOLVING BUSINESS	Faithfully,

Cordially yours and *Sincerely yours* express a warmth that is pleasing but which should also be consistent with the general tone of the letter. If the letter is reserved, the person addressed of great importance, or any doubt exists as to how much formality is required, choose the more conservative *Yours very truly* or *Very truly yours*.

HOW DO YOU SIGN YOUR BUSINESS LETTER?

If you are writing or dictating the letter, you will sign the letter simply without title and type your name beneath your signature. If you are a man, your signature will present no problems. You decide early in your career that you prefer to sign your name J. J. Astor, Jacob J. Astor, or Jacob John Astor; and you do so for the remainder of your professional life. You never attach a title of any kind to your signature. If you have a string of degrees or a title that your correspondent may need to know to be able to address his answer properly or to evaluate you as an authority, you still sign your name John Anderson. Then you or your secretary can type beneath your signature:

John Anderson, M.D. *or* Arthur McMurray
Sales Manager

The matter of a woman's signature is a bit more complicated. If you are unmarried, your proper signature is obviously your maiden name. If you wish, you may indicate *Miss* by placing it in parentheses before the typed signature. Either form below is correct:

Sincerely yours,

Agnes Head

Agnes Head

Sincerely yours,

Agnes Head

(Miss) Agnes Head

A married woman should use her given name in her signature, and, if she is known professionally by that name, in her typed signature:

Sincerely yours,

Agnes Head

(Mrs.) Agnes Head

In some business and social situations the woman may wish to sign her given name but to use her husband's name in the typed signature. If this is done, notice that the entire typed signature is placed in parentheses:

Sincerely yours,

Agnes Head

(Mrs. Frederick Head)

HOW CAN YOU MAKE THE TONE OF YOUR LETTER FRIENDLY?

The best way to make your letter friendly is to keep it reader-centered. The most important person in your world is you. The most important problems in your world are your problems. You are interested in other people, for the most part, only as they fit into your world and relate to you and your problems. Many people touch your life only as they are able to help you solve some problem. You aren't deeply concerned with how much time or effort they must spend to help you solve your problem so long as they do it successfully. And if they are paid to solve your problems, the problems which arise for them in the course of doing so are even less important to you.

If these facts are true for you—and you're very unusual if they are not—they are at least as true for the customers and clients of the company that will employ you. Your reader will respond to you as you make him feel that he and his problems are important to you. You convey your friendly interest in people with the warm smile and the firm handclasp with which you greet them, with the alert expression with which you listen to them, and with the pleasant tone with which you answer them.

When you write a letter, your reader can't, of course, see your smile or alert expression, feel your handshake, or hear your voice. Your words must convey all the warmth, friendliness, and eagerness to help that can be put into a smile, a handshake, and a pleasant voice.

HOW CAN YOU BEGIN A LETTER IN A FRIENDLY WAY?

Nowhere is warmth and friendliness more important than in the first sentence of your letter. Here you catch the reader's attention, express your interest in him, and show him that he and his problem are important to you. The opening sentence of your letter should be reader-centered and should establish the relationship between you and the reader as a friendly one.

A letter that begins with the following sentence is neither reader-centered nor friendly:

> This will acknowledge receipt of your letter of June 11 in regard to Order No. 892068, in which you asked about instructions for the installation of the hydrometer. In reply, I wish to say . . .

There is no warmth in this sentence. Nothing in the sentence highlights either the reader or his problem. Besides, it's wordy. Why not say, "The instruction sheet for the installation of the hydrometer which you asked about is being rushed to you today"? Now the reader knows what he wants to know, and he knows you're eager to help him.

The subject position of the sentence is one of the most important points in the sentence. Don't waste this important spot on an indefinite *this:* "This will acknowledge. . . ." Don't waste it on an inconsequential date: "Your letter of October 29 reached us and. . . ." The correspondent doesn't care when he wrote his letter. He can look in his files if he needs to know. He wants to know when he will get whatever satisfaction he is seeking. If possible, make the subject of your sentence the reader and his needs:

> The order you sent on June 23 is being filled at once.
>
> The data on the enclosed sheet will cover the question you asked in your letter of August 17.
>
> Here is the catalog on our special fall sale which you. . . .

That first sentence of your letter is the most important sentence in your letter because if it is not the right sentence, your reader may not really read the other sentences. Some letter writers aren't aware of this fact or they wouldn't waste those first precious words on empty participial phrases when they could plunge right into the really important matter at hand.

PARTICIPIAL OPENING	READER-CENTERED OPENING
Acknowledging receipt of and thanking you for your fine order, . . .	Thank you for your fine order.
Complying with your request of April 9 for a catalog, . . .	Here is the catalog you asked for.
Replying to your letter of January 18 in which you referred to information . . .	The information referred to in your letter . . .

Opening sentences should be interesting, gracious, and positive. They may do one of the following:

TELL WHAT YOU HAVE DONE FOR HIM

You should receive the data you requested by Friday.
Here is the report you asked about.
Your order for eight typewriter tables was shipped today.

ASK HIM A QUESTION

Did you receive our latest specification on . . . ?
Have you investigated the success experienced by the Wharton Company since they have installed . . . ?
Is there a way we could make our service more readily available to you?

MAKE A REQUEST

Could you let me know the results of your trial of . . . ?

Would you give me further information about . . . ?
Please give me the date and order number on . . .
Can you place my name on your mailing list for . . . ?

STATE SOMETHING OF INTEREST TO HIM

You will be glad to know the results of your trial of . . .
You are certainly right, Mr. Harcourt, when you say that . . .
The question you raised in your letter of September 3 is a good one and . . .

HOW DO YOU KEEP YOUR SENTENCES READER-CENTERED THROUGHOUT THE LETTER?

Throughout your letter, keep your sentences reader-centered by keeping your reader, his needs, and his interests in mind. The reader isn't interested in placing his order by June 15 so your company can clear certain items from its stocks, but he may want to place his order by that date if doing so will save him some money. He isn't interested in sending in a duplicate copy of an invoice to help you keep your records straight, but he might be persuaded to do so to insure prompt credit for his own account. Notice the difference of emphasis in the following pairs of phrases:

WRITER-CENTERED	*We* wish to announce . . .
READER-CENTERED	*You* will be glad to hear . . .
WRITER-CENTERED	*We* are enclosing our . . .
READER-CENTERED	*You* will find your check enclosed.
WRITER-CENTERED	*We* wish to point out . . .
READER-CENTERED	*You* will be interested to know . . .

It is not enough, however, to sprinkle a few *you's* through your letter. More important is the friendly spirit you express toward the "you," your concern with his problems, and your positive affirmation that he is an important, worthwhile person. Your sentences must center on the interests of the reader as well as on the word *you*. Notice the difference in the following sentences:

WRITER-CENTERED	*We* have received your order of July 18 which *we* have passed on to *our* special dealer in charge of *our* company in that area.
READER-CENTERED	*Your* check for $25 was received today. We are happy to credit it to *your* account.

HOW DO YOU CLOSE YOUR LETTER IN A FRIENDLY WAY?

If the first sentence of your letter creates the important first impression that makes the reader want to finish the rest of the letter in good will, the last sentence leaves the last impression which determines how the reader will feel about you and your letter in the future. Do not waste this valuable spot on insipid participial endings that say nothing. You can write the following phrases on slips of paper and place them in a hat to be drawn out when you need to close a letter. You can, but you will not be an effective letter writer that way.

Hoping this has not inconvenienced you . . .
Trusting this meets with your satisfaction . . .
Thanking you in advance . . .
Awaiting receipt of your reply . . .

How much firmer and friendlier is the goodbye in these sentences:

We are always glad to serve you.
We are very glad to have this new business.
When we can help you, let us know.
Thanks.

Sometimes you may want the reader to take some action. If so, tell him in plain English. Since the closing sentence of your letter is the sentence that makes the most lasting impression, it should be the one that tells your reader what to do. If what you want him to do requires a lengthy explanation, tell him earlier but repeat the main instruction in your last sentences. He will remember that instruction better if you keep it short.

Send us your check today, and your order will be shipped Monday.
Fill out the application and return it to us today, and your policy will be in force the first of the month.
Just put your okay on the bottom of this letter and mail it to me today.
By initialing and returning the enclosed order blank before the fifteenth, you will enable us to send you your stock in time for your January sales.

Notice that these requests are not vague. The reader knows exactly what the writer wants him to do. Moreover, he knows when the writer wants him to act. The words *today* or *at once* urge the reader to reach for his pen now, not after the letter has lain on his desk for a week. The reader will also act more promptly if you have simplified the action you ask of him. If questionnaires and other forms are involved, they should be self-explanatory and easy to fill out. The use of questionnaires or forms can save him the time and effort of writing or dictating a letter, and save you time in waiting for a reply. If he can check a *yes* or *no* at the bottom of your letter or attach his signature or okay to a sentence you have prepared, his answer may leave in the evening mail. And if he can slip that letter into a stamped, self-addressed envelope which you enclosed with your letter, his answer may go out the same day.

Sometimes you do not want your reader to do anything except finish your letter feeling friendly toward you. You might close with a sentence like one of these:

> For your sake and ours, we hope you will continue to have the kind of prosperity that prompted this fine order.
>
> If you are in Chicago for the trades convention, be sure to drop by our display room to say hello.

During the holiday season, you can add a friendly note by closing with such remarks as "Season's greetings and our best wishes to you" or "Best wishes at this happy season."

But however you close your letter, keep your closing sentence short, like the parting words of a visit with a friend. Do not stand at the door with your hat in your hand. When you are through, stop.

HOW DO YOU PROOFREAD A LETTER?

After you have written your letter, you are not through. The following steps will keep you from making many errors:

- Check the spelling of the reader's name.
- Check figures, facts, and enclosures.
- Check the spelling, grammar, and punctuation.
- Reread the letter you are answering to be sure you have answered it completely.
- Read carefully every letter you sign.

The letter in Figure 4 is filled with errors in form and content. Read the letter carefully and then study the comments which follow it.

8753 Gation Drive
Houston, Texas, 77211

4/17/74

Mr. Robert Pease, Credit Manager
Sav-a-Lot Department Stores
4010 Alfred Road
Houston,
Texas, 77001

Dear Sir,

    I am writing to let you know that you have my credit account all fouled up. I don't know what has happened because until this time I have always had good dealing with your company and have never had to write to anyone about anything before.

    I am really writing about my last statement. You say there that I owe you $45.78 and that I have not made a payment in two months and that you are going to close my credit account and report me to the credit association. I don't see how you can say these things.

    My wife sent you a check in February, about the 15th I think, for $10. We did not pay you in March because my little boy had to go to the hospital and be operated on. This all cost me $320, and I don't make but $435 in a month. You can see I didn't have much left.

    Anyway, you should know that I will pay you when I can and I hope that I will get paid this weekend and mail you a check. My credit has been good with you for five years.

    Besides, I don't know why we did not get credit for the $10 my wife sent you in February. Please let me know.

                                          Yours,

                                          Bill Rockton

Figure 4

How Do You Proofread a Letter?

Disregard for a moment the awkward sentences in this letter and look only at the content and form. Notice that Mr. Rockton is writing about his account but that his paragraphs do not move in an organized manner. Both his references to the ten-dollar payment, for example, should have been made in the third paragraph, rather than in two separate paragraphs. Specifically, notice the following errors:

line 2	No comma should separate the state from the zip code.
line 3	Only a lazy person uses this form for citing a date. Write the date out in full and do not skip a line between the date and the return address.
line 7	Keep the city and the state on the same line of the inside address. Do not separate state and zip code by a comma.
line 9	If you know the person's name, do not address him by general reference in the salutation. Follow the salutation with a colon, not a comma.
line 10	This is a wordy beginning to the letter. Actually you could strike this entire first paragraph and lose none of the meaning.
line 14	The letter should have begun here if this is what Mr. Rockton *really* is writing about.
lines 14–17	This is a very awkward sentence. It tries to do too much. Probably Mr. Pease does not need to be reminded of all that Mr. Rockton was told on the last statement.
line 19	Be exact. When was the check sent?
line 20	Mr. Rockton needs only to say that he had unusual medical expenses. Mr. Pease is a busy man and is not interested in the details of the boy's operation.
line 25	Be specific. When will a check be mailed?
lines 25–26	This sentence does not belong in this paragraph. It is intended to show that Mr. Rockton wishes to keep his credit rating secure, but it does not really say that.
line 27	This entire paragraph is badly stated and is misplaced.
line 29	*Yours* is far too casual a complimentary close. *Sincerely yours* would be much better.

Bill Rockton's letter could be rewritten to look something like Figure 5:

8753 Gation Drive
Houston, Texas 77211
April 17, 1974

Mr. Robert Pease, Credit Manager
Sav-a-lot Department Stores
4010 Alfred Road
Houston, Texas 77001

Dear Mr. Pease:

    I am writing about the last statement I received from your company. It showed a balance of $45.78 and indicated that I was two months behind in my payments.

    My wife sent you a check (our check No. 355) dated February 16 for $10. I do not think that we have been credited with this payment even though we have received the cancelled check from our bank. If you wish, I can mail you a copy of the check so you can examine it against your own records.

    I admit that I did not send my payment in March, and I realize I should have written to you then explaining why. I had such heavy medical expenses that month that I had to postpone several of my regular payments. But I do plan to make a double payment this month. I will be paid April 20 and will mail you a check for the last two months that same day.

    I have had an excellent credit rating with your company for five years, and I would certainly not want to lose it now.

                                         Sincerely yours,

                                         Bill Rockton

                                         Bill Rockton

Figure 5

ASSIGNMENTS

I. Letters 1(a) and 1(b), which follow, contain numerous errors in form and content. Using the line-by-line analysis which was used with Figure 4, list the errors that you find. Rewrite each letter so that it is acceptable. Remember that you might need to rephrase the entire letter to make it suitable.

II. Write letters for each of the following situations. Remember that you must include *your* return address and that you must sign the finished letter.

                                    1113 Pert Avenue
                                    San Francisco, Calif.
                                    Sept. 11, 1973

Mr. Fred Simpson
Manager
Oakwood Automobile Company
4414 Lamair
San Francisco, Calif. 94133

Dear Mr. Simpson

    You don't know me, but I bought a car from your company about three weeks ago. It was a brand new model. I traded in my 1964 work car for a down payment.

    The problem is that this new car is not running right. It gets too hot when my wife drives it around town. She said she had to keep the motor racing all the time to keep it cool.

    Also the front door on my side does not close good. It rattles a lot.

    I called the shop and they said they could not fix the car until next week. I just want you to know that I am not happy with it and that I am going to write the regional sales office to tell them that you are not giving me good service.

                                    Yours truly,

                                    Dan Paderson

Letter 1(a)

1. Write to the publishers of *Zme* magazine inquiring why you have not received the last two issues of the publication. Your annual subscription still has five months to go, and you have the receipt from your last payment.
2. Submit a letter to Plain-Clothes Dry Goods explaining that you cannot meet your monthly charge payment because of illness in your family. Indicate that you plan to make a double payment next month.
3. Write to the Credit Manager of Xert, Inc., inquiring why your charge account has not been approved. You submitted a credit application to them three months ago and have heard nothing. You have an excellent credit rating. (Include two or three good credit references in your letter.)
4. Prepare a brief letter to your mayor (or any other important official) expressing appreciation of some recent action for which he has been re-

3857 Avenue M
Boston, Mass.

Mr. Larry Gettron
Boston, Mass.

Gentlemen

    I just want to write you a short letter and tell you how much I appreciate the courtesy of your delivery man. I have done business with five different cleaners in the last two years, and I have not found anyone who is as good as your man.

    He always is dressed neat and clean. He is polite and courteous. He is ready to give me the right change when I pay him. He is real business like in everything.

    I also like the way he handles my clothes. He doesn't wad them up in a tight little bundle like some delivery men he keeps them on the hangars and treats them gently. When he brings them back home he always puts them in the front closet while I get the money for him.

    I just wanted you to know that he is a good man and you should be proud of him.

                                    Your customer,

                                    Louise McLoy

Letter 1(b)

sponsible. Remember that he is a busy man and that you want only to register with him your positive response.

5. Write a letter to the same official, this time briefly expressing disapproval of some action. Again remember that your purpose is to register your feelings and not to itemize details.

6. Write a letter to Improved Gasket Company asking if they have a replacement gasket to fit the manifold head of your 1949 Ford. You have been unable to find the gasket at a local supply house and have heard that they stock them. Order one of the gaskets sent C.O.D. if it is available.

III. In the previous section you wrote several letters to various persons. Assume now that you are on the receiving end of those letters and must respond to them. Write responses to at least three of the letters which you wrote for question II.

Assignments 43

IV. Each of the following letters is writer-centered. Rewrite each to make it reader-centered. You are given only the body of each letter, but your revision of it should include all of the necessary parts of a business letter.

Letter A

Replying to your recent letter, I am sorry that I am not able to send you information that you request regarding our new tomato plants.

Our supply of free brochures has run out, and we do not know when we will get any more from the printer.

Letter B

We would like for you to help us make a brief survey of working mothers. Our records show that you are one of the several thousand mothers in our city who hold a full-time job.

We are trying to determine several difficult things about working mothers and their contributions to the home and the job. If you complete the enclosed questionnaire for us, you will help to make our study more complete.

Letter C

We have been going through our customer records and have discovered that you have not made a purchase at our store in over a year.

We want to remind you that your credit is still good with us. We hope that you will come in soon and browse among the many new items that have been added to our inventory.

Our customers are important people to us. We want you to come see us again.

FOUR / Letters of Adjustment, Refusal, and Collection

WHEN DO YOU NEED TO PUT YOUR FOOT DOWN?

Frequently your errors or other people's errors will require that you write letters requesting adjustments of those errors or letters agreeing to make the adjustments that other people have asked of you. The kinds of mistakes that must be adjusted are multiple. Merchandise may arrive damaged. Errors may be made in filling orders. The terms of the sale may be misunderstood. The buyer may feel that the goods received do not measure up to the description. A mistake may be made in billing. In such cases and in hundreds of others, the buyer should ask for an adjustment. If you're the seller, you would appreciate the dissatisfied buyer's giving you an opportunity to straighten out the matter and win back his good will. If you're the buyer, you are entitled to satisfaction, and the seller will want to give it to you.

Letters asking for adjustment are frequently referred to as "claim letters." In writing, however, don't use the word "claim"; in fact, you should avoid claiming anything. Instead, give the facts and ask for what you believe is the proper adjustment.

HOW DO YOU WRITE A LETTER ASKING FOR AN ADJUSTMENT?

Whether or not you receive the adjustment you ask for may be determined more than you realize by the way you ask for it. The person who has made the mistake often reacts defensively. This reaction is most frequently found in the less important, less experienced worker. Mr. Vice-President-in-Charge-of-Red-Tape can always find some underling to blame, but the third assistant to the stock clerk has no office cat to kick. If you deal with him kindly, he may be so amazed and so grateful that he will put forth extra effort to see that your merchandise is properly packed and routed or that your statement is carefully checked.

You will be able to write more courteously if you are very sure that you yourself have made no error. So, first, you should do all you can to make sure that a mistake has actually been made by the seller and that you have all the facts. Then write your letter clearly, directly, and courteously. Show how you have been inconvenienced by the error and appeal to the self-interest and sense of fair play of the seller.

You will gain nothing by being irritable or quarrelsome. You may take some secret delight in displaying your wit through some sarcastic remark, but you may be embarrassed later when you discover that the error is really yours. And your sense of fair play should require that you give the seller the benefit of the doubt and assume he is honest, conscientious, and only slightly more subject to error than you. If you really are angry and must expel the venom that fills your soul, write an angry letter, then throw it away and write one that will get the kind of prompt, well-intentioned response you want.

There will be two parts to your letter. One part will give the information that the seller needs in order to make the adjustment. It will contain the date of the order or shipment, the order number, the stock number of the article if there is one, the exact nature of the complaint, and a description of the way in which you have been inconvenienced by the problem. The other part suggests to the seller the adjustment which you want him to make. You may make such a suggestion at the beginning of your letter in order to emphasize or clarify it, or you can give all the facts first. The order of the letter will depend somewhat upon the situation.

HOW CAN YOU SHOW COURTESY IN REPLYING TO A LETTER ASKING FOR AN ADJUSTMENT?

When you receive a letter from a dissatisfied customer, you can be sure that somebody has made a mistake. No matter who that somebody is, use this opportunity to build good business relations. Right or wrong, do your best to see that the customer is satisfied with the experience.

The adjustment letter, more than any other business letter, should be reader-centered. Realize first that the customer is unhappy for two reasons: first, he has been inconvenienced by some discrepancy, mistake, or product failure that he connects with your company; second, he has had to take the time to write to ask you to solve his problem, and he has had to place himself in the uncomfortable position of complainer or asker of favors.

You hope, of course, that all the letters that you receive asking for adjustment are as clear, accurate, and courteous as those you will write. Whether they are or not, you should answer them as though they were. Even if you wonder why the words of the letter you have received did not set the paper on fire, calm yourself and assume that the person who wrote it is intelligent and careful and that he is honest and conscientious, and that your company wants his business. Such assumptions will make him write more intelligently, carefully, and conscientiously next time; and such generosity will build good will and good business.

Avoid words or expressions suggesting that the person asking for an adjustment is careless:

You neglected to specify . . .
You failed to include . . .
You overlooked enclosing . . .

Do not use words that imply he is lying:

You claim that . . .
You say that . . .
You state that . . .

Be careful not to write sentences that belittle him or make him feel that you think he is ignorant:

We cannot see how you . . .
We fail to understand . . .
We are at a loss to know . . .

Avoid demanding phrases that arouse the reader's rebellion:

You should . . .
You ought to . . .
You must . . .
We must ask you to . . .
We must insist . . .

Some phrases that seem friendly or polite to you may be read as sarcastic or condescending by your reader:

No doubt . . .
We will thank you to . . .
You understand, of course . . .
Please respond soon . . .

Read these phrases aloud as though you were angry. Do you see that a sneer seems to be applied? Put your own letter to the same test.

No matter what action you may feel is proper in the case, there is one important thing you can do to help. You can answer promptly. Even if you can't take action without further examination of the facts, you can write the customer at once to tell him that you are looking into the matter. The customer has already been inconvenienced by an error or misunderstanding in connection with your company; he should not be further annoyed by your delay in caring for the matter. He will expect action as soon as he has dictated his complaint, and he would really like it sooner. The longer he waits, the greater his inconvenience and the hotter his temper. Whether you can make the adjustment the customer asks or not, you should show the customer that you understand his dissatisfaction and that you are really sorry about any inconvenience that he has experienced.

HOW SHOULD YOU HANDLE THE ERROR THAT IS RESPONSIBLE FOR THE LETTER ASKING FOR AN ADJUSTMENT?

Every adjustment that is asked for involves a mistake somewhere. One of three parties may be at fault: the seller, the buyer, or a third party such as the shipping company. If the buyer is at fault, you may have to tell him so; but you should do so in a way that will relieve him of embarrassment and displeasure. Remember, pointing out his mistakes puts him on the defensive. Even if he sees he is wrong and you are right, he will not like you better for making him feel stupid or incompetent. If a third party is wrong, don't blame him too harshly nor completely shift responsibility for settling the matter to the carrying agent or other intermediary. He may in a very definite sense be your agent. At the least, he is still associated in the customer's mind with your company, your product, and the immediate inconvenience. Even if you refer the matter to the third party, you should still make some check to be sure the customer is left satisfied. If the error was made by your company, assume the blame cheerfully and firmly and hasten to make a fair adjustment.

HOW DO YOU HANDLE THE REQUESTED ADJUSTMENT?

A fair adjustment is one that is reasonable and impartial. When you write an adjustment letter, you are judge, jury, and attorney for both parties. You will want to view the matter impartially for two very good reasons. First, your company is ethical and fair in its dealings. You wouldn't be associated with it if it were not, and it won't be there for you to be associated with very long if it is not. Second, no matter how tactfully and courteously you handle your letter, you will not make your adjustment appear fair if it is not.

You may be able to be unfair in the customer's favor, and you should probably investigate to see if you can afford to do so. Securing new customers costs money. It may be cheaper to make some concessions to hold an old customer than to court a new one. If at all possible, you should grant at least part of the request made by the seller.

Granting part of what the claimant asks is making a compromise and may require some negotiating. In such a case, explain why you can't make a full concession and what you are prepared to offer. You should usually offer only one plan of adjustment. Two or three plans are confusing to many people. However, always offer the compromise to the claimant as an arrangement that is subject to his approval. At the same time, take the positive, cheerful approach that you expect the customer to accept your suggested adjustment.

If you can grant all or part of the adjustment, do so cheerfully, even enthusiastically. If you act begrudging even in giving the claimant a fair adjustment, he probably won't feel really satisfied. When you give in, give in all the way. You are wasting a valuable opportunity if you don't use a favorable adjustment to get every ounce of good will that you can. Phrases like the following help to show the reader that your company is in business to serve him:

> We are pleased to return the amount enclosed.
> We are grateful you gave us the opportunity to correct our mistake.
> Thank you for calling this matter to our attention.
> We are glad to credit your account.
> We appreciate your frank letter.

HOW DO YOU SAY "NO" TO A REQUESTED ADJUSTMENT?

Saying *no* is more difficult. But if you are clever and tactful, you may be able to make your *no* sound almost like *yes*. If you must say *no*, try to surround it with *yesses*. Agree with him as much as you can:

> I would feel the same way if . . .

You are quite right when you say . . .
I don't blame you for . . .
I agree that you should be able to expect . . .
You certainly should receive . . .

No doubt you have an excellent reason for saying *no*. Your customer is entitled to know what that reason is. Don't dodge behind "Our policy will not allow. . . ." Give him the facts as briefly as you can. Assume that he is intelligent enough to understand and reasonable enough to see your side. Appeal to his fairmindedness, but don't argue.

HOW DO YOU SAY "NO" TO CUSTOMER REQUESTS?

It is easy to answer an order letter or letter of request when your answer is *yes*. In fact, usually no letter is required. The customer wants a part for his tractor, twenty-five dozen Christmas tree balls in time for his pre-Halloween display, or a selection of office supplies, not correspondence from you. But if you have to say *no*—if the tractor part is out of stock, a transportation strike delays your shipment, or the customer didn't include enough information with his order—then your answer will require tactful handling. Try to find some good news to include with your bad news. Perhaps the bad news won't seem so bad if you can find a positive way to state it. If you have good news, *don't bury it* among your *regrets* and *sorrys*. Bury the bad news. Tell the reader what you can do and perhaps he will shed few tears over what you can't do.

GOOD NEWS	BAD NEWS
We are sending you our latest model of the part you requested. We are proud of the many improvements we have been able to make over the older model.	I am sorry that the part you ordered is out of stock. Instead we are sending . . .
In spite of the transportation strike, you will be glad to know that we will be able to ship your order by October 8.	Because of the transportation strike, we will not be able to ship your order before October 8.
You will be happy to know that your shipment went out this morning. We filled your order as soon as we received your second letter containing the necessary information.	We are sorry that we did not have enough information to fill your order as promptly as you wanted it. Now that we have all the information, we can . . .

End your letter on a constructive note. Try to do something else for the customer. Suggest an alternative:

> The freshman text which you ordered is out of print, but we are sending you examination copies of two similar texts which might meet your needs.
>
> The winter catalogue and price list that you requested are being replaced by the new spring catalogue and price list which are now at the printer's. We shall send you the new ones as soon as they are available, possibly by the end of next week. In the meantime, we are sending you our latest sale catalogue. You may be able to find what you need there at a reduced price.

Show your appreciation of your reader:

> We appreciate the time and effort you and your associates spent in preparing your bid. We hope the fact that we cannot accept it will not keep you from bidding on our next job. We have enjoyed working with you in the past and hope that we can do so again.
>
> Your past patronage of our shop indicates that you had confidence in us. We appreciate that confidence and hope that this episode will not disturb that confidence in the future.

Offer to assist him in the future:

> The next time you need help with such a problem, we hope you will call on us.
>
> We hope that we can look forward to working with you on a future project.
>
> We certainly regret that this delay caused you inconvenience and hope that you will give us the opportunity to show you that we can do better.

Hold the door open for a *yes* in the future:

> Perhaps when we are able to expand our budget we shall . . .
>
> We are keeping your application on file . . .
>
> Possibly after the first of the year . . .

Figure 6 illustrates the type of adjustment letter you might write when you are able to grant exactly what the claimant wants.

If Mr. Allison had been unable to make a full adjustment on the merchandise, he might have offered Mr. Turner a compromise. Figure 7 illustrates how he might have written such a letter.

If Mr. Allison had been unable to make any kind of adjustment, he might have written a letter much like Figure 8.

811 Dobb Road
San Antonio, Texas 78200
April 20, 1974

Mr. Fred Turner
P. O. Box 87
San Antonio, Texas 78155

Dear Mr. Turner:

    We appreciate your frank letter stating that the suit which you purchased in our store during our March Clearance Sale was defective.

    Ordinarily we do not exchange merchandise bought during a sale, but we certainly do not want our customers to be unhappy with a product that is defective. Please return the suit at your earliest convenience, and it will be exchanged for any suit that is presently selling for the same price.

    You will realize, I hope, that we handle hundreds of suits a month and cannot always spot defective material until too late. We do want you to be happy with the service that you receive from us and to know that we will always do our best to serve you. As a token of appreciation to you and to repay you, at least in part, for your inconvenience, we want you to select a complimentary tie to go with your new suit.

    If you will contact Mr. Ralph Walker, Manager of Men's Wear, he will assist you in your selection of a suit and matching tie.

Sincerely yours,

Paul Allison

Paul Allison, Manager
Customer Relations

Figure 6

811 Dobb Road
San Antonio, Texas 78200
April 10, 1974

Mr. Fred Turner
P. O. Box 87
San Antonio, Texas 78155

Dear Mr. Turner:

    You are right when you state that no one likes to spend money for inferior merchandise. No one would like to buy a suit and discover that it had a stain on one pants leg.

    In part, though, the excitement of shopping at a sale lies in the possibility of finding something for a price below what you would normally pay. We could not have sold a first quality suit for such a low price. If you recall, the sign advertising the suit you purchased stated that those suits were seconds.

    Ordinarily we do not exchange items bought during a sale, but we want you to be pleased with the merchandise that you get from our store. We realize, too, that perhaps you did not see the "seconds" sign when you bought your suit. Let me offer you a suggestion. You bought your suit on sale for $79.35. A firstline suit by that same manufacturer sells for $124.25. If you will return the defective suit, I will arrange with Mr. Ralph Walker, Manager of Men's Wear, for you to purchase the firstline suit for only $99.50. You can readily see that this is still quite a bargain.

    Please call Mr. Walker within the next two weeks and make an appointment to be fitted for your new suit. We hope that you will be happy with your new purchase.

                                     Sincerely yours,

                                     Paul Allison, Manager
                                     Customer Relations

Figure 7

811 Dobb Road
San Antonio, Texas 78200
April 20, 1974

Mr. Fred Turner
P. O. Box 87
San Antonio, Texas 78155

Dear Mr. Turner:

You have always had confidence in our Men's Shop and have been one of our most consistent customers. We are, therefore, more than upset when you are upset.

The suit which you purchased during our March Clearance Sale was one of 500 which we received on a special factory order. Some were only slightly irregular; others were critically inferior. The prices were set according to the defects. Apparently you got one of the very bad ones, and we are sorry.

Unfortunately we cannot exchange items purchased during a sale. The suits were marked low because of the special purchase order. We cannot buy first-line suits for that price ourselves.

You have been a customer at our store for the last five years, and we hope that you will not permit this one experience to disturb your confidence in us. We are now receiving our Fall merchandise, including a new line of suits that is slightly less expensive than those we now stock. You will enjoy browsing among the new ones in the latest fall colors. These first-line suits sell for only $92.50.

Come to visit our Men's Shop again. We will do all that we can to make you happy.

Sincerely yours,

Paul Allison

Paul Allison, Manager
Customer Relations

Figure 8

WHAT ATTITUDE WILL HELP YOU WRITE EFFECTIVE COLLECTION LETTERS?

Letters that say *no* aren't the only letters that require you to exert tact, imagination, and the ability to put yourself in the reader's place. The letter that says *please* can be even trickier to handle, but *please* you must say if you are to keep accounts receivable receiving and not liquidated. When somebody owes you or your company money and you have the unpleasant task of asking him to pay, you may be tempted to take one of two approaches. You may, feeling embarrassed and apologetic, hold out a trembling hand like a beggar. You may, feeling angry and abused, bang your fist on the desk and rave at the thief. Neither action will get the results you want.

In the first place, you have nothing to apologize about. If someone owes you money, he has an obligation to pay and you have a right to ask him to. If you seem doubtful about his obligation to pay, he may hesitate or doubt that he is so obligated. Speak up. Point out boldly and clearly that the payment is past due and that you expect him to make amends.

On the other hand, you will lose more than you will gain if you write an angry collection letter. The reader does not consider himself thoughtless, inconsiderate, or dishonest; and your scolding, insinuating letter will not convince him that he is. In fact, you don't want it to. You want to convince him that he is a careful businessman who likes to keep his accounts straight, who needs to keep his credit clear, and who intends to write you a check for the specified amount as soon as he finishes reading your letter.

WHAT APPROACH SHOULD YOU USE IN YOUR FIRST COLLECTION LETTER?

When you write your letter to remind a delinquent customer that he hasn't paid his bill, take it for granted that he is an honest man who has shown a normal amount of forgetfulness. Allow him to save face and you will save the customer. Imply that the matter has merely been overlooked:

> Probably everybody misfiles or overlooks a statement at one time or another, and I wonder if that is what you did to our statement for June 1.

Maybe you misplaced our letter of April 27. Even the most careful businessman can do that sometimes.

A person as busy as I know you are might overlook a letter, and maybe you missed our letter of November 25 that way.

Keep your reminder friendly:

Just a reminder that your account for $93.95 was due on the first of the month.

We have been watching the mails for your check, but we have been disappointed.

Your check for $123.46 is not here. Where is it? In the mail? On your desk waiting for your signature? On my agenda is a letter to you saying, "Thank you for your check." Please help me get it in the mail and on your desk at once.

I am sending this friendly reminder because we have not received your check for $81.90 that was due on May 15.

The response to your letter will be made more quickly and cheerfully if you can point out the advantages of prompt action:

Just staple your check for $15.68 to this letter and mail it in the enclosed envelope to bring your account up to date and keep your rating clear.

Your check will be appreciated because it will maintain your superior credit record at Bailey's.

As soon as I receive your check, I will mail you the new catalogue for the spring clearance sale which I am sure will enable you to make big savings on several of the items which you usually buy.

WHAT KIND OF FOLLOW-UP LETTERS ARE USED?

Customers who have merely neglected to pay the bill will probably pay when they have received your reminder. A few will need to be urged a bit more strongly. You should send a second follow-up letter within the next fifteen days. Make this letter firmer and more insistent than the first, but still keep it friendly and courteous:

You will note from the attached statement that our January bill has apparently been overlooked. We are sure that we can rely upon you to take care of this matter at once.

We sent you a statement for $112.35 on June 26. This letter is dated July 18. We hate to annoy you with such reminders, but we would appreciate your check at once.

> We do not understand it. We still have not received the $59.70 that you owe us.
>
> According to the terms upon which you received your credit card, you agreed to pay upon receipt of your statement. The net amount, $89.70, was due on August 10. We did not hear from you. A second statement was sent to you on September 12, asking if there was some error. We have received no answer. Please be fair to us and yourself and mail your check at once.

Even now, when you want to be firm, and later, when you want to be firmer, you don't want to insult or anger the customer. Put yourself in the customer's place as you word your letter, and avoid any expression that could arouse hostility.

Most people ordinarily pay promptly, and delay only when they are in some sort of financial difficulty. They would like to pay now, but they think that nothing can be done to help them. If you write offering some solution to their problem, they may be able to meet their obligation and they will be grateful and loyal customers in the future. After two follow-up letters have failed to bring a response from a customer who has usually paid his bills promptly, you might write a firm letter which closes with a paragraph such as one of the following:

> If you cannot handle this matter now, please write us a note telling us when we can expect payment.
>
> We know a good customer like you must have some reason when he lets an account go unpaid for four months. If you cannot pay all or even part of the amount, please use the enclosed envelope to send us a note of explanation.
>
> If your circumstances are such that you cannot take care of the entire account at once, then please send us part of it and make some suggested schedule for payment of the balance.
>
> We are sure that something must have happened to you or you would have handled this matter as promptly as you have always handled your obligations. Please come by to see me, and let's talk this thing over. I'm sure we can make some arrangement that will allow you to keep your credit record clean.

When three or four follow-up letters have been sent out and two or three months have elapsed since the account was due, you will need to apply more pressure. Tell him firmly and definitely what you want him to do and what you are prepared to do if he does not. Create a sense of urgency. Set a date by which he must act. You need not become insulting or angry, however. Your purpose is still to save the customer as

What Kind of Follow-up Letters Are Used?

well as to collect the money he owes you. Note the firm but friendly tone in the following:

> We find it difficult to believe that you intend to evade completely your obligations in this matter. Yet the way you have continued to ignore this account forces us to ask you to mail us a check immediately. Although we dislike to resort to legal measures, we find a further extension of time impossible.
>
> Unless we receive your check for $243.67 within ten days, we shall be forced to turn your account over to our attorney for collection. This action is one we would like to avoid. Naturally, we want our money, but we do not want to embarrass you. Nor do we want to add legal fees to what you now owe us. All we want is your check for $243.67. Please help us avoid this action and save yourself embarrassment and added expense.

As you can see, collection letters follow a pattern of increasing firmness and urgency. The number of reminders that are sent before a company threatens and executes legal actions varies from organization to organization; but regardless of the number, they are arranged in this order:

1. Routine monthly statement of amount owed.
2. Simple reminder that account is past due.
3. Firmer reminder.
4. Appeal for immediate action or explanation.
5. Threat of legal action.
6. Notification of legal action.

Figures 9–12 are examples of a series of collection letters such as might be sent by a credit department. Note how the letters progress from simple reminders to increasingly insistent requests for payment:

RITE WAY PAPER MANUFACTURING COMPANY
9305 Sunset Avenue
Ostego, Indiana 81081
September 6, 1974

Ralph Waldo, Manager
Harold's School Supply
842 Austex Street
Pharr, Ohio 90332

Dear Mr. Waldo:

    We especially appreciated that fine order you placed with us July 8. We were glad, also, that you were feeling so prosperous and hopeful. When we did not receive your check after we sent your August statement for $186.90 and then when your September statement brought no return, we began to worry just a little. But we think we have the answer: with school starting and business booming after the vacation lag, you have been so busy selling that large order that you haven't had time to take care of our statement. We hope this is so and that after this little reminder you send us a check today.

    It isn't too early to be planning for the Christmas season. We have a specially designed assortment of Christmas wrapping paper with designs that are particularly appropriate for your customers. Under separate cover I am sending you our Christmas catalogue in which you will find a number of other attractive, new, fast-selling items.

    May you continue to have a prosperous season.

                        Sincerely yours,

                         Willard Penn
                         Collection Manager

Figure 9

RITE WAY PAPER MANUFACTURING COMPANY
9305 Sunset Avenue
Ostego, Indiana 81081
October 1, 1974

Ralph Waldo, Manager
Harold's School Supply
842 Austex Street
Pharr, Ohio 90332

Dear Mr. Waldo:

    I am enclosing this note in your monthly statement for $186.90 in order to point out that this bill is now nearly two months past due. This payment lag is not consistent with the prompt manner in which you have always handled your business with us in the past, and we do not believe that you really intend to be delinquent in your payments now. We hate to see you ruin your fine credit rating. So please, get your check in the mail at once.

                                        Sincerely yours,

                                        Willard Penn
                                        Collection Manager

Figure 10

RITE WAY PAPER MANUFACTURING COMPANY
9305 Sunset Avenue
Ostego, Indiana 81081
October 15, 1974

Ralph Waldo, Manager
Harold's School Supply
842 Austex Street
Pharr, Ohio 90332

Dear Mr. Waldo:

July 8 you placed a fine order for note books, paper, tablets, and other school supplies.

August 1 we sent you a statement for $186.90. No answer.

September 1 we sent you a second statement. No answer.

October 1 we sent you a third statement and a letter asking you please to care for this matter at once. Still no answer.

Don't you think we ought to hear from you? We are sure there must be a very good reason why you have not been able to pay, but we do not know what it is. Won't you please drop us a note and tell us what the problem is? Surely we can work something out. Perhaps you could pay fifty dollars now and the rest in three installments.

Please let us hear from you soon. We hate to have a good customer spoil his credit rating.

Sincerely yours,

Willard Penn
Willard Penn
Collection Manager

Figure 11

RITE WAY PAPER MANUFACTURING COMPANY
9305 Sunset Avenue
Ostego, Indiana 81081

November 1, 1974

Ralph Waldo, Manager
Harold's School Supply
842 Austex Street
Pharr, Ohio 90332

Dear Mr. Waldo:

It has been three months since you received the statement for $186.90 for your July 8 order. It has been fifteen days since I wrote and asked you to write us a letter of explanation or to offer us some plan for meeting your obligation. In all this time we have not heard from you.

We can not let this matter run on any longer. On the other hand, we hate to subject you to the embarrassment and expense involved should we be forced to take legal action. However, if we have not heard from you by November 15, we shall place this matter in the hands of our attorney, Adam Huntley.

                                            Sincerely yours,

                                            Willard Penn
                                            Collection Manager

Figure 12

ASSIGNMENTS

I. On May 18 Howard Hardcastle, manager and owner of Hardcastle's Hardware Store, ordered eight dozen meat presses from Handy Kitchenware Company. The presses were listed in a sale catalogue as Number 84653. The sale was to close May 31. On May 25 Mr. Hardcastle received his order and was billed in invoice number 432-192 for the sale price. On June 3 he received an unordered duplicate order, invoice number 432-275, for which he was billed the regular price of $9.25 per dozen instead of the sale price of $6.90 per dozen. The item was so popular that Mr. Hardcastle sold the second order also. Now he is writing the mail order manager of Handy Kitchenware Company, Mr. Arthur Allen, for an adjustment. Since the kitchenware company made the error, Mr. Hardcastle would like the second set of meat presses at the sale price of $6.90 per dozen. Write a letter from Mr. Hardcastle to Mr. Allen.

II. Write three answers to the above letter, one granting Mr. Hardcastle's request, one suggesting a compromise, and one refusing it. In the letter of refusal explain why you cannot grant the request and make some special effort to appease Mr. Hardcastle.

III. Mr. Hardcastle, following the adjustment letter which he receives from Mr. Allen, ignores his July statement and all following statements and communication. Prepare a series of five collection letters to be sent to Mr. Hardcastle.

FIVE / The Job Application Letter

WHY DO YOU NEED TO KNOW HOW TO WRITE JOB APPLICATION LETTERS NOW?

The first direct step in your career is applying for the job you want. If you write a letter applying for a job similar to the one you hope to hold when you finish your education, you can benefit from your instructor's objective criticism. If you are aware of the kind of experiences and aptitudes you will want to list in your letter of application in order to get the position you want, you can begin now to gain those experiences and abilities. Moreover, if you practice applying for jobs, even though the practice is in a classroom situation, you will gain confidence in the procedure. Many people are capable of holding much more important jobs than they are able to get. They lack both the knowledge of the techniques of getting a job and the confidence to use them. The object of this chapter is to help you acquire both.

WHAT IF THERE IS A JOB APPLICATION FORM?

Even though you write a letter of application, many companies may also require you to complete a job application form. Very often your application letter goes to one office and your application form, which contains more detailed information, to another. Do not approach the application form carelessly. It is an important record of many facts about you and your experiences, and it deserves close consideration.

Be certain you understand exactly what is being asked in each question of the form. Sometimes individuals fill in a certain bit of information and discover later that that information wasn't requested in the form they have used or that they misread the question. A good policy is quickly to scan the form, determining what it asks throughout so you can better structure your answers. One problem with forms is that they seldom give enough room to answer adequately; thus you must plan your answers carefully.

If possible, type your responses onto the form that you are given. If this is impossible, write clearly or print. And use ink!

Figures 13 and 14 represent the front and back sides of an actual job application form. Study them. Be certain that you know the exact information that is being requested in each blank.

WHY DO YOU NEED A LETTER?

A letter is much more personal than the application form, and because you compose your thoughts in the letter it also reflects more of your personality. In most instances your first contact with a potential employer is via letter even though he may subsequently send you a form for completion also.

Your letter, then, is your sales instrument. It should put your best foot forward, should reveal your most positive qualities. And since you are judged by your letter, it should be neat and orderly.

HOW SHOULD YOUR APPLICATION LETTER LOOK?

You should exercise the greatest care in preparing your application. Type neatly on a good grade of white bond paper, 8½ × 11 inches. Never use company letterhead stationery, hotel stationery, lined paper of any kind, or colored, gilt-edged, or decorated personal stationery. Follow an accepted form for business letters. Before you mail your letter, double-check your spelling, grammar, and punctuation and be prepared to retype your letter or even to rewrite it if it is somewhat less than perfect.

Your application for a job will be in two parts: a letter of application and a vita sheet [1] which gives an outline of your personal and professional background. The company may have a printed form on which they want the applicant to describe his qualifications in a prescribed space, but you usually have no such form when you first write. If you asked to fill one out later, you can do so. Some duplication of information

---

[1] A complete application folder is known as the *dossier* and includes the vita sheet, letters of recommendation, and any other important material.

How Should Your Application Letter Look?

APPLICATION FOR EMPLOYMENT

with the
DALLAS COUNTY HOSPITAL DISTRICT

Social Security Number:

Answer every question completely. Be accurate. Any misstatement of a fact that would prevent original appointment will result in dismissal later.

Title of position you are applying for _____

Will you accept temporary work? ☐ _____
Part time work? ☐ _____

Address _____
Phone Number _____

Last Name   First Name   Middle Name

Date of birth (Month)   (Day)   (Year)

Age _____
Mrs.
Miss.
Mr.

Color Hair _____   Weight _____
Color Eyes _____   Height _____

(Underscore) Married—Widowed—Single—Divorced—Separated

Number of Children: _____ Ages: _____

How long have you lived in Dallas County _____ Are you a citizen of the U.S.A. _____
Have you any physical defect? _____ If so, what is it? _____
Have you had any serious illness, injury or operation in last 10 years? _____
Describe and give details _____
Were you hospitalized? _____ Dates _____ Hospital _____ Location _____
My health is: (Underscore) Good — Fair — Poor: If poor, why? _____
Give residential address for past 10 years; give length of time at each location (City and State):

_____
_____
_____

Father's full name _____
Mother's full name _____
Full name of husband or wife _____

If husband or wife is employed, state where: _____

In case of emergency, notify _____

Have you ever been arrested for other than traffic violations? _____
If so, give records:

Date	Charge	Conviction or other disposition

Are you now, or have you ever been a member of any Communist organization? _____
Have you ever worked for the Dallas County Hospital District (Parkland or Woodlawn)? _____ If so, when? _____
What Position? _____ Reason for leaving _____
Do you have any relatives working for the Hospital District? _____ In what department? _____
Who are they and how are they related to you? _____
Have you ever filed suit against any of your former employers? _____ When _____
State details _____

Figure 13

The Job Application Letter

EDUCATION

High School Attended	CIRCLE LAST GRADE COMPLETED	DID YOU GRADUATE?	Give Date of Leaving or Graduation
	1 2 3 4 5 6 7 8 9 10 11 12	Yes _____ No _____	

College or University Attended	Years Attended	Major & Minor	Degrees Obtained	Give Date of Leaving or Graduation

Business College, Trade School or Correspondence Course	Years Attended	Course	Did you complete course? If so, when?

What professional or technical licenses, registrations, certificates, or memberships do you possess? _____

EXPERIENCE RECORD

Give complete information as to whom you worked for, the length of employment, and kind of work done. The time not employed must be shown. A complete record of your employment must be shown.

Date of Service		Length of Employment	EMPLOYED BY		Salary or Wages	Nature of Your Work
From	To		Name	Address		

May we communicate with your present Employer? _____
Use extra sheet when necessary to give complete employment record.

CHARACTER REFERENCES

	Name	Mailing Address	Business or Occupation
1.			
2.			

MILITARY STATEMENT

Have you ever served in the Armed Forces of the United States? _____ Component or Branch of Service _____
Dates of Service _____ Service Number _____ Reason for Discharge _____
Type of Discharge _____ Highest Grade or Rank attained _____ Have you ever been court-martialed, fined, or disciplined under any Article of War or Uniform Code of Military Justice _____ If answer is yes, explain fully.

Are you receiving disability compensation, pension, or disability retirement from the Veteran's Administration? _____
If answer is yes, explain fully, the nature, type and severity of this disability. _____

TO BE COMPLETED BY RN'S, TECH. NURSES & LVN'S ONLY

School of nursing from which you graduated _____ Location _____ Year of Graduation _____
Current Texas License No. _____ Other states currently registered in & Number _____
For Registered Nurses Only: Are you a member of the American Nurses' Association through membership in District or State Association: _____ Are you a member of the National League of Nursing? _____

NOTE:
I REPRESENT AND WARRANT THE ANSWERS I HAVE MADE TO EACH AND ALL OF THE FOREGOING QUESTIONS ARE FULL AND TRUE TO THE BEST OF MY KNOWLEDGE AND BELIEF.

AND FURTHER in order that the officials of the Dallas County Hospital District may be fully informed as to my personal character and qualifications for employment. I refer to each of my former employers and to any other person who may have information concerning me, agreeing, as this information is furnished at my express request and for my benefit, to hold such persons harmless and I do hereby release them from any and all liability for damage of whatsoever nature on account of furnishing such information.

Signature of Applicant _____

Date _____

Figure 14

will emphasize your apparent worth rather than detract from it. Moreover, by arranging the facts of your background to point up your specific qualifications for the job in question, you can make your vita sheet do a better job of selling your skills than a standard printed form will do.

HOW DO YOU MAKE A VITA SHEET?

The vita sheet is usually divided into four sections with headings for each: (1) personal information, (2) education, (3) work experience, and (4) references. Keep in mind the job for which you are applying as you arrange and word your information. You should be concise and exact so that the reader can see at a glance what your experience has been. Naturally, your arrangement of data will be neat, uncrowded, and balanced on the page. The four sections of your sheet should be separated slightly, and the headings which introduce them should stand out. Under each heading arrange the data in order from the most important information to the least important, chronologically from the most recent to the least recent. In describing your experience, be brief, using phrases rather than whole sentences, but give complete and exact information. Do not flatter yourself or try to represent your ability as greater than it is. By the time your future employer is ready to make a decision concerning you, he will have investigated your references and background enough to discover any discrepancies between your statements and reality. Nothing will insure your failure to get the job so definitely as the implication that you are not completely truthful.

Personal information should include age and date of birth, height, weight, health, and marital and Selective Service status. If you have children, you may include the number if you wish. Including your place of birth, nationality, or race is a matter of personal preference. Usually this information is not required. You can arrange the personal information as in Figure 15.

```
PERSONAL
                                  Height:     5'11"
    Name:             Robert S. Smith    Weight:     178
    Age:              22                 Health:     Good
    Sex:              Male               Address:    315 Pierce Drive
    Marital Status:   Married, one child             Fort Worth,
    Military Status:  II-S                           Texas 76119
                                  Telephone:  (817) 534-4455
```

Figure 15

Your educational preparation plays a more important part in securing the first job than it will after you have had several years of job experience. Therefore, you should not be satisfied just to name the school from which you were graduated. List any colleges or technical schools which you have attended, the dates of attendance, and the degrees or diplomas which you obtained. Then give your major field of study and list the major courses which you completed. If you had other courses which will make you a more valuable employee, name them even though they may not be directly related to the job for which you are applying. Give the specific course title. "Income Tax Accounting" will give your employer a more definite idea of the content of the course than "Business II." Give the name of your high school and the dates of attendance. Name any of your courses which particularly increased your qualifications. List also any honors or awards you received in school.

Your employer will want to know if you have demonstrated any leadership potential, if you have had opportunities to develop social poise, and if you have broad enough interests to make you an interesting person. Therefore, you should list any offices that you held and name extracurricular activities, hobbies, and special interests. If an employer has to choose between a young man with a 2.85 grade point average and the experience of having managed a Little League baseball team and a young man with a 3.00 average and no leadership experience at all, he may be inclined toward the Little Leaguer. The summary of your educational background might look like Figure 16.

```
EDUCATIONAL BACKGROUND

    Associate in Applied Science Degree, 1974

        Tarrant County Junior College
        Fort Worth, Texas
        Major: Business Administration
          Special courses:  Income Tax Accounting,
            Seminar in Management Problems

    High School diploma, 1970

        Paschal High School
        Fort Worth, Texas
          Honors:  National Honor Society  1970
            Letter in Basketball  1970
          Extracurricular activities:  Eagle Scout  1968
            Southside Baptist softball team  1968
```

Figure 16

Even though you may not have had any work experience in the area in which you are applying for a job, the section which lists your job experience is still very important. The fact that you have held a job, any job, indicates to your employer that you have initiative and are industrious. If you held a job for some reasonable period of time and left for some good reason, your employer will know that you are willing to work, that you are dependable and conscientious, and that you have been able to make the necessary adjustment to a job. List every job you have ever held, beginning with the last held and continuing in reverse chronological order. If you worked to help pay for your education, mention that fact. Show the dates for each job and briefly tell why you left. If you have had little experience working, do not omit this section or call attention to your lack of experience. Almost everyone has done some work some time which could be summarized by writing, "While I was in high school, I did baby sitting," "mowed lawns," or "worked for my father in his grocery store." The summary of your vocational experience can be arranged like Figure 17.

Applicants for a job are usually asked to give three to five names of persons who can be asked for references. Three kinds of references are usually given: personal or character references, credit references, and vocational or professional references.

The person whose name you give for a personal or character refer-

---

VOCATIONAL EXPERIENCE

1973-Present   Accountant   Wholesale Grocer Supply, Irving, Texas
                                                        Duties: Supervisor of accounts payable, Supervisor of four other accountants
                                                        Salary: $8400 per year

1971-72   Accountant   SuperTen Groceries, Fort Worth, Texas
                                                        Duties: Supervisor of all accounts under $10,000, Supervisor of two other accountants
                                                        Salary: $425 per month

1970-71   Assistant Accountant   SuperTen Groceries, Fort Worth, Texas
                                                        Duties: Routine Account Billing
                                                        Salary: $350 per month

Figure 17

ence should be your minister, your family doctor, or your family lawyer, someone who knows you well enough and who has enough experience in working with people to be able to make a reliable evaluation of your character.

For a credit reference you can name the bank where you have a savings or checking account or the name of some company where you have a charge account or a credit card. Your credit reference is important. Your prospective boss wants to know that you know how to manage your financial affairs and that you aren't going to have to take time away from your work to entertain your creditors.

If you have had job experience, list one or two employers as references. If you have only recently finished your vocational education, you should also list one of your instructors, preferably one in your major field who knows your scholastic ability and preparation. Include the complete name, job title, and address of each reference. Your list of references may be arranged as in Figure 18.

REFERENCES

Personal character
    The Reverend John T. Leggett, Minister, Southside Baptist
    Church, 2715 Ridglett Avenue, Fort Worth, Texas 76116

Credit
    Mr. Lawrence Billups, Vice-president, Neighborhood State Bank,
    P.O. Box 1741, Fort Worth, Texas 76116

Vocational
    Mr. Robert Jenkins, Manager, SuperTen Groceries,
    3415 Plain Tree Road, Fort Worth, Texas 76115

    Mr. William Heil, Chief Accountant, SuperTen Groceries,
    3415 Plain Tree Road, Fort Worth, Texas 76115

    Mr. Adolph Jenkins, Chairman, Department of Business Adminis-
    tration, Tarrant County Junior College, Fort Worth, Texas 76119

Figure 18

SHOULD YOU SEND A PICTURE?

Many companies ask that the applicant include a photograph. Doing so may help you to secure an interview. Application pictures should be small, should have been recently taken, and should show you dressed appropriately. If you enclose a photograph, fasten it with a paper clip or staple to the upper right-hand corner of your vita sheet.

HOW DO YOU WRITE THE APPLICATION LETTER?

Now that you have organized your thinking enough to make a vita sheet, you are ready to write your letter of application. Although in making your vita sheet you have been concentrating upon yourself and your abilities, you should have been doing so with an eye toward the job which you want. Your letter should be prepared with even closer attention to the desired job and the needs and attitudes of your prospective employer.

First keep in mind that he is a busy man. Do not waste his time. Get to the point of your letter immediately. The first paragraph of your letter should tell him that you are applying for a position, what position you desire, and where you heard about the job. A direct statement such as one of the following will serve the purpose of telling him what he needs to know and of getting you started in your letter:

> I am applying for the job of machine tester advertised in the *Times* yesterday.
>
> I am interested in the position of staff artist advertised in the *Daily Observer*.
>
> Mr. Hiram Freed, placement director of Hilltop Business College, has recommended your company as one with excellent opportunities to rise in the field of transportation management. I would like to apply for a position as manager trainee.
>
> Please consider me an applicant for the position of receptionist advertised in today's *Journal*.
>
> I believe my qualifications for a position as a medical secretary will interest you, and I would like to come in for an interview.
>
> I understand from my friend Mr. Ronald Cummings that you have a position open for a salesman in your furniture store. I would like to tell you why I think I have the qualifications which you need.

The second paragraph of your letter should tell the employer why you are a desirable candidate for the position. You should attempt to show that you have an understanding of the requirements for success in the job and that you, by training or experience, are prepared to meet those requirements. These examples should give you an idea of how you might write your second paragraph.

> A summary of my qualifications is enclosed. My training at the

Mercy Hospital School of Medical Technology was comprehensive and thorough. Because I was particularly interested in radiographic procedures, I not only took the regular course but also helped my instructor after classes on a special research problem in which he was engaged. Since your x-ray department is particularly well equipped for radiographic procedures, I am especially interested in working at your laboratory.

At Bosworth Business College, where I took the medical secretary course, I consistently placed in the upper third of my class. Besides the classes in the usual courses, I also took classes in advanced accounting and business psychology. Because I took advanced courses in English and journalism in high school, I am proficient in composition and can compose letters as they are needed for collection and referral purposes. I can type 75 words per minute and take dictation in shorthand at 115 words per minute.

Although I have had no direct experience in furniture saleswork, I am especially interested in working in that area. Saleswork, however, is not new to me. Last winter I worked at the Free Stride Shoe Emporium and this spring I was hostess at the display houses for the Safe Way Construction Company. I majored in home economics, and last summer I took some courses in interior decorating at the L. E. Gant School of Design. My discussions with Mr. Booker Shelby from your Main Street store about the many interesting areas of the furniture business have convinced me that it is a business that I would enjoy.

The employer is not interested in your need for a job; so don't take his time with a discussion of your financial problems or other difficulties. He will hire you not because you need the job but because he needs a worker and you seem to be the best-qualified applicant. Starting a new employee in a job costs the employer money. Someone must take time away from other work to teach the new worker, and he will work more slowly at first and make more mistakes than one who has been on the job awhile. Therefore, the employer will feel he is taking a smaller risk in hiring you if you can sincerely assure him that you are willing to learn and that you are genuinely interested in the job. Although you should not claim to have had more experience than you have had, you should not call unnecessary attention to your lack of experience. You might say something like the following:

> Although many of the procedures and routines will be new to me, I shall work hard to learn my job as quickly and as well as I can.
>
> I realize the importance of accuracy and attention to detail required in such a job, and I assure you that I shall do my best to do careful work at all times.
>
> In spite of my inexperience I believe I can perform acceptably in this

position. I learn quickly, remember what I learn, and enjoy the challenge of a difficult task.

The employer will not, of course, make a final decision on the basis of your letter alone. He will want to form a final estimation of your ability only after a personal interview. The last paragraph of your letter should ask that you be allowed such an interview. You should tell him when you can come in and how he can reach you, or you can state that you will call his secretary for an appointment.

> I shall be glad to come in for an interview at your convenience. I am available after 3:30 Monday through Friday and any time on Saturday. You can reach me to arrange an appointment by calling me at my home, 281-6633, or by writing me at the above address.
>
> If you are interested in my qualifications, I should like to come in for an interview. I shall call your secretary next Tuesday morning to arrange a time convenient to you.

Place your letter and vita sheet in a plain, unprinted, matching envelope of good quality paper. Include your return address in the upper left hand corner of the envelope. Follow the same neat and conventional style that you used in your letter and vita sheet.

Robert Smith's application letter will look like Figure 19 when he is through. Figure 20 is Robert Smith's completed vita sheet.

Perhaps your vita sheet will not be so long as Robert Smith's. If you are making application for your first important job, your letter and vita sheet might look more like Figures 21 and 22.

WHAT OTHER LETTERS MIGHT YOU NEED TO WRITE TO YOUR PROSPECTIVE EMPLOYER?

Other letters may be required in connection with your application. If a decision is not to be made soon by the employer, you may want to write a letter in order to keep him aware that you are still interested in the position. A letter thanking him for the interview and reminding him of some of the things you talked about is good strategy. If you are offered a position by mail, if the firm is out of town, or if you will not be reporting for work immediately, you should make your acceptance in writing. Remember that in some cases this letter might serve as a legal contract of employment. You should state briefly such terms of employment as salary and beginning date of work. If you decide not to accept such a job, write a courteous letter, giving solid, justifiable reasons for declining.

Figure 23 is an example of the letter you might write after you have been interviewed for a job.

The Job Application Letter

315 Pierce Drive
Fort Worth, Texas 76119
April 15, 1974

Mr. Ralph B. Dennis, Manager
Cler-Perk Coffee Company
5421 Terner Road
Houston, Texas 77027

Dear Mr. Dennis:

    I am applying for the position of chief accountant advertised in the April 13, 1974, Houston <u>Chronicle</u>. I believe that my qualifications and experience will interest you.

    You will notice from my attached vita sheet that I am employed as accountant at Wholesale Grocer Supply in Irving, Texas. I am quite happy with my present job, and I wish to move only because I am attracted to the Houston area, which was for several years my home. My three years of work as an accountant for two grocery supply houses have made me aware of many of the merchandizing and accounting problems that I am certain are shared by a speciality supply house. Supervision of other accountants for the last three years should also qualify me for the position of chief accountant, in which, I understand, I would be in charge of about ten accountants and the entire accounting department of your company.

    If you contact the references listed on the vita sheet, I believe that you will find that I have the ability to work well with others and the capacity to adjust easily to new procedures -- both personal qualities which I assume are demanded of a chief accountant. I am particularly challenged by the idea of helping your firm make the transition to a data processing system of accounting.

    If you wish to contact me, please call me at (817) - 534-4455. I am willing to come to Houston for a personal interview at a time most convenient to you. Thank you for your time and consideration.

                                        Sincerely yours,

                                        Robert S. Smith

Figure 19

DATA SHEET

PERSONAL

Name: Robert S. Smith   Height: 5'11"
Age: 22   Weight: 178
Sex: Male   Health: Good
Marital Status: Married, one child   Address: 315 Pierce Drive
Military Status: II-S   Fort Worth,
                                                   Texas 76119
                                        Telephone: (817)534-4455

EDUCATIONAL BACKGROUND

Associate in Applied Science Degree, 1974
    Tarrant County Junior College, Fort Worth, Texas
    Major: Business Administration
        Special courses: Income Tax Accounting, Seminar
        in Management Problems

High School diploma, 1970
    Paschal High School, Fort Worth, Texas
    Honors: National Honor Society - 1970
        Letter in Basketball - 1970
    Extracurricular activities:
        Eagle Scout - 1968
        Southside Baptist softball team - 1968

VOCATIONAL EXPERIENCE

1973-Present   Accountant   Wholesale Grocer Supply,
                                     Irving, Texas
                                       Duties: Supervisor of Ac-
                                         counts Payable, Supervisor
                                         of four other accountants
                                       Salary: $8400 per year

1971-72   Accountant   SuperTen Groceries, Fort Worth,
                                     Texas
                                       Duties: Supervisor of all
                                         accounts under $10,000, Su-
                                         pervisor of two other ac-
                                         countants
                                       Salary: $425 per month

1970-71   Assistant Accountant SuperTen Groceries, Fort Worth,
                                     Texas
                                       Duties: Routine Account
                                         Billing
                                       Salary: $350 per month

REFERENCES

Personal character
    The Reverend John T. Leggett, Minister, Southside Baptist
    Church, 2715 Ridglett Avenue, Fort Worth, Texas 76116

Credit
    Mr. Lawrence Billups, Vice-president, Neighborhood State Bank,
    P.O. Box 1741, Fort Worth, Texas 76116

Vocational
    Mr. Robert Jenkins, Manager, SuperTen Groceries,
    3415 Plain Tree Road, Fort Worth, Texas 76115

      Mr. William Heil, Chief Accountant, SuperTen Groceries,
      3415 Plain Tree Road, Fort Worth, Texas 76115

      Mr. Adolph Jenkins, Chairman, Department of Business Admin-
      istration, Tarrant County Junior College, Fort Worth, Texas 76119

Figure 20

The Job Application Letter

```
                                    3417 Penhelm Drive
                                    Fort Worth, Texas  76116
                                    April 15, 1974
```

Mrs. Alice Ward, Manager
Slim-Jean Dress Shoppe
4415 Letts Avenue
Fort Worth, Texas 76109

Dear Mrs. Ward:

    Please consider my application for the position of sales clerk that you have advertised on the college bulletin board.

    I am now finishing my freshman year at Tarrant County Junior College where I am enrolled in the mid-management curriculum. In high school I had two years of home economics, and in my second year one of my dress designs won first-place awards at our annual style show. During this year I have learned much about meeting the public and running a small business.

    The people listed for reference on the enclosed data sheet will tell you that I am dependable and honest. You will find also that I am always well-dressed and personable.

    If you are interested in talking with me, I would be happy to visit with you any afternoon. Please call me at my home, 738-9191.

```
                                    Sincerely yours,

                                    Ann Moore
```

Figure 21

VITA SHEET

PERSONAL

Name:	Ann Moore	Weight:	121
Age:	19	Health:	Good
Sex:	Female	Address:	3417 Penhelm Drive
Marital Status:	Single		Forth Worth, Texas 76116
Height:	5'4"	Telephone:	738-9191

EDUCATIONAL BACKGROUND

Freshman at Tarrant County Junior College, 1973-74
        Major: Mid-Management
            Special Courses: Advanced Typing, Accounting,
                Applied Communications

High School Diploma, Polytechnic High School, 1973
        Honors: Senior class secretary

VOCATIONAL EXPERIENCE

        I have held no full-time jobs, but during this year I have worked part-time as an assistant in the Registrar's Office.

REFERENCES

    Personal character
      The Reverend Ralph Gunter, Minister, Piedmont Methodist Church, 8495 North Gale, Fort Worth, Texas 76116

    Vocational
      Mr. Alfred Roy, Registrar, Tarrant County Junior College, Fort Worth, Texas 76119

      Mr. Raymond Blount, Professor of Mid-Management, Tarrant County Junior College, Fort Worth, Texas 76119

Figure 22

```
                              315 Pierce Drive
                              Fort Worth, Texas 76119
                              April 25, 1974


Mr. Ralph B. Dennis, Manager
Cler-Perk Coffee Company
5421 Terner Road
Houston, Texas 77027

Dear Mr. Dennis:

    I wish to thank you for the opportunity of seeing you last
Monday. Everyone in your firm seemed so pleasant and kind that
I look forward with greater anticipation to the possibility of
working there.

    At your request, I have talked with Mr. Frank Bobsey, my
present supervisor. He said that I could leave my position here
within a week after I have given him notice rather than after the
normally required two weeks. Therefore I could come to work for
you more quickly than we originally thought possible.

    I hope that by this time you have had some response from my
other references, and I look forward to some early word from you.

                              Sincerely yours,

                              Robert S. Smith
                              Robert S. Smith
```

Figure 23

To accept a position, you might write a letter somewhat like Figure 24.

If you cannot accept a position, a letter such as Figure 25 is appropriate.

SHOULD YOU ASK PERMISSION TO NAME A PERSON AS A REFERENCE?

Answering inquiries about you from a prospective employer takes time. Consequently, you should ask the individuals whom you would like to name as references if they would mind your doing so. Not only is it courteous to give them the opportunity to refuse if they do not have time,

Should You Ask Permission to Name a Person as a Reference?

<pre>
                                   315 Pierce Drive
                                   Fort Worth, Texas   76119
                                   April 28, 1974
</pre>

Mr. Ralph B. Dennis, Manager
Cler-Perk Coffee Company
5421 Terner Road
Houston, Texas 77027

Dear Mr. Dennis:

    I am pleased to accept the position that you offer me of chief accountant. According to the terms set forth in your letter, I will report to work May 13, 1974, and my monthly salary will be set at $875 per month.

    This new position offers me a definite challenge and an excellent opportunity. I hope that I shall be able to perform according to your expectations.

    My wife and I shall move to Houston the week of May 6-10. I will call the office sometime during that week to see if there are any other instructions which I might need before reporting to work.

<pre>
                                   Sincerely yours,

                                   Robert S. Smith
                                   Robert S. Smith
</pre>

Figure 24

but also you may save yourself the disadvantage of receiving a poor recommendation. If possible, telephone for such permission or ask the individual in person. Sometimes a former employer or teacher who should logically be consulted for information concerning your ability lives at some distance. To get his permission to name him as a reference, you will want to write a letter. Sometimes you may not have time to write him for permission to refer a prospective employer to him and then to wait for his answer. Moreover, if he has to write you a letter giving you permission to name him as a reference and then he has to write another letter to answer the inquiry, he will have to spend twice as much time for you. Under these circumstances be guided by your knowledge of the individual, the situation, and the urgency of your need. If you can, telephone to ask permission to name him as a reference.

    Whether you telephone or write for such permission, the person can give a more helpful and favorable recommendation if you give him cer-

315 Pierce Drive
Fort Worth, Texas 76119
April 28, 1974

Mr. Ralph B. Dennis, Manager
Cler-Perk Coffee Company
5421 Terner Road
Houston, Texas 77027

Dear Mr. Dennis:

    I am sorry that I cannot accept the position of chief accountant with your company which you have offered me. The terms which you specified in your contract letter were especially attractive, and the challenges of the job were certainly inviting.

    My present employer, Wholesale Grocer Supply, has made me an offer that permits me to finish my education, and I feel that I must not pass up such an opportunity. I will be given a two-year leave of absence, and the company will help me with some of my educational expenses.

    I do want to thank you for the time which you have personally given to my application. You were extremely helpful to me, and I looked forward to working with you.

                                                          Sincerely yours,

                                                           Robert S. Smith

Figure 25

tain information. Tell him something about the job you are trying to get, why you want that job in particular, and why you think you will do well in it. This information will allow him to focus on those qualities of yours which he has observed that will be especially important in this job. If you have not seen this person in some time, you may make it easier for him to write a recommendation if you bring him up to date on your vocational or educational activities. After you have been hired, you should write a letter of appreciation to anyone who helped you get the job.

    A letter similar to Figure 26 is appropriate if you must write to ask someone's permission to name him as a reference.

    Figure 27 is an example of one you would write to thank someone for his recommendation.

315 Pierce Drive
Fort Worth, Texas   76119
April 10, 1974

Mr. Robert Jenkins, Manager
SuperTen Groceries
3415 Plain Tree Road
Fort Worth, Texas   76115

Dear Mr. Jenkins,

    I am currently making application for a position as chief accountant of the Cler-Perk Coffee Company in Houston. Would you please permit me to name you as a reference?

    The position which I seek will involve direct supervision of several accountants, but the major task will be to update and program the entire accounting system for the company. You recall that when I worked for you, I supervised two other accountants and had direct responsibility for all of your accounts under $10,000. I feel that the experience I gained from that job will be a definite asset to me should I obtain this new position.

    I hope that you will not mind my naming you as a professional reference. If I do not hear from you to the contrary, I shall submit your name and address to Mr. Ralph Dennis, manager of the Houston company. If you prefer that I do not give him your name, please call me at 534-4455.

                                                Sincerely yours,

                                               Robert S. Smith

Figure 26

The Job Application Letter

> 315 Pierce Drive
> Fort Worth, Texas 76119
> April 28, 1974
>
> Mr. Robert Jenkins, Manager
> SuperTen Groceries
> 3415 Plain Tree Road
> Fort Worth, Texas 76115
>
> Dear Mr. Jenkins,
>
>   I wish to thank you for recommending me to Mr. Ralph Dennis. I have just received word that I am to begin work May 13 in the position for which I applied.
>
>   Mr. Dennis mentioned that you had given me an exceptionally good recommendation and that I was given the position largely upon that recommendation. You were generous to take the time from your busy schedule to write a letter for me. I hope that I am able to live up to the recommendation which you submitted. Thank you again for your time and personal attention.
>
>   Sincerely yours,
>
>   Robert S. Smith

Figure 27

ASSIGNMENTS

I. You should begin now to learn as much as possible about your chosen occupational area by talking to persons working in such jobs and by reading books, periodical articles, and pamphlets. However, you must be careful. Remember that the people you talk to may be seriously biased either for or against a job or an employer, and that promotional literature always presents an overly optimistic picture. Assume that you have narrowed your job possibility to one specific kind of work and even perhaps to one specific company. Answer the following questions:

1. What is the demand for employees in this area? How many were hired in your city last year?
2. What are the minimum and maximum age limits?
3. Will you be asked to join a union?
4. What are the opportunities for promotion? How long will you work before you will be considered for promotion?

Assignments

5. What is the average age of the persons now employed?
6. What is the average salary of the persons now employed?
7. What is the top salary paid at the level that most appeals to you?
8. What kind of insurance program is available? How much would it cost for you and your dependents?
9. What kind of retirement program is available? How much will it cost per month? When will it begin payment?
10. Are there any physical hazards closely connected with the work?
11. What is the policy for sick leave? How many sick days are you granted per year?
12. Do you get an annual paid vacation? How long?
13. Will you be expected to furnish any of your own supplies or tools? How much will this cost?
14. Will you be expected to wear a specified uniform or to dress according to a certain standard? How much will you have to spend to buy these clothes?

II. Following these assignments is a set of four letters written in application for the same position. Each letter has errors both in mechanics and content. Read each letter carefully and then use a chart somewhat similar to that on page 84 to indicate errors.

III. The following assignments are to be done under the assumption that you are applying for a real job in your professional area. You will increase your interest in the project by finding a suitable job opening and directing your letters toward that specific project.
1. Find three advertised job openings in your area of interest. If possible clip the advertisements from the paper and staple them to a fact sheet to bring to class. Which job offers the best pay? Which one has a comment about fringe benefits? Which one is in the best geographic location for your immediate needs? Arrange the three available positions in first, second, and third choice positions and be able to justify your preference.
2. Prepare a formal vita sheet, including listings for personal information, education, work experience, and references. Type the material neatly. Be certain to include all information that might help you secure the job.
3. Write a letter of application for the job that most interests you. Be specific and direct in your comments.
4. Write a brief note to one person whom you would like to name as a reference in your vita sheet. Advise him of your wish and ask his permission.
5. Assume that you have been hired by your desired employer. Write a brief letter of acceptance. Remember that in some cases this letter might serve as a legal contract of employment. You should briefly state such terms of employment as salary and beginning date of contract.

Letter _____ (indicate by alphabetical reference)

Errors in Mechanics
(For each error, list the line number and identify the specific mechanical error; then show how the error should be corrected.)

Errors in Content
(Indicate material that should be included but is not present. Indicate also any unnecessary material present in the letter.)

Errors in Organization
(Indicate any errors in organization within the letter. Do all of the paragraphs perform their intended function?)

315 Pierce Drive
Forth Worth, Texas
April 15, 1974

Mr. Ralph B. Dennis
Cler-Perk Coffee Company
5421 Terner Road
Houston, Texas   77027

Dear Mr. Dennis:

    I hear that you are looking for a new chief-accountant and I would like to apply for that job.

    I am working now at the Wholesale Grocer Supply in Irving, Texas, but would like to move because I like Houston.

    I have had five years of experience as an accountant and if you think you might be interested in me I can give you some references.

                         Sincerely yours,

                           Robert S. Smith

Letter A

315 Pierce Drive
Fort Worth, Texas   76119
April 15, 1974

Mr. Ralph B. Dennis
Cler-Perk Coffee Company
5421 Terner Rd.
Houston, Texas

Dear Sir:

    I understand that you have a position open for a new chief-accountant. Let me apply for that job.

    For five years I have worked with grocery supply houses, and I doubt that you could find anyone who is better qualified than me to do your work. I would be an honest, faithful worker. I have not been sick but three days in the last five years; so I would not lose time because of illness.

    My salery at the present time is $6400 per year. Please send me your salery list so I can see what you would pay.

    Also, what insurance company do you use for your employees?

    If you want me to, I will come to Houston next Friday to meet you and talk about the job.

                                   Sincerely yours,

                                   Robert S. Smith

Letter B

315 Pierce Drive
Fort Worth, Texas 76119
April 15, 1974

Ralph B. Dennis, Manager
Cler-Perk Coffee Co.
5421 Terner Rd.
Houston, Texas 77027

Dear Mr. Ralph Dennis:

    You need a new chief-accountant, and I am the man who you are looking for. I have been working in this kind of job for five years and know all about it. My boss here thinks I am the best accountant that he has ever had -- he told me so last week.

    The only reason I want to move is that Houston is my home. I went to school there before my family moved to Fort Worth, but I have always liked Houston the best. I would like to buy a home on the southeast side of town and settle down. My wife and I have saved a little money to use for a down payment for the home and we think that we could move to Houston and live if I could make a little more than I'm making now. I'm making $8400.

    I went to high school in Fort Worth and took an accounting course at a school in Dallas then I went to junior college two years. You can see I am qualified.

    If you are interested, call me and I will give you a list of people who will tell you about me.

                               Sincerely yours,

                               Robert S. Smith

Letter C

315 Pierce Drive
Fort Worth, Texas   76119
April 15, 1974

Mr. Ralph B. Dennis, Manager
Cler-Perk Coffee Co.
5421 Terner Rd.
Houston, Texas   77027

Dear Mr. Dennis:

    I would like to apply for the position of Chief-Accountant which you have advertised. You will find that I am a dependable, reliable worker.

    I have had five years of experience in grocery supply houses and feel that I know much about the accounting problems involved. I now boss other accountants and get along okay with them.

    The reason I want to move is that I like Houston so much and would like to live there.

    To learn more about you can write to Mr. Frank Bobsey, Personnel Manager, Wholesale Grocer Supply, Box 317, Irving, Texas; Mr. William Heil, Chief-Accountant, SuperTen Groceries, 3415 Plain Tree Rd., Fort Worth, Texas; or Rev. John T. Leggett, St. Paul's Methodist Church, 2894 Ridglett Ave., Fort Worth, Texas.

    I would come to Houston to visit with you if you are interested. My telephone number is 534-4455. I hope to hear from you before very long.

                                    Sincerely yours,

                                    Robert S. Smith

Letter D

SIX / The Employment Interview

WHY IS THE EMPLOYMENT INTERVIEW IMPORTANT?

An employer may receive dozens or even hundreds of applications to fill a particular vacancy. If so, he typically sorts through the application letters and vitas to isolate a small number of applicants who appear to have "paper qualifications." He then invites these individuals to an interview so he can personally determine if they are as good as they appear to be on paper.

The person conducting the interview may be the company owner, a personnel director, or a member of management; but he is trained to find out much about you in a relatively short time. Chances are that you do have the essential teachable skills that he wants; now he is examining to see if you have the sense of responsibility, degree of maturity, or whatever other personality traits he may think necessary.

You are at the interview to sell yourself, at least an image of yourself, to the potential employer. You should decide ahead of time just what your good points are and then be certain to talk about them during the interview. Do not just sit there and answer questions. Ask questions too. Appear interested in the job and the company. Obviously you can do much before the interview to prepare yourself to answer anticipated questions and to phrase intelligent questions of your own.

HOW DO YOU PREPARE FOR AN EMPLOYMENT INTERVIEW?

You cannot know what qualities will be important to the employer unless you know something about his company. You should find out all you can about the company's history, size, policies, and product. Some of these things you can learn from your Chamber of Commerce or the local chapter of your union. Your library will probably have some of the excellent reference books on American industries.[1] From employees of the company you can learn about working conditions, compensation, treatment of employees, and opportunities for promotion.

You will also want to learn as much as you can about the man who is going to interview you so that you can present the information about yourself in the best light. If he is a college-trained man, he will be more interested in your educational background. If he learned his skills on the job, he will be less interested in your education than in your actual experience. If he is a technical man, he will talk the language of a technical man and will expect you to be prepared to establish your technical qualifications and to show that you understand the technical angles of the job. If you and he have any background or experience in common, particularly vocational or educational experience, you can use this fact to establish common ground on which to begin the interview. If you know that he holds high standards for workmanship and you hold similar standards, you can find some opportunity in the interview to emphasize your standards. To find out as much as you can about this man, you can ask employees of the company. If your local newspaper office keeps an index to back issues and your prospective employer is prominent in the community, you may find some information there. Your librarian may also be able to help.[2]

[1] *Thomas' Register of American Manufacturers* (New York: Thomas Publishing Co.). Lists manufacturers alphabetically by product and trade name.

Moody's Industrial Manual (New York: Moody's Investors Service). Lists 4,400 companies and their subsidiaries; describes operations, lists officers, products, size of company, and other data.

MacRae's Blue Book (Chicago: MacRae's Blue Book Co., issued annually). Classifies 40,000 manufacturers by type of product and trade names.

Industrial Research Laboratories of the United States, National Research Council (Washington, D.C.: National Academy of Science). Descriptive listing of nearly 3,000 laboratories, indicating personnel and outlining research activities and resources. Includes subject and geographic indexes.

Sources of Information on American Firms (Washington, D.C.: U.S. Department of Commerce). Describes local sources, mentions business guides, gives addresses.

[2] Two books that may be helpful are:

Poor's Register of Directors and Executives (New York: Standard & Poor's Corp., issued annually). Classifies over 26,000 American and Canadian firms by industry and products, gives officers and number of employees, includes brief descriptions of about 75,000 executives and company directors.

Directory of National Associations of Businessmen. Lists over 2,000 national associations, giving number of members, size of staff, name and title of chief executive, and mailing address.

WHAT INFORMATION SHOULD YOU BE PREPARED TO GIVE AT THE INTERVIEW?

Whether he asks you the question or not, your prospective employer will want to know why you want the job for which you are applying. He may think you will adjust to the job more quickly, work better, and stay satisfied longer if you take the job for some special reason than if you will merely accept any job you can get. Moreover, you will seem to be a more desirable job candidate if you can afford to look for a particular job. You will do your best work, enjoy your job more, and satisfy your employer better if your particular abilities and aptitudes match the requirements of the job. Analyze your personal and professional qualifications and decide why this job is the one you want and why you are especially well qualified to hold it. Then be prepared to convince the interviewer.

Of course, you don't want to appear conceited. But facts are facts. If you can type seventy-five words a minute with a minimum of errors, you would be lying to claim a poorer speed; and if you neglect to mention your typing speed at all, you may be omitting information the interviewer needs. If you have had experience that should prove valuable in this job, that experience is a fact that the interviewer won't know if you don't tell him. If you honestly know that you have the ability to put people at ease and to deal with them tactfully, that ability is also a fact and one that you should mention.

SHOULD YOU APPLY FOR A DEFINITE JOB?

Obviously, since it is important to convince the interviewer that you are especially well qualified for one particular job, you should not tell him that you are looking for just "anything." Nobody is exactly suited to do "anything." If you really don't know exactly what kind of work the employer has available, describe your qualifications for the two or three jobs you think you can do well.

Sometimes after hearing you outline your capabilities, the employer may decide you are better qualified for a different job than the one you have in mind. He may be right. On the other hand, he may be describing the second job to test you, to see if you will change your analysis of yourself to prove that you are just the person for this second job as well. The only insurance you have against such a trick is your own sincerity. If you have made an honest self-analysis in the beginning, you will not misrepresent yourself to get either the first job or the job described as a test. Remember, if you get the job, you have to work at it. If you are not really suited for it, you will not be happy in it. You may have heard stories about people who bluffed their way into jobs for which they were not prepared but in which they made good, but you do not hear about the nerve-racking days they spent while they were learning the job and covering up their ignorance. Nor do you hear about the bluffers who do not make good, or who succeed in their work but are unhappy because they are not psychologically fitted for the job.

WHAT SHOULD YOU SAY ABOUT YOUR PAST JOBS?

Your prospective employer will want to know why you left other jobs you have held. You can volunteer the information or you can wait for him to ask you. If you wait to be asked, he may get the impression that you lost the jobs for some reason you would rather not mention. Don't wait. Give a complete history of your work experience, job by job, including your reasons for leaving each one. Since you are probably not perfect, you may have left some of these jobs for reasons that are not flattering to you. Don't criticize your past employers or try to place the blame on others. The interviewer knows that complaining workers do not change their habits with their jobs. He probably has enough gripers on his payroll already and is not looking for more. If you were wrong and deserved to lose your job, admit it and explain what you have learned from the experience. Everyone makes mistakes, but not everyone learns from them.

Have the facts and dates of your past employment memorized and ready to give as you discuss your experience. You may have sent these facts to your prospective employer already, so he probably has them before him as he questions you. He will notice any discrepancies between what you wrote on your vita sheet and what you say. There is no need to lie about your age or any of the periods of time involved in describing your past experiences. Most interviewers can put two and two together often, quickly, and accurately enough to estimate the actual facts.

WHAT SHOULD YOU DO ABOUT YOUR WEAK POINTS?

If you were honest in the self-evaluation that was part of your preparation for the job interview, you discovered that there are weak spots in your experience and ability. You hope that your prospective employer will not also discover these weaknesses, but discovering them is one of his purposes for interviewing you. As you answer his questions, he will seek to uncover these defects and estimate how they might cause you to fail if he employed you. In your preparation for the interview you should consider your weaknesses carefully so that you can concentrate on your strong points and make your weak points seem slight in comparison.

WHAT SHOULD YOU SAY IF YOU ARE ASKED HOW MUCH PAY YOU EXPECT?

If the prospective employer asks you what salary you expect to make, don't be disturbed. Neither should you hedge while you try to find out what salary he has in mind. You may try to avoid giving a definite answer for fear that if you ask too much you may miss the job and if you ask too little you may work for less. But don't let the question surprise you. Before you report for the interview, do some investigating. Find out what a person with your background of experience and education usually makes in your field and what salary can be expected for such a job as this. If you have some unusual abilities that deserve more compensation, evaluate them also. Then when you are asked the question, you will be prepared with a reasonable, justifiable answer. If you really prefer not to answer this question by naming the salary you expect, you might say something like the following:

> I am not as interested in my starting pay, Mr. Matthews, as I am in the chance to show you my real ability. I will start at whatever pay you think is fair if you agree that as soon as you judge my value to you, you will pay me what I am really worth.

But whatever you answer, show your prospective employer that what you ask is based upon your honest evaluation of your potential as an employee.

HOW MUCH INITIATIVE SHOULD YOU TAKE IN THE INTERVIEW?

It is clear that if you are going to present your story in the most favorable light, you will have to tell that story without waiting for the interviewer to drag the facts out of you answer by answer. Moreover, your prospective employer will be favorably impressed by your ability to communicate readily and well. Speak with assurance. Be alert and interested. Of course, you should not be too talkative. Don't talk just to keep the interviewer from having time to ask questions. Make a brief but complete statement of your qualifications, your background, and your interest in this job. Then answer whatever questions the interviewer puts to you in a confident, businesslike way.

If, after you have told your story, the interviewer seems to be unable to think of any questions to ask you, you may have failed to make any definite impression on him. Tell him something about yourself and your background. You may thus stimulate some questions to which you can reply in a way that will make a favorable impression. Or you might ask him some questions that will lead into a discussion of the area in which your qualifications are strongest.

If the interviewer has a definite pattern to his questions, go along with him. But if you feel that he is leading the interview in a way that is unfavorable to you, you may be able to answer his questions in a way that will lead the discussion back into areas in which you are stronger. Be careful, however, not to make him think you are being evasive. If he thinks you are trying to steer him away from your weaknesses, he will become persistent in his efforts to uncover them.

HOW SHOULD YOU CONDUCT YOURSELF DURING THE INTERVIEW?

Throughout the interview be courteous and pleasant. Greet the interviewer with a pleasant "Good morning, Mr. Matthews," and tell him who you are and why you are there. Do not offer him your hand, but be prepared to shake hands if he offers you his. Stand erect and wait for an invitation to be seated. Take the chair he offers and sit erect but relaxed. Do not prop your knee against the desk or slouch in your chair. You don't want to appear lazy, bored, or in need of medical attention. Try to keep your hands folded calmly in your lap; but if you can't keep them still, put them out of sight. You may find it difficult to appear calm when your stomach is full of butterflies, but use your will power to do so. If you can give the appearance of confidence, the interviewer will give you credit for having more ability than he will if you look as though you are scared he will uncover some awful secret.

Although you want to appear confident, you don't want to seem cocky. There is a difference between productive aggressiveness and objectionable boldness. Look into the eyes of the interviewer as he talks to you and as you answer his questions. Do not interrupt him while he is talking, but do not refuse to answer when he asks you a question.

Even if the interviewer does not treat you courteously, you have nothing to gain by acting rudely. If you remain unruffled and respectful, he may calm down. He may even be testing your self-control, trying to find out how flexible you are in an unpleasant situation.

When the interview has come to its logical conclusion, get up and leave. Even if you have not been offered a job, remain pleasant and courteous. Thank the interviewer for his time and bid him "Good-bye." If you have not impressed him with anything else, you can impress him now with your self-control and good nature. You should not, however, shrug your shoulders as though failure to get a job was what you expected. Be just as positive and confident as you take your leave as you were when you made your entrance.

HOW SHOULD YOU DRESS FOR THE INTERVIEW?

Just as the package helps to sell the product, your appearance is important in selling yourself to your prospective employer. Moreover, you will feel more confident if you look your best. You should not appear for the interview dressed as though you were going to a party. A business suit is appropriate for a man. A woman should wear a suit, skirt and blouse, or a neat, tailored dress; walking shoes, hose; and where it is customary to do so, gloves and a hat. Your clothes need not be expensive, but they and you should be neat. Just as your prospective employer drew some conclusions about you from the appearance of your letter of application, he will draw further conclusions from your appearance. If the heels of your shoes are run over or your shoes need polishing; if your hair needs cutting, washing, or combing; if your face needs shaving or careful make-up; your nails need cleaning; or your clothes need pressing, he will probably decide that he does not wish to hire you.

WHAT DOES THE INTERVIEWER WANT TO KNOW ABOUT THAT HE DOES NOT ASK?

The answers to many of the questions the interviewer will ask you may already be in your application letter or vita sheet. Your answers to other questions that he asks may not seem relevant to you at all. But as your prospective employer listens to you, he will be hearing answers to questions that are in his mind but which he will not ask you. He will have questions about how you will fit into his organization. Will you get along with the other workers? Will you be a good team worker? Will you be loyal to the company and to your fellow workers? Will you be able to grow and advance in the organization? He will also reach some conclusions about your work habits. Are you alert and observant? Are you open-minded and flexible? Are you able to learn? Do you have common sense? Do you take a real interest in your work and a pride in good workmanship? Do you do your work promptly and thoroughly? Do you have initiative and enthusiasm? He will also listen for answers to his questions concerning your character and personality. Are you honest and trustworthy? Are you reasonably mature and well-adjusted? Are you able to control your emotions and your actions? In short, are you a person who will be an asset to his company?

How will he find the answers to these questions? He will find them as he examines the details of your personal appearance; as he observes the way you respond physically to the stress of the interview; and as he listens to you describe your past educational and vocational experience, your relationships with your past instructors, employers, and fellow workers, and your plans and hopes for future work.

WILL ANYONE ELSE GAIN IMPORTANT IMPRESSIONS OF YOU DURING YOUR INTERVIEW?

You will probably come in contact with several people employed by the company in connection with your interview. You may talk to the secretary of your prospective employer when you arrange for the interview, and you will certainly meet her in the outer office when you arrive for the interview. Other employees may enter the outer office while you wait or come into the office while the interviewer talks to you. He may show you about some area of the company and introduce you to some of the workers. Before they come to a decision about hiring an employee, many employers like to have someone else's opinion. So your prospective employer may ask his secretary what she thinks of you, or he may ask the opinion of someone he introduced you to, or even of someone you didn't even notice. Obviously then, you ought to treat everyone you meet with the same courteous respect and pleasantness as you treat your prospective employer. Some of them may have a very important influence on whether you get the job or not. And if you do get the job, the good impression you have made will be still more important because these people will be your fellow workers.

ASSIGNMENTS

1. You will be more relaxed during your interview if you have carefully planned some of your responses. Make a list of the most important facts which you might use in an interview. Include, for example, summary statements about

Assignments

your training, experience, and qualifications. What weak spots do you have that might affect your prospective employer's decision?

II. Your instructor may invite to class employers from the community who represent several occupational areas. These men will interview several members of the class in exactly the same manner that they would use in a legitimate interview. If you are one of these interviewed, put to use the ideas you have gained from this chapter. If you simply watch others being interviewed, be prepared after the interview is completed to discuss both the strengths and weaknesses the applicant demonstrated.

III. A good way to prepare for an interview is to think what types of questions you would ask if you were on the other side of the desk. Work with another student in your class and prepare a five-minute interview dramatization. Be realistic. If you are the interviewer, ask questions that seem really important. If you are the applicant, answer as seriously as you would at an actual interview.

SEVEN / Preparation of Memos and Short Reports

WHY DO YOU NEED TO KNOW HOW TO WRITE REPORTS?

Reports of all types—long and short, formal and informal, technical and general, handwritten and offset-printed—help to keep the business world turning. You can hardly think of a single job at which you would not be required to do some writing as a part of the job process. The doctor keeps his charts, the auditor summarizes his records, the mechanic presents a diagnostic report to the car owner and writes his own weekly activity report, and the sales clerk maintains a sales record.

Some of these reporting jobs are admittedly formulaic: the writer is given a prepared form and blanks to complete. But even many of these blanks require sentence and sometimes paragraph responses. You may need to prepare the minutes from a departmental committee meeting, write a memorandum to the shipping department, post a notice on the bulletin board, deliver a report on a meeting or convention you attended, dictate a letter containing your recommendation for the new salary scale, prepare a detailed cost breakdown on the proposed expansion of the sales office, or issue a progress report to your immediate superior. All this communication can be classified as report writing. Most reports will remain within the company; sometimes they will not leave your immediate department. But the fact that the public doesn't see a report doesn't mean that such intracompany communication isn't important. The smooth operation of your company or department will depend upon clear and accurate communication within your department and between your department and other departments. No longer is the average company so small and cozy that requests, recommendations, and reports can be passed on by word of mouth. They must be carefully worded, filled out on a prescribed form, recorded in triplicate, stamped and approved by someone in the various offices through which they pass, and stored safely in the sanctity of some official's filing cabinet. Modern businesses are so large that the chain of command through which an employee report must pass may be very complicated.

When thousands of dollars are at stake, a company cannot afford to act on the basis of vague verbal reports and hurriedly jotted notes. The expert who has been asked to record the present state of his department or his recommendations for the new year has applied all his professional knowledge to the gathering of accurate information. The ability to communicate his findings with appropriate accuracy and clarity is just as important as the ability to gather accurate information. Somebody will read his report and base a decision on it. That somebody can understand that report and decide wisely only if that report is written well. Yet according to a survey made recently among prominent American organizations, the handicap that keeps most industrial engineers from advancing is their failure to communicate their ideas effectively. And there is no reason to suppose that engineers have more communication difficulties than members of other professions.

WHAT FORM IS USED FOR THE COMMUNICATION OF INFORMATION?

Your communication of information will normally take the form of a report. Reports fall roughly into two kinds: informal and formal. Both kinds of reports contain the same basic parts, and the chief difference between them is length. The informal report may be only a paragraph long or it may be as long as two pages. Anything much longer is considered a formal report.

WHAT IS A MEMORANDUM?

A common type of informal report is the memorandum or memo. Each company has its own memo style and many have printed memo forms. All memos contain four essential items of information, normally given in the heading of the form: (1) the date; (2) the name of the person to receive the memo, referred to here as the addressee; (3) the sender; and (4) the subject of the memo. Figure 28 is an example of typical memo headings:

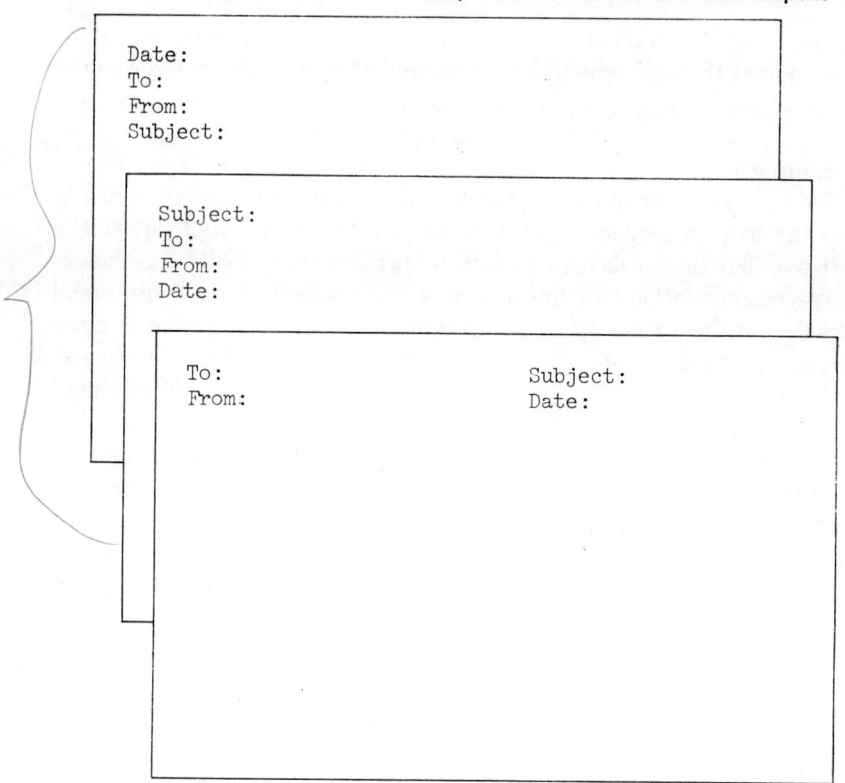

```
        Date:
        To:
        From:
        Subject:

            Subject:
            To:
            From:
            Date:

                To:              Subject:
                From:            Date:
```

Figure 28

Figure 29 is a typical memorandum:

```
                        Memorandum

Date:      October 18, 1970
To:        Joe B. Bush
From:      Al J. Clark
Subject:   Purchase order #1332

    Three items were omitted on the first order: AX 20485, AX 21120,
and B2 1158. Please have a new order made out including these items.
Get the signature of the department foreman, and have the order on
my desk to be signed for a rush order by Wednesday.
```

Figure 29

Such a form may be filled in on the typewriter, or it may be handwritten. It may be sent to another employee by special messenger, carried through interoffice mail, or posted on a departmental bulletin board. If the memorandum is important enough and contains information needed by a number of employees, it may be mimeographed and sent to each one. A memorandum may be destroyed as soon as it has served its purpose, or it may be filed for future reference.

WHAT ARE THE MOST COMMON KINDS OF REPORTS NOT MADE ON A PRINTED FORM?

Letters, which of course use standard business letter form, and handwritten notes are also common kinds of informal reports. Although they are not written on a printed form with labels for the four essential pieces of information, that information is still included. Examine the short handwritten note in Figure 30 to see how closely it resembles the memorandum in Figure 29.

```
(Date)                                    Oct. 18, 1970
(Addressee)    Joe,
(Subject)      About that purchase #1332 for Oct. 15,
               items AX20485, AX2110, and BB21158
               were left out. Please include them
               on a new order, get Jake to
               sign it, and leave it on my
               desk so I can sign it and
               mail it Wed.
                                          Thanks
(Sender)                                    Al
```

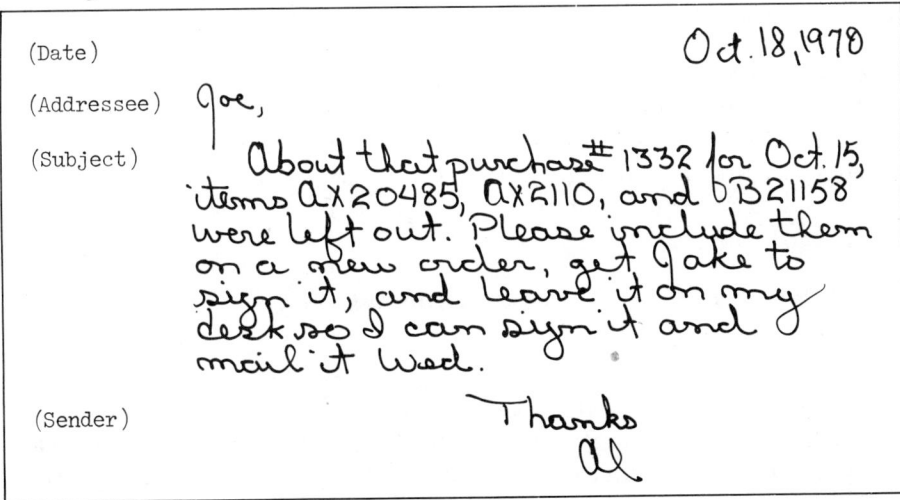

Figure 30

WHAT ARE THE MAIN PARTS OF THE MESSAGE OF THE REPORT?

Although the message carried by reports is brief, each contains some of the basic parts of all reports: introduction, summary, body, conclusions, recommendations, and appendix. Notice how the contents of this brief note break down into three of these parts:

INTRODUCTION	About that purchase #1332 for Oct. 15.
BODY	Items AX 20485, AX 21120, and B2 1158 were left out.
RECOMMENDATIONS	Please include them on a new order, get Jake to sign it, and leave it on my desk so I can sign it and mail it Wed.

An informal report may omit some of the basic parts, may combine some of them, or may contain all of them separately. In this case the conclusion—these items should have been included on the order—is implied by the statement of the problem and by the recommendations. No summary is needed in such a brief report.

WHAT OTHER KINDS OF REPORTS ARE MADE ON PRINTED FORMS?

There are also a number of specialized reports required by an individual company. The form and content of these reports vary from company to company. The most common ones are forms for accident reports, travel expense reports, supply requisitions, sales reports, operation expense reports, and progress reports. The purpose of all such reports is to give information in a uniform, easily read, easily understood form.

WHAT ARE THE STYLISTIC REQUIREMENTS OF REPORT WRITING?

Writing short reports, whether they take the form of memos, of letters, of notes, or of longer reports, should not create any problem. The form and content requirements are simple enough and are frequently identified for you on the sheet or blank provided for that purpose. But an examination of some of the memos and directions that pass through the interoffice mail of any large company will reveal that many people who write such informal reports do not find the task easy at all.

An analysis of a large number of these reports reveals that the writers have a real problem in communication. They know what they want to say, and they would know how to say it in simple, straightforward English if they thought that simple, straightforward English would do the job. But somehow they have an idea that company memos and directives should be written in some kind of special gobbledegook that is at best misunderstood, at worst completely unintelligible. Such communication or lack of communication must cost American industry thousands of dollars yearly because the men who receive it don't know what they are expected to do after they have received it.

Figure 31 is a memorandum that was issued with some urgency

To: All Department Inspectors

Subj.: Processing of G.I.A.'s

There seems to be some confusion as to whom is to clear final operation complete, and going forward stamping applicable G.I.A. operations in subsequent stations as instructed in the G.I.A.

This is evident in Pre-Delivery Station when G.I.A.'s are ran prior to going to customer. Approximately 80 to 90 percent of ships arriving in this station have one or more operations open.

Effective immediately, all inspectors that release ships from one station to the next less shortages or whatever, will stamp these operations as such.

Two other problems are also evident. (1) Stamps not legible and dated, (2) Ship numbers not entered on appropriate bottom block of operation clearance form.

Effective immediately all inspectors stamps will be legible and dated. The inspector will be responsible for seeing and placing ship number on operation clearance form.

                                        S. R. Hardy
                                        Supervisor,
                                        Flight Inspection

Figure 31

and evidently considered important. If the writer of this memorandum had thought through exactly what he wanted the department inspectors to do and had tried to describe those operations clearly and simply, he might have written something like Figure 32.

WHAT KINDS OF WORDS SHOULD YOU AVOID IN A REPORT?

Proper word choice is important for the exact kind of writing required for instructions and reports. For one thing, you should avoid words with high connotative value. Remember that some words call highly personal pictures to the reader's mind, and such pictures may not be the

```
To:      All Department Inspectors

Subj.:   Processing of G.I.A.'s

    Eighty to 90 percent of the ships that reach the Pre-Delivery
Station are incomplete. All inspectors releasing ships from one sta-
tion to the next are responsible for the following:

    (1) Stamping each incomplete operation legibly on the operation
        clearance form that accompanies the ship.
    (2) Dating the stamp accurately.
    (3) Entering the ship number in the appropriate bottom block of
        the operation clearance form.

                                              S. R. Hardy
                                              Supervisor
                                              Flight Inspection
```

Figure 32

same as those you connect with the same words. Such words will not help you to write clear instructions that will be followed without error.

Remember also that emotionally loaded words may cause the reader to react with his feelings just when you want him to keep a clear head. Theoretically, a lawyer examining prospective jurors tries to select individuals who have no preconceived ideas concerning the guilt or innocence of the individual on trial and who also have had no personal experiences that might cause them to feel emotionally involved in the outcome of the trial. Such an impartial attitude is also needed by the secretary recording the actions of the school board, the policeman gathering the facts about the need for a stop sign at Highway 83 and Plaza Boulevard, and the researcher establishing the relationship between the use of tobacco and the common cold.

Just as such individuals should try to keep open minds, they should describe their findings with words that allow the reader to remain equally objective. The reader of the policeman's report should not be able to tell whether the writer wants the stop sign installed or not; but he should know how many vehicles use the streets, whether traffic is heavy at certain hours, whether school children use the intersection, and how many accidents have occurred at the corner. The tobacco-common-cold researcher should write a report that gives no hint as to how many packs he smokes a day or whether he is employed by American Tobacco Company or the American Medical Association.

WHAT KINDS OF WORDS SHOULD YOU USE IN A REPORT?

You will also communicate more accurately and exactly if you choose words that mean exactly what you intend them to mean. Some words have meanings very close to those of other words and yet they suggest a fine shade of difference. *Old lady* and *old woman* might identify similar females, but the first shows a little more respect and suggests that the person referred to has a higher social position or more money. A matron may be younger than a dowager, but she has less personal dignity. A crone is an old woman, but the word *crone* calls attention to wrinkles and a bent posture. A hag, like a crone, is withered, but she may entertain evil and malicious thoughts. A witch not only entertains malicious thoughts, but also carries them out by supernatural means.

Because some words have several meanings, they can lead to misunderstanding. If you declare that the day is nice, that your neighbor's daughter is not a nice girl, and that your mother looks nice in her new hat, you may know what you mean, but others might be confused. *Overlook* means both to inspect or survey and to neglect or pass over without criticism. *Peculiar* has a number of meanings that appear unrelated: belonging to an individual, privately owned, not common, characteristic or distinctive, different from the normal or usual, singular, special, particular, queer, or eccentric. If you think that any of your words may be misunderstood by your reader, define your terms.

WILL THE ARRANGEMENT OF THE WORDS IN YOUR SENTENCE HELP YOU TO WRITE MORE ACCURATELY?

The arrangement of words in a sentence is very important if you are to say exactly what you mean. If you write, "Still he stood by the window," your meaning is quite different than if you write, "He stood still by the window." The sentence "The little boy nearly walked ten miles," actually means that the little boy came very near to taking a walk ten miles long but he did not really walk at all. If in fact he walked nine or nine and a half miles, the sentence should read, "The little boy walked nearly ten miles."

Note the differences in the following pairs of sentences:

Almost everyone had finished eating when the band began to play.
(Most people had finished eating, but some had not.)

Everyone had almost finished eating when the band began to play.
(Probably no one had finished eating, but everyone was nearly finished.)

People who exercise frequently keep physically fit.
(Frequent exercise promotes physical fitness.)

Frequently people who exercise keep physically fit.
(Exercise commonly promotes physical fitness.)

The student council met to discuss vandalism in the student center.
(The vandalism occurred in the student center.)

The student council met in the student center to discuss vandalism.
(The council met in the center. There is no statement concerning the site of the vandalism.)

Sometimes such poorly arranged sentences can be almost amusing:

The judges presented the trophy to the owner of the horse which had been engraved in gold.

The car can be seen at the garage which was in the accident.

The float moved slowly down the street with artificial flowers covering the top and sides.

There was loud applause when the speaker said he was in favor of the program at the back of the hall.

She returned the dress to the store that didn't fit.

We have a booklet on our new underground sprinkler system which we will send you on request.

You will also fail to say what you mean if you leave out necessary words. Be especially careful in your use of pronouns. Notice how confusing these two sentences are:

Mr. Hartley told Joe that he needed to complete the filing before he made out the paychecks.

The secretary showed her assistant the office in which she would be working.

Directives and instructions are frequently indirect and hard to follow because they are written in the passive voice. Compare the directness and clarity of these two sentences:

When you are the recipient of a call which is answered by your secretary, her name and your office should be stated for identification.

When your secretary answers the phone for you, she should identify herself and your office.

How Can You Achieve Brevity?

Here is a summary of the above suggestions for clear and accurate report writing:[1]

Use the most accurate and exact word you can find.
Avoid words that don't say anything or that repeat other words.
Arrange the order of your sentences so that they say what you intend them to say.
Don't leave out anything your reader needs to know.
Don't suppose that he will know what the words *this*, *which*, and *it* refer to if you don't tell him.
Do not use passive verbs unless you can't avoid them.

SHOULD YOU ALWAYS USE THE FEWEST WORDS?

Although your statements should be direct, you will not communicate clearly if you do not include all the necessary details. The sentence "The man entered the building" really doesn't give much information. The following are much more specific:

The rookie staggered into the bar.
The burglar pried open the window and crawled into the jewelry store.
Santa Claus slid down the chimney.

If the plumber asking his helper for a small tool has in mind a ⅝-inch wrench, he may not be able to use a screwdriver. If the millionaire promises his girl friend "a small memento of this occasion," she may be disappointed with a postcard. Cooks once baked cakes by using a pinch of baking powder, a squidgin of spice, several eggs, flour, and enough milk to hold the batter together; but today's homemakers would rather measure with graduated spoons and cup measures and use a tested recipe. Laboratory-trained experts work with even more accurately defined amounts.

HOW CAN YOU ACHIEVE BREVITY?

Your writing will not be clear if you clutter it up with words that don't say anything or that just repeat other words. Find the simplest,

[1] Additional examples of style and usage can be found in the Handbook section of this text.

shortest, most direct way to say what you have to say. Notice the difference in the following pairs of sentences:

54 WORDS	11 WORDS
It is the responsibility of each and every department head to make the arrangements necessary to provide personnel replacement in order to ensure the efficient continuation of operation in his area in the case of absenteeism resulting from the illness of any salaried employee ordinarily involved directly in the activities of his department.	Each department head is responsible for hiring substitutes for ill employees.

WHAT SPECIAL PROBLEMS WILL YOU MEET IN WRITING INSTRUCTIONS?

Writing instructions that can be followed correctly requires using all of the techniques of good technical writing. You will also need both forethought and discipline. Before you start to write, think through exactly what you have to say and decide on the best order in which to say it. If you have to back up and explain something that you should have said earlier, you will only confuse your reader. Moreover, don't try to tell your reader too much at once. The more complicated your material, the more you must break it down into small, simple parts. Finally, don't make your instructions any more complicated than necessary. If the operation is relatively simple, keep your instructions simple. Don't expect the reader to read your mind, but do give him credit for some common sense.

Compare the following statements of instruction to a firm's new employees.

Because of the excessive amount of paperwork and the problem in scheduling, it has become impossible for us adequately to process your insurance papers in our usual way. Those desiring insurance should report to Mr. Lyons, Office 257–B, on either Monday or Tuesday of next week (March 20–21).	New employees are responsible for filing their own insurance application forms in Mr. Lyons' office (257–B) on either March 21 or 22.

You will assume responsibility for the satisfactory completion of your own papers.

A typical problem in writing instructions is presenting too much material at once, thereby confusing the order of action. Notice how confused the instruction at the left is as compared with the one at the right.

To start a fire in your new home grill, place the charcoal on the grill floor and make certain that the grill vents are all open. After soaking with charcoal lighter, ignite with a match, and then wait five to ten minutes before beginning to cook.	To prepare your new home grill for cooking, first open all of the vents on the bottom and the sides. Then place charcoal evenly on the grill floor and apply a small amount of charcoal lighter evenly over the charcoal. Wait five minutes, and then light with a match. Let the charcoal burn five to ten minutes before beginning to cook.

HOW DO YOU HANDLE ABBREVIATIONS AND FIGURES IN REPORT WRITING?

Writing reports frequently involves the use of more abbreviations and figures than ordinary writing does. Although different businesses have their own rules for using figures and abbreviations, there are certain practices that are standardized throughout much of the business community. A rather complete listing is given in the English Handbook section of this text. Consult it if you have questions.

HOW ARE LONGER INFORMAL REPORTS WRITTEN?

Figure 33 is a longer informal report on the findings of the committee that investigated the problem of the employees' cafeteria. Notice that it contains all of the basic parts of a report but that it is short enough to be classified as an informal report. Notice also that the body of the report states and analyzes the problem, locates the causes, and suggests and examines the solutions. The order in which each part of the problem and each part of the solution are handled is consistent.

	Date: December 10, 1968
	To: B. R. Frederick
	From: A. W. Frazier
	Subject: Findings of the special committee authorized to investigate the employees' cafeteria.

(Summary) All information indicates a need for remodeling the cafeteria cold room, opening two doors into the serving area, and purchasing a new oven for the bakery.

(Introduction) This report will give the findings of the committee authorized by B. R. Frederick to investigate the causes for the complaints concerning the food and service in the employees' cafeteria.

(Body: Analysis of the problem: baked goods, salads, service) The complaints lodged against the food in the employees' cafeteria chiefly concern the quality of the hot breads and baked desserts, the temperature and freshness of the salads, and the slowness of the food service.

(Cause of the problem: cold room, poor arrangement of entrance to serving deck) Investigation of the cafeteria facilities reveals that the bakery ovens were purchased in 1952 and that the thermostatic controls and timers are inaccurate and undependable. The cold room, measuring 6 by 8 ft., was built in 1948 when the cafeteria served 300 employees. It is inadequate today when an average of 750 employees are served daily. The present serving area is crowded and inefficiently arranged. The waitresses replenishing the steam deck must pass through the dishwashing area and through the same door as the busboys returning from the dining area with trays of dirty dishes.. The resulting bottleneck slows the progress of food to the serving deck.

How Are Longer Informal Reports Written?

(Solution: buy new ovens,	Repair of the oven thermostatic controls and timers seems impractical as the cost would be only slightly lower than the replacement of the ovens with newer and more efficient equipment.
enlarge cold room,	A consultant of the ColdWay Commercial Refrigeration Company recommends enlarging the cold room to 6 by 18 by 18 ft. Two rows of shelves down the center as well as along the back and sides of the room would not only take care of present needs but would also be adequate for any expected increase in personnel.
	Space for the enlarged cold room could be taken from the adjoining dishwashing area which is larger than necessary now that new and more compact dishwashing and drying equipment has been installed.
rearrange entrance to serving deck,	Two new double doors cut into the wall behind the steam deck would allow for efficient service in that area.
(Conclusion)	It is the conclusion of this committee that the complaints concerning the cafeteria food are justified and that the problems responsible for these complaints can be solved by purchasing new ovens for the bakery, enlarging the cold room, and making two double doors behind the steam deck.
(Recommendation)	It is the recommendation of this committee that these actions be taken as soon as possible.
(Appendix)	Here is a sketch of the proposed cold room and the reduced cleanup area. A breakdown of the necessary costs follows.

Figure 33

ASSIGNMENTS

I. Prepare the following memoranda:
   1. A memo from you to your school librarian requesting permission to keep two books out a week longer than is normally allowed. Give the specific titles and call numbers of the books.
   2. A memo from you, acting as secretary for your professional group on campus, announcing a club meeting. Be certain to indicate the name of the club, the time and place of the meeting.

II. Write the following brief notes:
   1. A note from you to your communication instructor asking that he remember to bring you a specific book which he has in his personal library.
   2. A note from you to your employer (real or imaginary) asking that you be permitted to have next Saturday off. Cite the exact date. Give a brief reason for your request.
   3. A note from your employer responding to your note and giving permission for you to take the requested time off.
   4. A note from your employer denying you permission to take the requested time off.

III. Work with a group of your fellow students and identify an important local problem, either related to your campus or your local community. Identify what you feel to be the issues and then address a formal report to the appropriate governing body. Structure your report similarly to the one in Figure 33.

EIGHT / Serving on the Problem-Solving Committee

WHY DO YOU NEED TO LEARN HOW TO SERVE ON A COMMITTEE?

You may find that much of your work time will be spent in committee meetings and that some of your most important work will be done at a conference table. For all that has been said against them, committees often work successfully. Two heads are better than one in problem-solving; consequently, a committee of three or five or seven ought to be even more effective. Certainly the multiplication of heads produces a multiplication of opinions. Committee members take sides and discussion becomes heated. Discussion takes time, but it is part of the democratic process by which America and American business and society operate. Generally speaking, an intelligent person's mind is like a bed: it can be made up better when there is someone on either side. If the five members of a committee always agree, four of them are unnecessary.

A committee room is not an arena for a verbal free-for-all, however. There are well-established, generally accepted rules by which business is conducted. And there are certain skills and attitudes that will help you become an employee who is more valuable because he works well with others.

ON WHAT KINDS OF COMMITTEES WILL YOU SERVE?

Committees, conferences, and similar meetings are organized to solve problems. Some committees are *temporary*, called to handle one specific problem. Others are *standing* committees that exist to deal with all the problems of a certain type with which the organization is concerned. There are also *executive* committees to which the top administrators of the organization belong. Such committees make decisions of policy and delegate other committees to handle problems in various areas. You may serve on a committee because the person in your particular job always serves on that committee, because you have some needed specialized skill, or because you are thought to have clear judgment.

WHAT ARE THE REQUIREMENTS FOR A COMMITTEE MEMBER?

Problem-solving requires informed thinking. The problem facing the committee may be a new one in which you have no background at all, or you may have had considerable experience with similar problems. Since no two problems are exactly alike, in either case you will need all of the information that can be gathered on the subject.

Sometimes the chairman or someone he has appointed will bring the necessary information to the group. Sometimes a number of such reports will be necessary. Although you can usually count on being filled in on certain aspects of the problem, you ought to do some work in preparation for the meeting yourself. When the meeting is not a regularly scheduled one, you will probably be notified of its purpose. For regular meetings an agenda or list of matters to be discussed is usually sent to the committee members before the meeting. If the chairman informs you ahead of time of the subject of committee business, he wants you to have time to think about the subject and perhaps learn something about it on your own. If you think the information you have gathered about the subject before the meeting or at the meeting is not enough for you to make an intelligent judgment, say so and ask that any action on the problem be postponed until more facts can be learned. Members of the committee may then be assigned to make further investigation and report to the committee at a later meeting. Never let a committee on which you serve act upon inadequate information just because the hour is late and the members are tired.

The second requirement for problem-solving is an objective mind. Facts are worthless if the people who examine them have already made up their minds about what they think and what they intend to do before they know those facts. You may not be able to do much about the prejudices and preconceived ideas of other members of the group, but you are responsible for your own objectivity. Examine your own ideas and thoughts honestly. Recognize your biases and try to guard against their influencing your decisions. Don't be manipulated by emotionally charged words, and don't use them to manipulate others. A free discussion is not a debate or a power contest. You should want the group to find the best answer to its problems more than you want to persuade it to do something your way.

WHAT KINDS OF PROBLEMS ARE SOLVED BY COMMITTEES?

Problems of Fact

Three types of problems are handled in discussion: problems of fact, problems of value, and problems of policy. Obviously the best method for solving problems of fact is to consult experts who have already investigated the matter or to assign the best-qualified members of the group to investigate it. Your group should not waste its time discussing a question which could be settled by referring to an almanac, a government bulletin, or a personnel officer's survey.

Usually the problems of fact that are brought to committee contain several parts; in other words, the information sought is made up of many separate facts. The committee may decide what individual facts are needed; or they may, because of their different backgrounds, be able to supply these various needed facts. Problems of fact include such questions as these: Will the present steam deck in the employee cafeteria be adequate if the lunch hour is decreased ten minutes? What are the causes of the decrease in production in the x-ray department? What changes in process will have to be made if the top of the hygroflam bottle is made of plastic foam? How much will such changes cost? Solving a problem of fact is frequently the first step in solving one of the other kinds of problems.

Problems of Value

A problem of value is similar to one of fact except that it allows for some difference of opinion. Facts may be the basis of the discussion, but the question will be settled finally by the judgment and preference of the group. The best decisions of value are reached when the group withholds judgment and remains uncommitted until its members have heard *all* the facts. Such a situation is ideal and exists more often in textbooks than in groups made up of real people. You can help your group to make fair judgments by guarding your own objectivity and by making a tactful suggestion if the decision seems to be affected by personalities.

Problems of value concern questions such as these: Is one twenty-minute coffee break more valuable for employee morale and efficiency than two ten-minute breaks? Will changing the color of the top of the hygroflam bottle from navy blue to seafoam green increase consumer appeal enough to offset the temporary increase in production costs?

Problems of Policy

Most of the problems that face your committee will be problems of policy. Problems of policy concern the actions that might be taken to meet a given situation. In any business, circumstances are constantly changing. Such changes create problems. Solving those problems may require other changes. When a committee faces a problem of policy, it must consider all of the possible solutions and decide which one is best and most practical. Problems of policy are as varied as the businesses and committees that consider them. The variety of the solutions considered is limited only by the imagination of the group considering the problem.

WHAT IS THE MOST INFORMAL TYPE OF PROBLEM-SOLVING COMMITTEE?

One of the most productive ways of approaching the problem of policy is the "brainstorming" session. Such a session is quite unconventional in its organization since the one who calls the group together is not looking for obvious or conventional answers. He hopes at the session to bring out every solution that pops into the minds of the inventive men and women he has invited to the meeting. At a brainstorming session everyone is expected to speak out without inhibition or restraint. The point is not to consider the merits of the suggestions at the moment, but to try to think of everything even distantly connected with the problem. No solution should be considered too impossible or ridiculous to suggest.

The group will probably have no leader. Someone will be needed to take down all the suggestions, preferably on a blackboard, since the sight of what has already been suggested may stimulate other ideas. Usually none of the ideas are evaluated or discarded at this meeting. Each member of the group may be assigned a certain portion of the suggested solutions for investigation. No solution should be discarded as foolish or impractical until it has been examined carefully. After a complete examination and fair evaluation, an answer which originally sounded quite silly may turn out to be the best one. Therefore, give each idea a chance. What good are fresh ideas without fresh minds to consider them?

Although this kind of meeting is not usually very orderly, it stimulates originality and draws ideas from many who are otherwise too shy to let anyone know how creative they can be. Such meetings frequently yield new and workable solutions and are therefore growing in popularity among progressive organizations. If after an active brainstorming session the problem still seems insoluble or soluble only by some faulty method, you and your colleagues will know that at least you gave a fair hearing to every possible solution.

WHAT DO YOU DO WHEN YOU ARE A COMMITTEE MEMBER?

An ordinary committee meeting has a chairman and is conducted a bit more formally than a brainstorming session. At a formal meeting, as at any other discussion group, you should observe the ordinary rules of courtesy. You will listen to what others say, really listen, taking care to hear exactly what is said and to understand what is meant. You should even develop the habit of taking notes so that you can keep in mind the different points that are made. Of course, you will not interrupt a speaker or talk to those about you while someone else is speaking.

When it is your turn to speak, don't talk as though you had all the answers and don't start an argument or take sides in one somebody else has started. You are not there to get your way, to show how stupid someone else is, or to impress others with your powers of public speaking, reasoning, or sarcasm. You are there to help solve a problem which can be solved more easily if everybody stays cool and objective.

The ability to be tactful when you disagree is a trait that will help you in both your professional and personal life. Use expressions such as "I would like to hear more on this subject" or "I may be wrong but it appears to me . . ." Assume that other speakers are as intelligent and are striving as sincerely for objectivity as you are certain you are.

Don't think, on the other hand, that you have fulfilled your purpose on the committee just because you have answered to roll call, looked intelligent, and refrained from insulting anybody. The strong, silent committee member is frequently sitting there shyly worrying what others would think if he had the spunk to get up and say what he wants to. After the meeting he may voice his opinions loudly and critically, but they will serve no useful purpose then.

Consider the problem before the committee to be yours. Face it thoughtfully. If you have a thought that is pertinent and has not already been expressed, ask for recognition in whatever manner is customary in the group and speak loudly enough to be heard, without mumbling, droning in a monotone, or gesticulating wildly. Don't worry about what others will think about your ideas. You like them, and you are there because somebody in authority thought your ideas worth hearing.

But you don't have to speak on every question. Sometimes your opinions will be the same as those already expressed by others. Sometimes it is possible that you honestly have no preferences in the matter. Every group usually has at least one member who has an opinion on every subject. Frequently it is the same opinion. He may even express it in the same words. His colleagues know what he is going to say when he gets up. Another unpopular member is the fellow who talks too long, who has trouble staying on the subject, and who can't tell a relevant fact from one that is completely beside the point. If you notice that your fellow committee members frequently grow restless when you rise to speak, review what you said and what others said before and after you spoke to see if any one of these faults is yours.

WHAT DO YOU DO WHEN YOU ARE THE CHAIRMAN OF A COMMITTEE?

If you are the committee chairman, you have a very important job. Whether or not the group accomplishes its purpose will be largely up to you. As committee chairman you send out an agenda to the members of the group a few days before the meeting so that they can come to the meeting prepared to discuss the questions at hand. Give reasonable attention to matters which other members ask to have considered as well as to those which you feel are important. If some special information will be needed, secure it or ask some other member to do so. You should also take care of any other preparations, such as announcing the meeting, arranging for a meeting place, preparing ballots, making minutes of past meetings available to the members, and seeing that a record will be made of this meeting.

At the meeting you will introduce topics to be discussed according to your agenda and you will lead the discussion. Although you will allow anyone to speak who asks for permission in the customary way, you should exert some guidance in keeping the discussion on the problem and moving toward a solution. To be fair, you must see that everyone is allowed free expression, but you should not allow a troublesome or fervent minority to take over the whole meeting. Naturally you will never use your office to gain special advantage for your desires or ideas.

HOW IS THE BUSINESS OF A COMMITTEE CONDUCTED?

In small, informal committees decisions may be made by general consent. Sometimes no formal vote is necessary, although informal opinions may be voiced. The business of larger committees, however, is conducted more formally and according to standard parliamentary procedure. In such meetings you or someone else may suggest a decision or an action. You should ask that the proposal be stated as a formal motion. The person who made the suggestion, or perhaps someone else, will then say simply, "I move that . . ." Another person must then say, "I second the motion." If no one seconds the motion, then no one except the person who made the motion is in favor of it, and the motion dies for want of a second. After the motion has been seconded, you will restate the motion or, if its wording is difficult, have the secretary read it. Then you will ask if there is any discussion of the motion. When no one has any more to say about it, you call for a vote, taking care that everyone understands the motion. The vote may be taken by a simple *yes* or *no* given in unison, by a show of hands, by roll call, or by secret ballot. The manner of voting depends upon the importance of the question and the customs of the group. You will always restate the motion three times: before you call for discussion, before you call for the vote, and after the motion has been voted.

The kind of motion that concerns the usual business of a meeting is referred to as the *main motion*. Two main motions cannot be handled by a group at the same time. After a main motion is made and seconded, the group must accept, reject, or in some way dispose of the motion before another main motion can be considered.

Improving or Changing a Motion

If there is a motion to change or amend the main motion, it must be discussed and voted upon before attention is returned to the main motion. Be sure to state the motion to amend a motion three times: before the discussion, before the vote, and after the vote. It is especially important that everyone understands that it is the *motion to amend* the main motion and not the main motion that is being considered. After the motion to amend the motion has been accepted, the main motion can be discussed and voted upon in its new form. The motion to amend a motion is amended by a similar procedure, but usually it is simpler if the person who made the original motion withdraws his motion and the group starts over.

Referring a Problem to Some Other Group

Sometimes someone in the group may feel that the problem involved in a motion requires further study or action by some smaller group that can give the problem more specialized attention. He will *move to refer* the matter to a standing committee or to a special committee. The motion may name the standing committee, or it may describe the kind of new committee desired: "Mr. Chairman, I move the question be referred to a committee of five members to be elected by this group and that the committee report its findings at the next meeting." A majority vote is required to pass this motion. Naturally, if it passes, no further attention is paid to the original motion at this time.

These three motions—the *main motion,* the *motion to amend* a motion, and the *motion to refer* the question—are the principal ones used in most meetings. There are, however, a few other motions which you may need to know about. These motions are all subsidiary motions because they pertain to main motions which have been made and seconded and which are before the group at the time.

Postponing a Motion

A *motion* may be made *to postpone* a motion until some definite, stated time. Such a motion is usually made to allow the members of the group time to give more thought to the matter and to get some more information. This motion is a fair and useful one because it can be discussed, and it does not keep the matter from being considered again at an appointed time. This motion requires only a majority vote.

A motion may also be made to postpone a main motion indefinitely. The purpose of this motion is to kill the main motion. The opponents of a main motion may also use this method to test the popularity of the main motion. This motion is a fair one because it can be discussed. Only a majority vote is required to pass it.

Reconsideration of an Indefinitely Postponed Motion

At some later time a motion that has been postponed indefinitely can be brought up for reconsideration. Someone who was present when the main motion was postponed moves that this main motion be reconsidered. The *motion to reconsider* requires a second, it can be discussed, and it passes with a majority vote.

If someone who was not present when the motion was made to postpone a motion objects to that postponement, he cannot move to reconsider the motion. He can, however, move that the postponement motion be rescinded or taken back. A two-thirds vote is required to pass the motion to rescind. To keep from confusing these last two motions, remember that you can't move to reconsider a motion that you didn't consider in the first place.

Another Way of Postponing a Motion Indefinitely

A rather unfair motion—and one that is frequently misunderstood—is the *motion to table* the main motion or to lay the main motion on the table. This motion requires a second, but it cannot be discussed. It requires only a majority vote to pass. An undebatable motion kills free discussion, which is important to the democratic process. Therefore, a motion to postpone indefinitely is a much fairer motion and one which serves a similar purpose.

A motion which has been placed on the table can be returned to consideration only after other business has intervened. Anyone can move to take the motion from the table and return it to consideration. A second to the motion and a majority vote are required.

Keeping a Motion from Vote

A motion may be kept from vote in two ways. Someone may *move to object to consideration of a question or motion*. This motion requires a second. It is not debatable. If it passes with a two-thirds vote, the matter is closed indefinitely. If a motion has been made but not discussed, someone, frequently the person who made the motion in the first place, may say, "I move that the motion to . . . be withdrawn." No one need second this motion, and no vote is required. But if the original motion has been discussed at all, the *motion to withdraw* it must be seconded, voted upon, and passed by a majority vote.

Closing the Discussion

After a motion has been under discussion for some time, someone may think that those discussing the matter are repeating themselves or each other or wasting time. Or he may wish to bring the question to a vote before he loses some of his support. He may say, "I move to close the debate." Someone must second him. Discussion of his motion must be allowed. And his *motion to close the debate* must pass by a two-thirds vote.

Motions Especially Concerning Parliamentary Procedure

There are two motions that concern parliamentary procedure. Someone may *move to suspend a rule* of the organization. A two-thirds vote is required to pass such a suspension. Clauses of bylaws of the constitution of the organization cannot be suspended.

If someone thinks that a mistake is being made in the procedure with which a motion is being handled, he makes a *motion on point of order*. The chairman may accept or reject the point. No second, discussion, or vote is necessary; but the chairman's ruling may be appealed.

The *motion to adjourn* must be considered and seconded whenever it is made, regardless of what business is already before the group. Since only a majority vote is required to pass it and since it must be voted on when it is made, it should not be used as a means to close a discussion or prevent fair consideration of a problem. The *motion to fix the time* for the next meeting has priority over even the vote to adjourn.

Most organizations have their own methods for nominating officers and the procedures are specified in their bylaws. If they are not, a motion suggesting procedure is necessary. Nomination may be made by a committee, from the floor, or both. Nominations do not require a second. A motion to close nominations requires a two-thirds vote and should not be used to restrict the rights of the members. A motion to reopen nominations requires only a majority vote.

The various types of motions are outlined for you in Figure 34. Reference to this chart will familiarize you with the types of motions, when each may be used, and what vote is necessary for passage.

WHAT ATTITUDE TOWARD COMMITTEE WORK AND RULES IS HELPFUL?

At first, all this discussion of motions and procedures may seem a bit complicated. If you reread it, however, and give the matter a little thought, you can see that most of the rules of parliamentary procedure are matters of common sense, courtesy, and justice. They are designed to ensure order and democracy. If you frequently serve as chairman of committees or as an officer of an organization or if you are placed on the constitution committee of a new organization, you will find a book explaining parliamentary law in greater detail to be quite helpful.[1]

But don't allow natural timidity or awe of procedure to keep you

---

[1] A very helpful book is *Sturgis Standard Code of Parliamentary Procedure*, by Alice Sturgis (New York: McGraw-Hill Book Company, 1966).

What Attitude Toward Committee Work and Rules Is Helpful?

from being an active, contributing member of the groups and organizations in your professional and personal life. Although you should not use your membership in such groups merely for your own personal advancement, you will find that if you sincerely try to make a real contribution when you are asked to serve on a committee, you will benefit both in your professional prosperity and in your personal satisfaction.

Figure 34. A Simplified Chart of Parliamentary Procedures

PRINCIPAL MOTIONS

Type of Motion	Comment	Vote to Pass
Main Motion	Principal business before the group; only one main motion may exist at a time	simple majority
Motion to Amend	Adds to or changes the main motion; must be voted before returning to main motion	simple majority
Motion to Refer	Refers a main motion to a committee or some other group for further study; must be referred to a definite group	simple majority

SUBSIDIARY MOTIONS

Type of Motion	Comment	Vote to Pass
To Postpone	Postpones action on principal motion until another time; may postpone until a designated time or indefinitely but must state which; may be discussed	simple majority
To Recall	To discuss again a motion which has been postponed or referred; must be made by someone present when motion was postponed; may be discussed	simple majority

Figure 34 (cont.)

Type of Motion	Comment	Vote to Pass
To Rescind	To discuss a motion which has been postponed; used by someone not present when motion was postponed; may be discussed	simple majority
To Table	Postpones a principal motion indefinitely; may not be discussed	simple majority
To Object to Consideration	Objects to further discussion and voting on main motion; may not be discussed	two-thirds
To Withdraw (before discussion)	Withdraws a motion from any further action	no second; no vote; motion automatically withdrawn
To Withdraw (after discussion)	Withdraws a motion from further action; must be seconded	simple majority
To Close Discussion	Ends discussion on a motion and calls for immediate vote; discussion allowed	two-thirds
To Suspend Rules	To suspend a rule temporarily, usually to get faster action; may not apply to by-laws	two-thirds
To Call Point of Order	Questions procedure of another member or of chairman	no vote; ruled on by chairman
To Adjourn	Must be considered as soon as made	simple majority
To Fix Meeting Time	Sets time for next meeting; must be voted even before a motion to adjourn	simple majority

ASSIGNMENTS

Most committees meet to solve a problem, and the solution to that problem is usually presented as a report to the individual or group that authorized the committee. The following assignments, done in order, will take you through the usual tasks of committee work.

I. Assume that your class is an organized body of some type and that it is presently involved in working toward the solution of some important problem. Elect one person from the class to function as chairman. This person should be someone who has some definite leadership ability and who can devote some extra time to his special assignment.

II. The chairman should lead the group in a discussion to select a topic. The following suggestions are given as guides, but perhaps you have a more pressing problem to suggest.
   1. The college library should be open longer hours.
   2. Students should not be required to take a general orientation course.
   3. The fee for the use of the Student Center should be lowered.
   4. The college should sponsor a book exchange at which students may trade texts between semesters.
   5. Some changes need to be made in the existing structure of the student government.

III. After you have selected a subject, your chairman should conduct a group discussion aimed at identifying the specific problems involved. This discussion should also lead to the development of a list of persons or sources which should be contacted for information.

IV. The chairman should appoint subcommittees with responsibility to conduct interviews and research to gather needed information. These subcommittees will probably need to meet with their chairmen to plan the exact course of their business.

V. At a later meeting the chairman should ask for reports from the various subcommittees. Conflicting evidence will probably be presented and will have to be discussed.

VI. After sufficient discussion, someone should propose a motion which contains the statement of the problem and the proposed solutions. Vote on the major motion.

NINE / Solving Problems Logically

WHAT IS THE FIRST STEP IN SOLVING A PROBLEM?

The first step in solving a problem is to find the problem. That statement, of course, sounds silly. You don't go looking for problems. If you sit still, problems will find you soon enough. Besides, you know what the problem is. The problem is brought to your attention or to the attention of a committee to which you are assigned and a solution is asked for. But the immediate, referred problem may not be the real problem. For example, suppose you are serving on a committee at your plant that is asked to investigate employee complaints about the food in the company cafeteria. Knowing that the food from the company cafeteria is bad is not knowing what the problem is. Tasting the food may prove that there is a problem, but you don't sit in the committee room and complain about the food and then take a vote asking the dietitian to improve it. Members of the committee are asked to gather information about the cafeteria. Then that information is brought back to the committee for it to evaluate and pinpoint the problem or problems responsible for the poor food.

Some individual on the committee—maybe you—must gather all the information that is relevant to the case, not just that which is easiest to find. You don't, for instance, just go down to the kitchen and talk to the cook. The cook, no doubt, has a long list of grievances, but he may not know what the real problem is either. You listen to the cook, all right, and take notes on what he says; but you also talk to other people and gather information from other sources. You find out if the equipment in the kitchen and serving deck is adequate and arranged efficiently. You may have to call in an expert in this line to give an opinion. You may talk to both the dietitian and company personnel director to find out if there are enough people working in the cafeteria, if they are well trained, and if they work well. If there are not enough employees there, you find out why. Maybe the budget for the cafeteria is too small to allow for enough workers or for well-qualified ones. Perhaps the working conditions are so unpleasant that good kitchen workers won't stay. Perhaps the cook is too hard to get along with. You will also investigate the wholesalers who sell to the kitchen. If the dietitian is buying a poor grade of produce, you must find out why. As you make your investigation, you will uncover other questions that you must answer before you will have all the facts. But you must have all the facts before you or the committee is ready to put them together and decide what the real problem is.

WHAT IS THE SECOND STEP?

Recognizing the problem may be all that is necessary in order to find a solution. Usually, however, there is more than one solution to the problem; and the best solution is not the first one that comes to mind. All the possible solutions must be thought through and evaluated before the best one will be found.

Suppose, for instance, that you or the committee find that the problem is inadequately trained personnel, but they find also that the wage scale by which the workers are paid is good. One solution would be to fire all workers, or at least the poorest ones, and start over with a new group. Another solution might be to start an in-service training program with increases in pay as the employee advances through the training offered and demonstrates his proficiency in his job. Perhaps the final solution will be a combination of these two: firing the poorest workers and beginning a program to train the others.

WHAT IS THE THIRD STEP?

After you have identified all the possible solutions, you must evaluate them. It is important that you withhold judgment on any one solution until all the possible solutions have been identified and all the facts involved in each solution gathered. A solution that at first appears to be impractical or even ridiculous may, upon investigation with an open mind, prove to be the best.

Having an open mind is essential if you are to weigh all the possible solutions fairly. You shouldn't try to persuade yourself or anyone else that one solution is the best because it will be more convenient for you or because you happen to be the one who thought of it. You are looking for the best solution, not some solution that will further your own personal interests.

Examining the solutions may require as much gathering of information as was required to locate the problem. It may require more. But you won't be ready to evaluate the solutions until you have gathered that information. Then you will consider all the facts.

WHAT IS THE LAST STEP?

Solving a problem involves making changes. Changes take time, cost money, and create personnel problems. Some people don't want to change their work patterns; they like things the way they are, they prefer the status quo. Before you ask employees to change their habits and the employer to spend money, you must test your solution by these questions:

- Is the problem great enough to justify all that is involved in making the changes required by the solution?
- Will the solution work, and is it practical and realistic?
- Are you certain that the solution will not create more problems than it will solve?

In the light of these questions you may find that the ideal solution isn't the one that should be chosen at this time or that some compromise must be made. You may even find that although the problem can be solved, solving it is so costly or difficult that matters will just have to remain the way they are for a while.

Now you can see that problem-solving involves four steps:

1. Locating the problem.
2. Locating all the possible solutions.
3. Evaluating the solutions.
4. Choosing a solution.

HOW DO YOU EVALUATE THE INFORMATION YOU GATHER?

The first three steps require you to gather information. All four steps require you to evaluate that information. Statements of facts can be checked to see whether they are true or false. The truth or falsity of a statement is not a matter of opinion or judgment. However, evaluation of the facts after you have gathered them is an act of judgment. To make a judgment, you draw a conclusion from the facts. Facts do not vary; but judgments vary because the people who draw the inferences from the facts vary in the manner in which they examine the facts and draw their conclusions.

There are two ways of drawing inferences: by deduction or by induction. Therefore, we say there are two kinds of reasoning: deductive and inductive.

WHAT IS DEDUCTIVE REASONING?

When you use deductive reasoning, you are thinking by classes. That is, you are working from a general idea about everything in one particular class to a specific statement about one individual thing within that class. The term *deduction* itself comes from two Latin words meaning to lead from something to something (specifically, from a general statement to a conclusion).

Suppose that a friend tells you about his dog Fido and a rabbit hunt. You do not need necessarily to be told that Fido is a dog with four legs. Because you have seen other dogs that had four legs, you have assumed that all normal dogs have four legs, and thus you assume that Fido is a normal dog and must have four legs. What you have done is to think from the general statement to the specialized—in this case about Fido. The movement of your thought process can be grouped into classes, each becoming more specialized. Class 1 includes all things with four legs. Within that class is a subclass of dogs, and within that division is Fido. A sketch of the deductive scheme looks something like Figure 35:

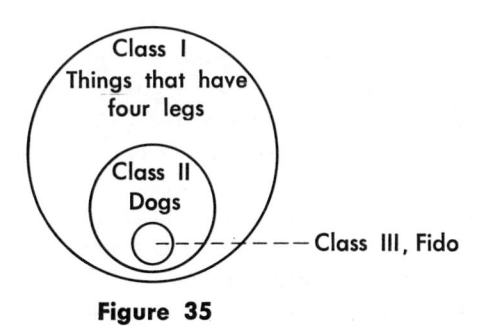

Figure 35

In each instance in the process the smaller class must be capable of being fitted into the larger and being one of its component parts.

Perhaps you are an avid jogger. If so, you jog because you think it is good for your health. Other exercises are also good, but jogging is the specialized one you have selected. Your deductive process might be sketched to look like Figure 36:

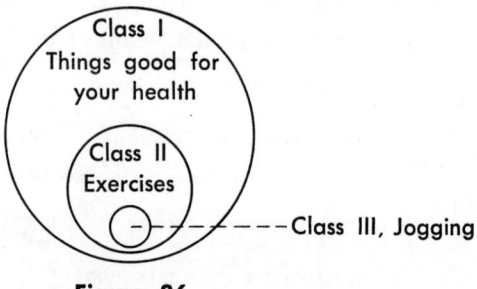

Figure 36

What you are saying, in effect, is that exercise is good for your health, jogging is a form of exercise, thus jogging is good for your health. You would have violated the deductive process of thinking by classes had you thought something like this: exercise is good for your health, eating is good for your health, thus eating is a nice form of exercise. Look at the sketch in Figure 37:

Figure 37

Obviously eating cannot be fitted into the circle that includes exercises. Both are a part of Class I, "things good for your health," but each is a member of a separate division within Class I. In the first example about Fido, you cannot begin thinking about things that have four legs, examine the Class II, dogs, and then decide that the animal you see is a dog because it has four legs. You may be looking at a cat, a horse, or an elephant. Deductive reasoning demands systematized organization of classes within their appropriate groupings.

Throughout the day you make evaluative statements about persons and things. Many of these are made on the basis of knowing traits of the general group and then applying those traits to your specific object. Be certain, as you make these decisions, that your classes are in their proper order.[1]

[1] The formula for deductive reasoning is the syllogism, but it is not the purpose of this text to review its complicated structure in detail. A good book on logic will provide further information if you are interested.

WHAT IS INDUCTIVE REASONING?

In deductive reasoning you apply a general statement to a specific case. To reason inductively, you reverse the process. You examine one specific case, several specific cases, or many specific cases to reach a conclusion. There are three kinds of inductive reasoning: reasoning to reach a generalization, reasoning from analogy, and reasoning by considering causal relationships.

WHAT IS REASONING TO REACH A GENERALIZATION?

The deductive reasoning that you have just been considering begins with a major premise. A major premise is a general statement. In order for that general statement to be true, it must be universally true as it is stated or implied in the syllogism. Universally true major premises are not so plentiful as is sometimes supposed. It is easier to take the statement of a major premise as truth than to question it and check it out, especially if you have heard it repeated often enough. Consequently you may be ready to base your deductive reasoning on statements such as these: "All redheads have quick tempers," "All fat people are jolly," "People from (Peoria, Russia, the South, Addis Ababa) are (civic-minded, enemies, religious, ignorant, irresponsible)," or "People who (drink, smoke, wear beards, vote Republican, go to church) are (stupid, irresponsible, wicked, enemies, good)."

But your major premise was first arrived at by a type of inductive reasoning called *generalization*. Generalization is the process of examining a number of individual cases, finding that a certain fact is true of all of them, and stating that fact as a generally true conclusion. To make the perfect, absolutely infallible generalization, you would have to examine every case—everywhere in all time, past, present, and future. Obviously the opportunity to make such a generalization doesn't occur very often. Normally you will have to be satisfied with something less than a total count.

You will rely on examining a number of selected samples, drawing a conclusion, and then applying that conclusion to the whole. All political, sociological, and scientific examination is based on this method. The method has its limitations, however—limitations that you don't always recognize when you see figures and statistics. The percentages and *alls* and *mosts* that you hear the experts toss about so glibly are not based upon an actual count of all the doctors, decayed teeth, or upset stomachs under discussion. Such a total survey would be impractical if not completely impossible.

HOW DO YOU TEST A GENERALIZATION?

If you are a careful researcher, you must observe two rules in selecting and examining your samples and in drawing your conclusion. First, you must examine a large enough sample. How large is large enough will depend upon what you are measuring. If a certain antibiotic placed on a dozen plates of bacteria under carefully controlled conditions kills all of the bacteria, the scientist might be justified in deciding that under those same conditions the antibiotic would always destroy the bacteria. He would, however, need hundreds of tests before he could draw a conclusion about how the antibiotic would act on bacteria found in a human being. There is a greater difference in the physical make-up of people and the conditions under which they are living when they receive the antibiotic than there is between the plates in a carefully controlled environment. The researcher would need a larger sample when he is drawing a conclusion about people simply because there is more room for variation. You can safely say that the larger the number of variables or differences between the individual members of a class, the larger the number that must be examined before a generalization can be safely made.

The second thing you must be careful about is that the samples you examine are typical of their group. Naturally, if the generalizing hair-counter had included a few bald heads in his hair count, his final figures wouldn't have been very reliable.

If you examine a sample which is too small or which is not typical, you have made the fallacy known as *hasty generalization.*

Whenever you, in your research for information, draw a conclusion about any group of people or class of materials, or whenever you read or hear such a conclusion, you are probably not handling an absolute fact but a generalization. Test it by asking two questions:

- Did the researcher examine a sample which was large enough to allow for the variables in its class?
- Is the sample typical of its class?

WHAT IS AN ANALOGY?

A second type of inductive reasoning is reasoning by analogy. Analogy means similarity. When you reason by analogy, you infer that if two things are alike in several important ways they will also be alike in certain other respects.

The members of the committee that was looking for an answer to the problem of the poor food served in the company cafeteria all bring to that problem experiences they have had with similar problems elsewhere, and they may reason that because a solution worked for a similar problem, it will work for this one. One man, for instance, remembers that when he did KP duty in the army, he observed that the food was poor because many of the workers didn't care whether they did a good job or not. He suggests that probably these kitchen workers serve poor food because they don't care. Another man says that he hasn't eaten in the company cafeteria very much but that he complains about the food his wife serves at home whenever the meal contains food left over from another meal. He suggests that perhaps the dietitian is buying and cooking food in too large amounts and that warmed-over food or rehashed hash is what the employees are complaining about. One woman says that in a company where she worked once there was a similar problem which was solved by getting a new dietitian.

All these persons are reasoning by analogy. They all see similarities between the present problem and other problems they have met. They are wise to do so. Few problems are completely unique. Each experience you meet is in some ways like some other experience, and you reason that the manner in which you handled the earlier experience successfully will be equally effective this time. If you handle this experience the same way you did the last one and the method doesn't work, you compare the two experiences to see how they are different as well as how they are alike.

HOW DO YOU TEST AN ANALOGY?

To a baby, the dissimilarities between the objects that are good to eat and the objects that are not good to eat are not as evident as the similarities. But he is learning what he can eat and what he can't eat by reasoning by analogy. He learns to test the inferences he makes in his analogies with the same question that the committee members will ask in testing their analogies:

> Are the two things (marbles and candy, household bleach and milk) similar in the characteristics that are important for this analogy?

While no situation is unique, no two situations are exactly alike either. In other words, there are no perfect analogies. The first committee member must remember that the men on KP might have lacked interest in their work because they had drawn KP duty as punishment, whereas the cafeteria workers can quit and get other jobs if they dislike kitchen work. The second committee member should investigate to find out if the cafeteria serves leftover food. The situation in the cafeteria and the situation at his home might be similar in that food is bad in both places, but quite dissimilar in the way it is bad. The situation the woman describes is analogous only if the fault for bad food in this cafeteria lies with the dietitian, as it did at the other company cafeteria.

Finding a solution for a problem by analogy is a very useful method, but it is not perfect. You should always test the analogy to be sure that the two cases are analogous in the ways that matter in this situation. To make such a test you will have to gather information and use some of the other kinds of reasoning.

WHAT ARE THE KINDS OF CAUSAL RELATIONS?

Reasoning according to causal relations is another very useful kind of inductive reasoning. In this type of reasoning you relate two events to see if one caused the other. In solving problems you might reason by considering causal relations in three kinds of problems:

1. Two conditions exist that suggest that one may in some way be responsible for the other, and you need to find out if they are so related:

    You pushed the button of the dashboard, and the glass cover fell off.

    There is a $5,347 error in last month's audit; and last Monday the bookkeeper, who makes $125 a week, traded in his ten-year-old jalopy on a new convertible with all the trimmings.

    The cafeteria food is poor, and the equipment for the kitchen was bought in 1955.

2. A condition exists, and you need to find out what caused it. Here you know the result or effect, and you are trying to find the cause. You are reasoning from effect to cause:

    Mr. Sparks is lying dead on the floor in front of his open library wall safe. What killed him?

    The electricity is off in the cafeteria's refrigeration locker. What is wrong?

    There is a bottleneck in the shipping department. What is responsible for it?

3. A condition exists and you need to know what will be the probable result. Here you know the cause, but you are trying to find the result or effect. You are reasoning from cause to effect:

    Old Moneybags is dead. Will his step-nephew inherit his money?

    The electricity is off in the cafeteria's refrigeration locker. Will the food spoil before the current can be restored?

There is a bottleneck in the shipping department. Will the special government order go out in time?

Sometimes you will find a whole chain of causes and effects so that there will be several steps in your reasoning. An effect of one cause becomes a cause of another effect and so on until you have a long line of such causes and effects:

Bill Dennis overslept last Monday;
Therefore he was late leaving for work;
Therefore he ran a red light on the way to work;
Therefore his car was hit by a truck at the intersection;
Therefore he was injured;
Therefore he is in the hospital;
Therefore he has not worked in the shipping department this week;
Therefore there is a bottleneck in the shipping department;
Therefore the special government order probably won't go out on time.

A sufficient cause is one which can produce an effect without the aid of any other factors. You may find more than one sufficient cause operating at the same time. You may also find several causes, none of which are sufficient when found alone but which can produce the effect when they occur together. In either case, you could express this relationship with an equation like the following:

$$A_1 + A_2 + A_3 + A_4 \longrightarrow B$$

You can test your reasoning concerning causal relationships by asking a few questions:

1. Is it possible or even probable that the cause you are considering could produce this effect unaided?
2. Could the cause you are considering be one of several causes which, operating at the same time, could produce this effect?
3. Does some condition exist which could alter the relationship that you would normally expect between the causes and effects which you are considering?

ARE THE KINDS OF REASONING USUALLY FOUND ALONE OR IN COMBINATION?

Although there are two kinds of reasoning—deductive and inductive—and three kinds of inductive reasoning—generalization, analogy, and causal relation—you will not often employ any of these methods alone. You might make a survey from which you make a generalization. Then you might use this generalization as a basis for your deductive reasoning. Generalization is frequently used in reasoning from cause to effect or from effect to cause. When you test your causal reasoning to see if the cause you are considering could be responsible for the effect in question, you will weigh the possibility on the basis of past experience. If you have a large number of experiences from which you have drawn a conclusion that a certain cause could produce a certain effect, you will probably form a generalization. If your experience has been more limited, you will probably use analogy as the basis for judging the relationship.

But whatever kinds of reasoning you use, you should be certain that you have gathered all the facts. Then as you organize those facts to arrive at your conclusions, you should test each step of your reasoning with the appropriate questions.

ASSIGNMENTS

I. Use circles to structure the deductive reasoning suggested by the following examples. Mark as *invalid* the one example that does not correctly fit the pattern.
  1. Every man must die, and since John is a man he must die.
  2. All actors are creative. Larry is creative so he must be an actor.
  3. I think all novels are exciting. *Another Country* is a novel so I think it is exciting.
  4. Green walls always depress me. This room is painted green; therefore it depresses me.

II. Qualifying words like *all, some, only,* and *most* are very important to generalizations. Look at recent issues of a popular magazine or a local newspaper and find examples in which the use of a qualifier makes a generalization acceptable. Find examples in which the generalization is either invalid or questionable because no qualifier is used. Clip your examples, tape them to a full-sized sheet of paper, and bring them to class.

III. You habitually reason by analogy, and sometimes you are guilty of setting up faulty comparisons. List three specific instances when you have reasoned by analogy and in a brief statement about each explain whether the reasoning was justified and why.

IV. A big danger in causal reasoning is the assumption that one cause alone is responsible for one effect. Indicate an incident when you have been guilty of falsely reasoning that A alone caused B. Show that B was really caused by numerous factors, and list them. Then set up an equation that might be indicated as

$$A_1 + A_2 + A_3 + A_4 \longrightarrow B$$

TEN / Avoiding Common Fallacies

WHAT IS A FALLACY?

Combining and presenting information in such a way that an incorrect conclusion is drawn is called an error in reasoning or a *fallacy*. Such reasoning is called *fallacious reasoning*. Sometimes fallacies are made unintentionally; sometimes they are made deliberately. Sometimes they are easy to recognize; sometimes they are very subtle. Fallacies that are used deliberately to mislead you are the principal devices of propaganda. It is important that you learn to recognize these devices so that you can evaluate intelligently the information which you gather and so that you won't make these errors yourself.

In the last chapter you learned that the first three steps in solving a problem require you to gather information. Some of this information you will find is contradictory. Some will be hard for you to believe. Some will be obviously untrue. Some, after careful study and research, you will find to be only partly true. You need to know how to evaluate this information so that you won't be fooled either by those who deliberately want to fool you or by those who have been fooled themselves. The reports that you bring to committees, give to your superior, or pass on to clients will be of value only if you are able to examine your material and identify and remove the information and conclusion that are false or misleading.

WHAT ARE THE MOST COMMON PROPAGANDA DEVICES?

Here are some of the most commonly found propaganda devices. They all have fancy Latin names, but you probably prefer these easier and more widely used terms:

Hasty Generalization
Name Calling
Glittering Generalities
Plain Folks
Bandwagon
Card Stacking
Poisoning the Well
Red Herring
Transfer
Testimonials

WHAT IS THE HASTY GENERALIZATION DEVICE?

As you will remember from what was said in the chapter on problem solving, the ability to make generalities about whole classes of objects is essential if you are to deal efficiently with the individual sample. The shoemaker labors under the assumption that most men have two feet; the bricklayer, that mortar made by a given formula will hold most bricks together; and the department store manager, that most people will buy an assortment of toys, knickknacks, and baubles at Christmas time. But the hasty generalization, the generalization which is made before a large enough sample has been examined carefully and objectively, causes you to deal with the individual too quickly; you reach a conclusion about the individual sample without thinking about it. This fallacy, which was described at length in the previous chapter, can be made honestly by the careless or untrained researcher. But it can also be made deliberately by the propagandist who hopes you will accept his "all" without questioning the means by which he reached such a generalization.

WHAT IS THE NAME CALLING DEVICE?

Sometimes you draw a hasty conclusion because you have reacted automatically and emotionally. Feeling is easier to do than thinking, and feeling is even easier to do when you have been patterned or conditioned to feel a certain way in response to certain symbols or labels. George Orwell's book *1984* depicts a society which set aside a period of time each day known as the "Two Minutes Hate." Each day the workers gathered together before a screen on which were flashed pictures and words pertaining to the enemy of their country. The group responded

What Is the Name Calling Device?

with a wild demonstration of hate which lasted for two minutes. The enemy changed from time to time, but the reaction remained the same. The viewers didn't stop to analyze the pictures or the words or to remember that this year's enemy was last year's ally. They were conditioned to respond with hate to the verbal symbols and they responded according to that pattern.

The only difference between the "Two Minutes Hate" in *1984* and your set responses to certain words is that the people in the book had a warning that they were expected to respond in a particular way to certain words. Propagandists, advertisers—and even you when you aren't thinking—use certain words and labels to get expected responses. The labels change, but the response remains the same. You hate what you in your generation have been taught to hate, and you identify it easily and quickly by its label. This propaganda device is called Name Calling.

During the Victorian period any word suggesting that mankind was created male and female was labeled immoral, and people who used such words were regarded as lusty, sinful people. The emotional reaction against such words was so strong that the taboo was extended to include any words that referred to human anatomy. Thus women had *bosoms* rather than *breasts* and *limbs* rather than *legs;* even the parlor table wore a long skirt to cover its offensive appendages lest some lecherous male in the presence of both table and lady should be reminded that ladies, like tables, had legs.[1]

In wartime, emotions must be stirred if citizens are to enlist, buy war bonds, face personal inconvenience, and support the national cause. During World War I feelings against the enemy were transferred to any item or word that was Germanic in origin. The names of streets were changed, men who had inherited German names found it difficult to get jobs, and it was unpatriotic to call wieners and sauerkraut anything but Hot Dogs and Liberty Cabbage. In World War II the label *Nazi* suggested not only the enemy but the enemy's concentration camps, its totalitarian denial of human rights and liberty, and its torture chambers, gas showers, and crematory ovens.

During the McCarthy Senate investigation of un-American activities in the 1950s, the labels *Red* and *Communist* could keep a man from getting a job, cause him to lose the job he had, and alienate friends and voters. Labels are always used in political campaigns, and the reaction to the labels varies according to a person's political philosophy. Some labels that are used today to brand candidates and ideas are *reactionary, right wing, left wing, radical, conservative, labor, capitalist, racist,* and *rebel.*

[1] Henry Louis Menken, *The American Language* (New York, 1960) II, 650.

HOW CAN YOU DETECT THE NAME CALLING DEVICE?

Propagandists engage in Name Calling because they know that most people make an immediate emotional connection between the label and a whole set of distasteful ideas without thinking. To those who have been conditioned to make the connection, the labeled individual or idea stands accused and found guilty of all the unpleasantness that the label implies. Because the accusation is implied rather than spoken, the person so labeled has no opportunity to deny it. The propagandist wants people to react without thinking so that he can manipulate them into acting as he wants them to act. Unless you want to be a puppet who moves whenever some clever name caller pulls verbal strings, you should learn to spot the labels that are used. When you meet such a label, stop and analyze the situation. Ask two questions:

1. What does the label really mean, apart from the suggestions that popular opinion has taught you to attach to it?
2. Is the label in either its real sense or in its popular enemy-branding sense important or correct?

WHAT IS THE GLITTERING GENERALITIES DEVICE?

Just as labels can be used to signal that certain people and ideas should be avoided, they can also be used to secure approval for people and ideas. In either case, they cause people to act hastily without proper evaluation of the situation.

Words that are used to secure blanket, automatic approval are called virtue words. To use them in place of careful reasoning and analysis is to commit the fallacy of Glittering Generalities. Virtue words are not so much subject to fads and temporary conditions as are the labels used in the propaganda device of Name Calling. Americans are always in favor of patriotism, liberty, Christianity, motherhood, the girl next door, and apple pie. And they can be depended upon to execute whatever action is called for in honor of these sacred institutions. Office seekers, commencement speakers, and dedicators of park statuary can string together terms like *noble, forefathers, progress, achievement, this modern age, our homes, the man of tomorrow,* and *the common man* for thirty minutes and be certain to be rewarded with approval and applause. Such words are calculated to be translated from the notes of the speaker into desirable action by the hearers without any mental activity on the part of either. Parrots can learn to say such words; dogs can learn to roll over at command; and Americans will stand, cheer, die, or vote for anything draped in a flag, topped by a cross, or suggested in the name of Dear Old Ivy. After all, anybody that likes kids, dogs, and baseball can't be all bad.

HOW DO YOU DETECT THE GLITTERING GENERALITIES DEVICE?

The questions that you ask when you hear a virtue word and feel your eyes blinded by a Glittering Generality are the same as you ask when you spot an enemy-branding label:

1. What does this label really mean?
2. Does it have any importance here?

WHAT IS THE PLAIN FOLKS DEVICE?

The propagandist uses one particular group of virtue words so well that they deserve a separate heading of their own, Plain Folks. The labels of Plain Folks are implied as often as they are stated. Americans favor people who use simple language, even make a grammatical error now and then; who come from poor but honest, hardworking parents; and who eat beans and potatoes for supper, fried chicken on Sunday, and hot dogs and hamburgers on picnics and at baseball games. These people are just plain folks like you and me. You can trust them. They understand you. They won't try to put something over on you like those people who use big words with a stilted accent and order food from a French menu; people who don't know what it is to work for a living; people, in short, who aren't like you and me.

Americans honor the hometown boy who made good, the dime store clerk who became a movie star, and the little boy who grew up in a log cabin and became President. The poor boy's success is part of the American tradition, one with which everybody identifies. So no one admits to being lower class or upper class in America today. We fall into the lower middle income bracket, the upper middle, or the middle middle.

HOW DO YOU DETECT THE PLAIN FOLKS FALLACY?

When you meet an appeal on behalf of a man or idea that is dressed even slightly in words or symbols that remind you that this candidate deserves your support because he is just an ordinary man, ask yourself two questions:

1. Is the Plain Folks label sincere?
2. Would the man or idea have your approval without the Plain Folks label?

WHAT IS THE BANDWAGON DEVICE?

The ordinary American favors a leader who is "a man of the common people" because he can identify with such a man and with his success. Such a man has risen through difficulties to success, and his rise encourages the voter to believe that he could do the same if he wanted to. Nobody, however, wants to identify with a failure, or be reminded that the goblin of defeat will "get you too if you don't watch out." The propagandist appeals to this natural desire to be a winner when he invites you to hop on the bandwagon and go along with the crowd.

He appeals also to another basic human desire, the desire to belong, to be one of the group. The fellow who disagrees with the crowd stands alone and is lonely. Few have the courage to be lonely. You feel safe when you are part of the crowd, when you vote with the majority party, attend the largest church, belong to the most popular club, watch the television show with the highest ratings, brush your teeth with the tooth paste preferred by nine out of ten, and wear your skirts and hair at the length that is "in."

The Bandwagon device is used to encourage you to take a certain action because "Everybody's doing it." Thus it is natural that the propagandist using this device sees you not as an individual with individual tastes and opinions but as a member of groups that already exist for other purposes. As a member of organized groups, you have characteristics and interests in common with other members; you have a loyalty to your group and its interest; and you have a strong desire to act in accordance with other members of your group so that you can maintain your membership and acceptance by that group.

So the propagandist appeals to you as a student or teacher; as a Catholic, Protestant, or Jew; as a Black or White; as an American; as a member of a party, profession, or union; but never as a member of the human race. He flatters you that members of your group are superior. He arouses your prejudices, your hatreds, and your fears against those who do not belong to your group. They must remain inferior if you are able to remain superior. Since such superiority lies with the group that is in power and thus can name which group is superior, you are invited to vote for the candidate who is sure to win, to attend the show that everybody is talking about, to read the book that is on the best-seller list, and to listen to the song that is in the "top ten."

WHAT IS THE CARD STACKING DEVICE?

When the propagandist uses the device of Card Stacking, he stacks the cards in favor of the idea, product, or person he is trying to sell. He may be satisfied with overemphasis of the facts that favor his side and underemphasis of those on the other side, or he may distort the evidence completely, using lies and censorship of truth to make sure that the picture the public sees is one that will make it seem unreasonable for anyone to favor the opposite cause.

WHAT IS THE POISONING THE WELL DEVICE?

The device of Poisoning the Well is one form of Card Stacking. The propagandist using this device states his proposition in such a way that the listener takes sides against the opposition without thinking. When the businessman is favored in an election because he is not "a dirty politician," when you are asked to vote against a bill that will "allow gambling and syndicated vice in your fair city," or when you are asked to buy a product because it will protect you from upset stomachs, heel marks on your kitchen linoleum, or bad breath in dogs, the propagandist is poisoning the well by the subtle assumptions that politics and dishonesty go together, that syndicated vice must accompany legalized gambling, and that we lie awake at night worrying about our digestive systems, kitchen linoleum, and dog's breath.

WHAT IS THE RED HERRING DEVICE?

The Red Herring device is the introduction of information that really is not relevant to the question at hand but which the propagandist hopes will catch your attention so completely that you will miss the real issues. He tells you that the other candidate is divorced, is wealthy, or belongs to some unpopular church. He reminds you that his product is "imported." He hopes that you will be so distracted by his startling but wholly irrelevant information that you won't get around to asking the very logical question, "So what?"

WHAT IS THE TRANSFER DEVICE?

When the propagandist uses the Transfer device, he relates the thing that he would have you accept to something which already has your respect and favor. He pictures a handsome young man offering his girlfriend a cigarette or admiring her hair color or clean breath and hopes you will assume that you are really being sold romance in a package. The good men wear white hats; the man in the white coat is a scientist or doctor; the official photographed in front of the church is a religious man; the office seeker pictured visiting wounded soldiers is patriotic.

The Transfer device can also be used against a cause or idea. The enemy is shown abusing old women and little children. Brand X leaves a dark ring on your clothes or causes your boy friend to tell you goodnight with a handshake instead of a kiss.

WHAT IS THE TESTIMONIAL DEVICE?

The Testimonial device is really an abuse of a legitimate form of evidence. This is an age of specialization in an ever-increasing number of highly technical fields. You will never have the training or the time to become well-informed in all the many areas that are related to your professional and private life. You must rely upon authorities who have the education and experience to give you the information you need about their particular fields. You should, however, learn how to evaluate the authority of the individual who gives the information so that what he says won't influence you more than it should. When you are faced with disagreement between two authorities, you should be even more careful to examine their backgrounds, qualifications, reputations in their fields, and personal prejudices.

HOW DO YOU EVALUATE A TESTIMONIAL?

When information comes to you from one who claims to speak as an authority, you should examine that authority by asking two questions:

1. What is the background of education and experience upon which this person is basing his information or judgment?

2. Will your acceptance of this person's information or judgment benefit him in any way?

If you make the effort to learn the identity and background of the individual who is offered as an authority, you will usually place the proper emphasis upon his testimony. The propagandist, however, doesn't want you to make such an effort. He hopes you will be so impressed by the importance of the celebrities he uses to endorse his ideas and products that you won't ask whether these celebrities qualify as authorities on the question at hand. Sometimes an individual who has gained prominence and fame in his own field will express an opinion in another area in which he is no more an authority than any other man on the street. The nuclear physicist has a right to an opinion on religion, the war hero to his own ideas about American education, and the famous surgeon to his personal attitude toward our foreign policy. The propagandist is trying to mislead you when he expects you to accept these ideas, opinions, and attitudes as being important because of the people who hold them. Frequently such people have spoken as private individuals with no thought of having their personal ideas accepted as authoritative, but the propagandist has used the words and the prominence of the speaker to support his own cause.

Frequently, however, the celebrity has been paid directly or indirectly to endorse the product or idea. Dazzled by Mr. Famous Star, you fail to wonder why he is a better judge of the taste of a brand of orange juice, diet beverage, or cigarettes than ordinary mortals.

Sometimes you even accept anonymous testimonials: "Authorities have found," "a leading laboratory has proved," and "a prominent health journal has published the facts." In the face of such convincing proof, who are you to quibble about identity? You dose yourself with the approved pain killer, scrub your bathroom with the acceptable disinfectant, and start your days with the recognized corn flakes, serene in the knowledge that every move in your daily routine bears the stamp of the Better Businessman's Bureau, the Good Housekeeping Institute Seal of Approval, and the blessing of the National Council of Dental Hygiene.

A famous authority and prominent American writer once said that there is no limit to how far a man will go to escape thinking. Propaganda plays such a prominent part in the modern world that you need not go very far to find such an escape. But if you want to reach your professional and personal goals, down the roadway of sound judgment, you will learn to recognize the propaganda escape hatch as the trap that it is—so say nine out of ten leading propaganda detection experts.

ASSIGNMENTS

I. Using the labels given in this chapter, label each of the following fallacies.
   1. I use Ztergen fertilizer for my roses. Barbara Zane, who is a national television personality, recommends it highly. *Testimonial*
   2. After staying overnight in New York City, I decided that I definitely do not like big cities. *Hasty generalization*
   3. We should all support Candidate Smith for the state senate. He is gaining votes every day. *Bandwagon*
   4. The modern welfare program is dangerous to our moral fiber.
   5. My brother bought a new car because everyone else at his office had one. *Bandwagon*
   6. I would never drive a Lampex automobile because Ziggs Turner drives one. *Name calling*
   7. Surely such a faithful church member could not be guilty of so major a crime. *Poisoning the well*
   8. Nearly half of the doctors in our city buy their clothing at Sam's Smart Shop. *Red herring or Bandwagon*

II. Purchase a copy of your local newspaper. Read carefully the editorials and the letters to the editors. Study the ideas set forth by the popular syndicated columnists. Bring clippings of your material to class and be prepared to discuss and label any fallacies present.

III. Advertisers often use the propaganda devices described in this chapter to sell their products. Look through several recent magazines and find at least *ten* advertisements that use these devices. Clip these and paste each on an individual sheet of paper. Mark the words and items in the pictures that are propaganda and label the device. Bring your clippings to class for discussion.

ELEVEN / Data Collection

WHERE IS HERE AND THERE?

As you have seen, to locate a problem and investigate all the possible solutions, you must gather all the related information you can. You can gather information from four sources: on-the-spot observation, personal interviews, public speeches, and written material. Sometimes you may need to use only one of these methods, but if you are a thorough worker, you will usually gather information from many sources. Some people can't see the facts even when they are right under their noses. But the person who locates the real problems and finds the best solutions is the person who leaves no source of information unexamined.

HOW DO YOU GATHER INFORMATION ON THE SPOT?

How you will conduct on-the-spot observation depends upon the kind of problem you are considering. The medical researcher observes the action of bacteria, viruses, drugs, and vaccines on the specimens in his laboratory. The social scientist studies the conditions in an area and the actions of its inhabitants. The anthropologist lives in a primitive village and observes the customs of the natives. The motion study expert follows the progress of a product through a factory and notes the movements of the workers involved in the manufacturing process. But regardless of the methods used by researchers, these men all have three habits in common: (1) They are alert to all that occurs. (2) They keep an open, objective mind. They draw no conclusions until they have gathered all the facts, and they don't try to arrange the facts to lead to a desired conclusion. (3) As they observe, they take careful and complete notes. They don't depend upon their memories. They know that nobody can remember everything and that their personal biases may cause them to forget something because they don't want to remember it or because they thought at the time it was unimportant. If their notes are complete, later when they reread them, they may see a relationship between the facts that they didn't see at the time.

HOW DO YOU GATHER INFORMATION FROM AN EXPERT?

If you talk to people to gather information from them, you should exercise the same caution you would in on-the-spot observation. Don't overlook anyone who might have information or a valid opinion. Sometimes you will gather information from an individual during an informal chat. At other times the person is a stranger to you, has a tight schedule, or is generally unavailable. When any of these conditions exist, you should make an appointment to interview him about the matter.

WHAT PREPARATIONS SHOULD YOU MAKE FOR AN INTERVIEW?

If you interview such an expert, you should make some preparations before you arrange the meeting. Read all the information available on the subject. Naturally, you should take notes. It may be that you will learn everything you want to know in this way. If not, you will have the basic information and can concentrate when you talk with the expert on the data which he has that you could not find anywhere else. Never take the time of an expert while you try to get him to give you information that is freely available elsewhere.

If you don't know the individual, find out his particular qualifications and prejudices. It may be that the man you planned to ask for information is really qualified in a slightly different field and is not the best person to approach for what you want to know. If you find that he is the man to help you, surveying his background before you meet him will enable you to know how to phrase your questions in a diplomatic way and how to evaluate his answers. Some careful researchers include even the hobbies and avocational interests of the person to be interviewed in their preparation. They believe that finding any common interest with the expert may cause him to be more helpful than he might otherwise be.

HOW DO YOU ARRANGE TO INTERVIEW SOMEONE?

When you have decided that a particular expert has information you need and can't obtain from published material, call for an interview. Introduce yourself; give your company, the project on which you are working, and your qualifications for doing so. It may be that you can find out all you need to know in a telephone conversation.

A face-to-face interview is necessary when the information is complicated, when you will need to be shown something or to show something, or when there is a possibility that the person won't want to release the information to you. When any of these circumstances exist, you will, of course, ask the secretary for an appointment. Don't quibble over time. If at all possible, take the hour offered you, making note of whatever time limits are set. Unless the matter is confidential or there is some question that your party may not want to help you, be certain that he will understand ahead of time what you wish to know. He may save his time and yours if he can gather certain facts or papers before your arrival.

Sometimes it is better to write for an interview. If there is a possibility that he won't see you or if you need to establish your qualifications at any length, it may be better to write, stating the nature of your investigation and mentioning other similar work you have done.

Joe Quickly and Anne K. Pable were separately engaged in research that required them to examine some rare manuscripts that were in the possession of Dr. Centrik. Joe wrote a pleasant letter identifying himself and his project and asking to see the manuscripts. He received no answer at all. Anne wrote, enclosing the unfinished typescript of the section that related to Dr. Centrik's manuscripts, an explanation of why she needed to see the collection, and a copy of an article she had published on a similar project. Dr. Centrik replied immediately, offering Anne the use of his library and his time and enclosing a copy of an article he had written on a related subject.

HOW DO YOU PLAN AN INTERVIEW?

After you have made your appointment, you will still have some preparations to make. Decide exactly what questions you should ask in order to find out what you need to know. Memorize the questions. Think about all you know about the person and about the subject. If you try to plan now for the possible turns the interview might take, you will be able to use the time of the interview better.

You should arrive for your interview exactly on time or perhaps five minutes early. If you are meeting him at his office and you have to wait, use the time to observe your surroundings. Pictures, diplomas, maps, or charts on the wall, the furnishings of the room, books and magazines on the tables and shelves, and the general atmosphere of the waiting room may give you some clue to his personality that will help you to communicate with him better.

HOW DO YOU CONDUCT AN INTERVIEW?

When you meet, it isn't necessary to engage in social pleasantries such as commenting on the weather or admiring the view of the trees from his office window. He is probably a busy man who is in the habit of attacking problems directly. Of course, if he wants to talk about something else, you will have to let him. Don't, however, allow his temporary interest to distract you from your subject for more than a few minutes.

He can help you better if you tell him briefly what you are doing, what general information you need from him, and how you expect to use it. Then you can use your questions to get the specific information. Although you have planned your questions and memorized them, you need not phrase them exactly as you planned. Try to work them into your conversation easily and gracefully. As a carry-over from their school days, many people are made uncomfortable by a steady stream of formal questions.

He may answer many of your questions without your asking him. Perhaps, in spite of your careful forethought, he will open up areas that are entirely new to you. You may find this new information vital. On the other hand, it may merely be a distraction from what you need to know. You will have to judge hastily whether to allow him to continue talking about his new area or to try to bring him gently and politely back to the problem.

HOW DO YOU TAKE NOTES?

If the information is too detailed to remember, ask if you may take notes. Even if he says no he doesn't mind, he may be disturbed if you write while he talks. Therefore, you should write as inconspicuously as possible, keeping your eyes on his face as much as possible. Certainly you won't try to take dictation. When you begin to write, he may begin to talk less freely. If he does, you will have to quit taking down any but the most difficult material. More than likely, however, he will know that you need to be accurate and will be glad to help you get the facts straight. If any of the information is so complicated that you are afraid you didn't record it accurately, ask him if you may read it to him for him to check. Your notes should be dated and documented with the name of the person interviewed, his title or position, and the place in which you interviewed him.

HOW DO YOU CLOSE THE INTERVIEW?

When you have taken as much of the person's time as you were promised, bring the interview to a close, thank him for his time, and leave. If the secretary didn't tell you how much time you could take, judge how busy he is from the number of people waiting to see him and the number of phone calls and interruptions, and limit your interview accordingly. Even if he seems relaxed and unhurried, don't stay more than half an hour unless he has become so much interested in your project that he urges you to stay. Even if he does, you still shouldn't stay much longer.

WHAT DO YOU DO WITH YOUR NOTES AFTER THE INTERVIEW?

Immediately after the interview you should go over your notes, completing by memory any information which seems fragmentary. As soon as possible, work your notes up into the form in which you will use them for your report or project. You should be very careful in this writing to keep the meaning and purpose of the person's remarks as he intended them. If you are writing an article in which you use his name and quote him either directly or indirectly, you may wish to send him a copy for approval before you submit your article for publication. File the notes from the interview with the notes which you took during your preliminary reading.

ASSIGNMENTS

I. In Chapter One you were asked to gather information about your occupational area by visiting with someone presently employed at such a job. For that first interview you were given some general questions to guide you, but these questions were related more to the importance of communication skills than to the more detailed aspects of the work itself.

You should now conduct another interview with a different person employed in your occupational area. This time you should find out as much as possible about the exact nature of the jobs performed, specific working conditions, and opportunities for advancement. If some other subject for an interview has come out of your committee work or your preparation for your formal report, you may want to use this assignment to gather material relevant to that subject. The following assignments are directly connected with this second interview:

1. Prepare a set of at least twenty questions that you want answered. Remember, though, that a good interview is much more than just a question and answer session.
2. After your interview, sit down with your own question sheet and see if you can answer all of your questions.

II. Organize the material which you have gathered during your interview into a carefully unified 500-word theme.

TWELVE / Gathering Information at Professional Meetings

**WHY ARE PROFESSIONAL MEETINGS
A VALUABLE SOURCE OF INFORMATION?**

When you begin to work in your chosen field, you will probably be invited to join the official organization of that profession. One of the most important advantages of such membership is the privilege of attending the meetings, conventions, and workshops that the organization will hold. These gatherings will offer you one of the best ways of keeping up with the latest developments in your field. The information gained at professional meetings is frequently well in advance of that which you can get from other sources.

The world moves so fast that you can't keep up with the latest knowledge in any given field if you rely entirely upon books and other published material. By the time a new drug or machine or product or process has been researched, reported, and published in a book and that book has been purchased by the library, accessioned, and placed on the shelves to be examined by you, patients have developed allergies from using the drug, the machine is in need of repairs, the product is on sale at the local discount house, and another area has been voted federal aid because the new process put the men of a community out of work.

Not only is the information gained at professional meetings more up to date than that found elsewhere, but it may also be more directly related to your needs. Other companies have faced problems similar to those your company faces, and they have found solutions. As you hear them discuss these solutions, you may find some of the answers you are seeking. Sometimes your company will send you to a professional meeting in order to find the answer to a specific problem. Sometimes you will go just to learn about the most recent developments in your field. What you learn at a meeting may be of no immediate use to you, but sometime in the future what you have learned may be important to you. In none of these cases will you want to depend upon your memory. You may need to recall what you have learned to make a report to some individual, committee, or larger group. At other times you need the information for your own immediate use in a large report or paper. You will also want to record information to keep in reserve for future, undefined use. For all these purposes you will want to know how to gather the most useful information in the most efficient way.

WHAT PREPARATION SHOULD YOU MAKE BEFORE ATTENDING A MEETING?

If you want to gather useful information efficiently, you must prepare for the occasion. Usually you know something about a public address before it is given. When the professional organization to which you belong holds its annual meeting, you will receive a brochure listing the speakers, their topics, and the time for their addresses. If the meeting is local, your newspaper will have an article announcing it. You will read all this material carefully. But you shouldn't stop there. If the meeting is important enough for you to attend and for your company to pick up the check for your expenses, you will want to go prepared to get the maximum benefit from the occasion.

After you have studied the program and selected those meetings which you think will be the most valuable to you, you should try to learn as much as you can about the speakers and their subjects. All the material that you read before you attend a meeting should be examined with two purposes in mind: (1) to give you the background you need in order to understand the material which will be presented and to benefit from it; (2) to allow you to evaluate what you hear with an informed and unbiased mind.

All learning moves from the known to the unknown. If you have already learned as much about the subject as you can, you should be able to add to that knowledge the fine points that the speaker knows and that aren't such general knowledge. Sometimes, unfortunately, the speech will be little more than a rehashing of the information you have already gathered. Sometimes you can foresee this kind of performance and use your time more valuably by attending some other meeting held at the same time, by meeting some speaker who has especially interested you, or by visiting some of the exhibits. If the speaker is an active, alert man, still making real contributions in his field, and not some old-timer who has been asked to speak because he is famous for work he did twenty years ago, he will probably have some information beyond what you have been able to learn. And you will be able to make better use of it if you have taken the trouble to get a thorough background in the subject.

HOW DO YOU EVALUATE WHAT YOU HEAR?

You don't go to workshops and conventions to swallow completely all that is dished out to you. Frequently, you will find that the speakers disagree with each other, with what you heard at a similar meeting elsewhere, or with what you already know. You should, therefore, be prepared to evaluate intelligently what you hear. As you listen, you should examine the logic of the speaker's reasoning; you should also be on the alert for propaganda devices. Whether the speaker employs these devices intentionally or unintentionally, you shouldn't be fooled by them. If you learn as much as possible about the speaker before the meeting, you will be able to make a better judgment about what he says. What is his professional background? He may be identified in the brochure that announced the meeting. If he is prominent enough, you may find a brief biography in *Who's Who* or in a specialized *Who's Who* for your profession or section of the country. An issue of one of your professional journals may identify him in some way. Has he written any books or articles? Find and read them if you can. As you read, make some judgment of the writer. Does he seem to approach his subject objectively or does he seem inclined to oversimplification, excessive enthusiasm, or oversight of some pertinent facts or considerations? Is there anything in his background or present position that could logically cause a bias in his attitudes? Unless you are aware of his prejudices, a dynamic speaker can persuade you to accept ideas that are not completely sound. Your employer may spend money on the basis of your report of the speeches. He has a right to expect you to weigh carefully what you hear. Even if the speaker is a famous authority in his field, you should know what other authorities have thought and written about the subject. There may well be some valuable aspects of the matter that your speaker has overlooked, or there may be another reasonable, though less popular, side to the question. Naturally, you will take notes on this background material. You may need to summarize this background briefly in your report. Moreover, you can review your notes quickly before you attend the meeting.

HOW SHOULD YOU LISTEN TO A SPEECH?

To get the most from a public speech, you should arrive a few minutes early and find a seat near the front. Try to sit where you will not be disturbed by latecomers or by groups who use such gatherings to visit with old friends. Attend the meeting alone or with someone who is also serious about gaining from what he hears. Don't worry about how you can leave early. Meet that problem when it comes. For the time being concentrate on the speech.

Spend the few minutes before the speech in rereading your notes on the speaker's subject or in reviewing in your mind what you have learned about it. Then when the speaker begins, you will be ready to tune in on his wavelength at once because you will already be thinking with him. While the speaker is acknowledging the introduction and engaging in a few opening pleasantries, compare the man you see and hear with what you already know of him. But don't be misled by the speaker's presentation. You aren't here to be entertained. Unless you are attending a convention of comedians or toastmasters, there may be little relationship between the speaker's ability to hold an audience and his professional knowledge. The people in the audience are there presumably to learn something which the speaker knows, and he shouldn't have to resort to tricks in order to hold their attention.

The problem of attention is your concern, and it isn't always an easy one. One of the reasons that listening is difficult is that you are capable of thinking many times faster than the speaker can talk. While he is explaining to you why alphodiesel engines are inclined to coagulate when operated under high pressures and at low altitudes, your mind has time to wander. Those mental wanderings might be fine if you could always be certain that your mind would get back in time. Since you can't, it would be better if you confined its wandering as closely as possible. If you must think of something else while the speaker discusses the coagulation tendencies of the alphodiesel engine, you might make a brief review of what you already know about alphodiesel engines, about coagulation, or about any other fact that seems relevant. Your mental wanderings will then aid your understanding of the speech rather than interfere with it.

While you listen to what the speaker is saying right now, try to connect it to what he has already said. Summarize the speech to this point and try to anticipate what will follow. If the speaker draws the conclusions which you expect, you will understand them better because you have drawn them yourself. If he does not, you can listen for his explanation or be prepared to reexamine what you have heard to see why his conclusions are different from yours. Remember, your physical presence is not enough. You are there to listen to what is said. Intelligent listening isn't an oral sponging-up process. You can benefit from what you hear only if you listen actively, questioning and evaluating what you are told, measuring it by what you already know, and applying it to the problems and questions that you have already found. On the other hand, you should suspend complete judgment of the material the speaker is presenting until he is finished. It may be only later, when you are reviewing your notes in your room, that the full impact of what he has said will reach you. Be careful, also, to hear what the speaker really says and not what you think he says or what you think he should say.

HOW SHOULD YOU TAKE NOTES ON WHAT YOU HEAR?

You will listen better if you take notes on the speech. You will also need notes to prepare your report. Even if no report is expected of you, you should have some record of what you have heard since you don't always know what pieces of information you will need later.

Probably your notes will be more useful to you if you take them on full-sized typing or notebook paper. Such sheets will fit well into a folder in your filing cabinet and can be filed with other material on the same subject. Arrange the material on the page to show the relative importance of various items and their relationship to each other. If you take notes in a small pocket notebook or on file cards, you may be tempted to take less than complete notes. Your purpose here is to cover one lecture as a complete unit, and you don't want to break up information into bits and pieces. Later, if you want to extract various ideas or facts from your notes to be used in a paper, you can do so more accurately if you have a complete resumé of the lecture to draw from. Since the notes will go into your file, the first thing you should put down is the date, the occasion, the place, the name of the speaker, and the title of his speech. Then if you use the material at some later time, you won't have to depend upon your memory.

Some speakers are well organized. You can almost hear the *I* and the *A* under *II* that must be in their notes. If so, take your notes in outline form with proper indentations for subheads. If you are able to take most of your notes in outline form, don't be disturbed if occasionally there is a block of material which you prefer to summarize with whole or nearly whole sentences. If the lecture isn't organized well enough for you to take your notes in outline form, you may still be able to indicate by indentation that certain material seems to come under some heading which has already been indicated. Perhaps the speaker will indicate with the words *second* and *third* that he is enumerating, and you can number some items. If he indicates by voice, gesture, or repetition the importance of some term or fact, you can underline it.

Leave a wide margin on the left-hand side of your page for additional comments that may occur to you or for anything you might want to add to make your notes more useful. Don't fill up the margins or corners with aimless doodling that distracts you as you take your notes and will distract you as you use them.

Don't try to take down everything the speaker says. He may tell stories as illustrations. He may repeat points for emphasis. Some of his remarks may just be padding. Your notes will be more valuable to you than a transcript of his speech because you will have omitted such extraneous material and preserved only the real meat of the address. For this reason it isn't wise to try to take the speech down in shorthand or to employ a tape recorder. A tape recorder is useful at a convention to catch an address which you are unable to hear, but it can't take the place of your notes. If you rely upon your tape recorder, you will have to listen to the lecture again in order to pick out the most pertinent information. So instead of saving time as you had intended, you will have to spend more time because you will have to listen to the lecture twice. Tape recording a lecture may seem very thorough, but it is unnecessary. Actually you won't listen as well the first time if you are relying upon a machine.

ASSIGNMENTS

I. Although you may have gathered some of the information called for here in an earlier assignment, find the answers to the following questions:
   1. What is the name of the most important national organization in your field?
   2. When and where does this organization hold meetings?
   3. Who may attend these meetings? What fees are charged?
   4. What are the names of any regional, state, and local organizations within your field?
   5. When are their meetings held?
   6. Who may attend these meetings? What fees are charged?

II. Perhaps now or some other time during the semester your instructor will ask you to attend a nearby convention. If so, you should submit to the instructor the following information:
   1. When was the convention held? Where? What dates?
   2. What professional organization was the sponsor?
   3. How many delegates were in attendance?

Assignments

4. Was the program largely composed of general sessions with important speakers, or was it a workshop program with smaller study groups?
5. Exactly what sessions of the convention did you attend?
6. Who was the keynote speaker?
7. What are his qualifications?
8. Write a brief summary of his important statements.
9. Write a short reaction to his statements. Did you agree with him? Did you find him convincing? Did you find him interesting?
10. If you attended any small workshop groups, indicate the subject discussed.
11. Who was in charge of the workshop group? What are his qualifications?
12. Was the subject treated in a panel discussion, with a debate or forum, or in a general discussion by everyone present?
13. Write a brief summary of the discussion within this workshop group.
14. Write a brief evaluation of the discussion. Did the subject receive fair treatment? Did any opposition present have an adequate voice? Was the subject handled in such a way that it gave you any new ideas or changed any that you already had?

III. Perhaps it will be impossible for you to attend an actual convention. If so, obtain a set of written reports (often published in a professional journal) from a recent convention and answer as many of the questions in II (above) as possible.

THIRTEEN / Using the Library

**WHY DO YOU NEED TO LEARN
HOW TO USE THE LIBRARY?**

In the fast-moving professional world you are about to enter, knowledge in each field is changing and multiplying so fast that you will constantly find that much that you know is no longer so. Of course, you will do your best to learn all that you can about your field while you are in school; and you will also try to keep up with the advances that are made later. Nevertheless, you will soon realize that you can't know everything about your field and that you need to be able to locate the information that you don't have.

If you become really successful in your profession, libraries will play an important part in your life, not only in college but throughout your career. This is true even if you haven't chosen one of the professions usually considered to be "bookish." Once you learn to use a library and to depend upon its facilities, you won't think you have adjusted to a new community until you have become acquainted with its local library. Fortunately, once you have learned to use one good library well, you will find you know how to use other libraries also; for they all have their materials organized in a similar manner.

HOW IS A LIBRARY ARRANGED?

Whether they are located in an abandoned armory or on a university campus, most libraries divide their facilities into three sections. There will be a corner, a section, a room, or a floor devoted to *periodicals;* a section or room where *reference books* are found and used; and a section, room, wing, or floor reserved for the rows and rows of books which are normally referred to as the "stacks."

HOW ARE THE BOOKS ARRANGED?

The area of the "stacks" may be closed to public admission. If so, you will have to ask for the book you want at the desk reserved for that purpose. The library may have "open stacks" so that you can go among the shelves of books, find your own book, and perhaps even sit down at a desk close by to use it. Some libraries allow their patrons free access to fiction books and biographies but maintain "closed stacks" for other books. Whether you find your own book or ask the librarian for it, you will need to understand the way books are arranged in a library and how they are designated so they can be found.

All the books in a library are arranged according to one of two systems. The *Dewey Decimal System* divides knowledge into ten divisions, easily subdivided by decimals. Its main divisions of subject classification are as follows:

000–099 General Works
100–199 Philosophy and Psychology
200–299 Religion
300–399 Social Science
400–499 Languages

500–599 Pure Science
600–699 Applied Sciences
700–799 Fine Arts and Recreation
800–899 Literature
900–999 History, Travel, Collected Biography

Fiction in English may be classified under *F* and arranged alphabetically according to author, or it may be under the appropriate number in the 800s. Individual biography may be classified under *B* and arranged alphabetically according to the name of the subject, or it may be arranged under the numbers appropriate to the subject's field. Public and high school libraries are more likely to use *F* and *B* headings than are college and university libraries.

The *Library of Congress System* uses letters for general headings and offers twenty categories. Although the Dewey System has been in general use longer than the Library of Congress System, more and more libraries are converting to the Library of Congress System as they increase their holdings and need more subdivisions to locate one book among hundreds of its class. Here are the main divisions of the Library of Congress System:

A. General Works (including Encyclopedias)
B. Philosophy and Religion
    BD. Metaphysics
    BF. Psychology
    BJ. Ethics
    BL. Religions
    BM. Judaism
    BR. and following—Christianity
C. History (General, including Civilization, Genealogy)
D. History—Old World
    DA. Great Britain
    DC. France
    DE. Classical antiquity
    DF. Greece
    DK. Russia
    DS. Asia
    DT. Africa
E. American History and General United States History
F. American History (Local) and Latin American
G. Geography, Anthropology, Folklore, Sports, and other
H. Social Sciences
    HA. Statistics
    HB. – HD. Economics
    HF. Commerce
    HG. –HJ. Finance
    HM. Sociology
    HQ. Family, marriage, home
    HV. Social pathology (alcoholism, criminology, penology)
J. Political Science
K. Law
L. Education
M. Music
N. Fine Arts
    NA. Architecture
    NB. Sculpture
    ND. Painting
P. Language and literature
    PA. Classical language and literature
    PB. Celtic languages
    PC. Romance languages
    PD. Germanic languages
    PE. English languages
    PN. Literary history and collections
    PQ. Romance literature
    PR. English literature
    PS. American literature
    PT. Teutonic literature
    PZ. Fiction and juvenile literature

Q. Science
  QA. Mathematics
  QB. Astronomy
  QC. Physics
  QD. Chemistry
  QE. Geology
  QH. Natural History
  QK. Botany
  QL. Zoology
  QM. Human anatomy
  QP. Physiology
  QR. Bacteriology
R. Medicine
  RD. Surgery
  RS. Pharmacy
  RT. Nursing
S. Agriculture, Forestry, Animal culture, Fish culture, and Hunting
T. Technology
U. Military science
V. Naval science
Z. Bibliography and library science

Each book has a Dewey number or a Library of Congress number and, below it, a "book number" consisting of a code number for the author's last name followed by a digit or digits and a small letter. Below the book number may be the date of the book if the library has more than one edition and the copy number if the library has more than one copy. The Dewey number or the Library of Congress number and the book number make up the complete *call number.* The complete call number belongs to only one book in the library and is, consequently, the most accurate designation of that book in a library. You will use it to call for a book at the library desk or, if the library has open stacks, to locate the book for yourself.

WHERE ARE THE BOOKS LISTED?

All of the books in the library are listed in two places. The "shelf list" is a catalog of the books as they stand on the shelves. Books are entered on 3 × 5-inch cards arranged in trays. Because the books are arranged on the library shelves by numbers assigned them according to their subjects, the shelf list, which is arranged by these numbers, can also be used as a subject catalog. You won't use the shelf list often; but when you do need it, you will find it useful.

Usually you will locate books in the card catalog. This catalog also consists of cases of trays containing 3 × 5-inch cards. The cards are here arranged alphabetically; a label on the front of the drawer indicates the alphabetical range of that tray, and guide cards indicate alphabetical divisions within the tray.

Within the trays are three kinds of cards: *subject cards, author cards,* and *title cards.* Figure 38 is an example of these cards:

Subject card

```
     E         KENNEDY, JOHN FITZGERALD, PRES.,
   842.9         1919-1963 ----ASSASSINATION
    .M35


              Manchester, William Raymond, 1922-
                  The death of a president,
                November 25, 1963. (1st ed.) New
                   York, Harper & Row  (c 1967)
```

Title card

```
     E          The Death of a President
   842.9
    .M35


              Manchester, William Raymond, 1922-
                  The death of a president, November
                25, 1963. (1st ed.) New York,
                Harper & Row  (c 1967)
```

Author card

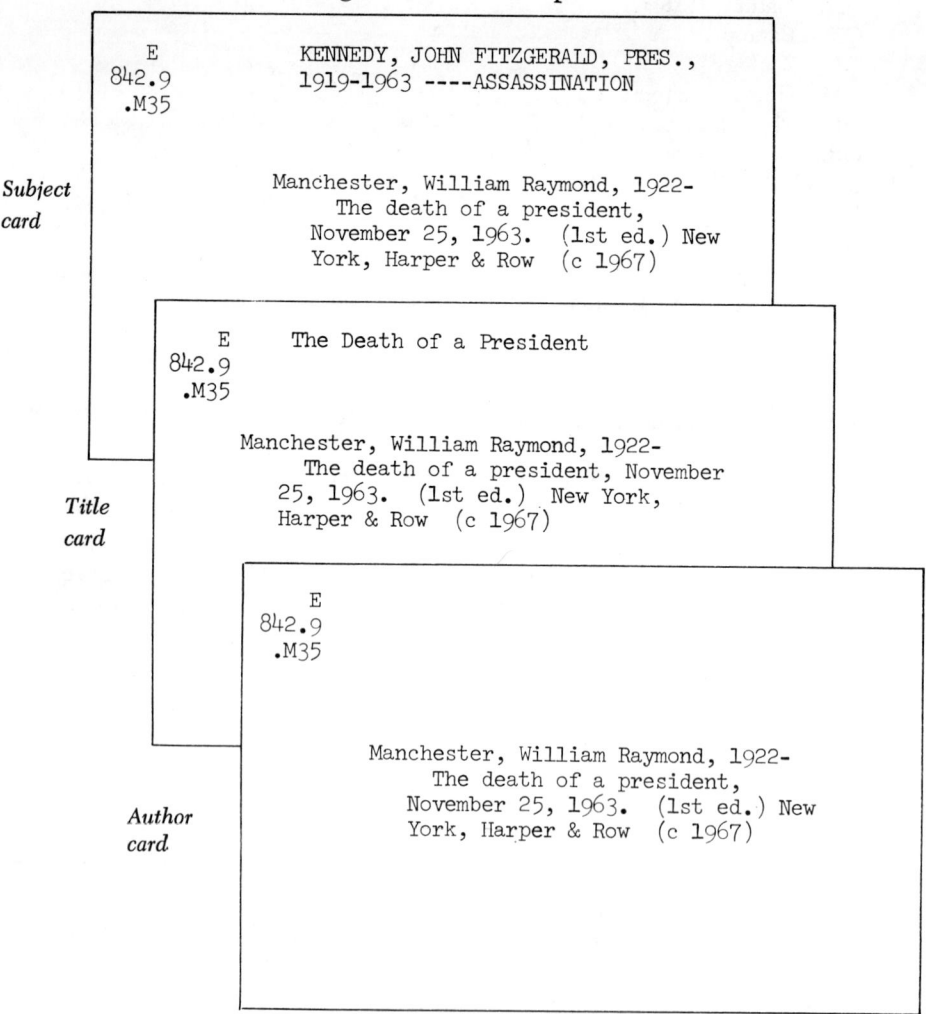

```
     E
   842.9
    .M35


              Manchester, William Raymond, 1922-
                  The death of a president,
                November 25, 1963. (1st ed.) New
                   York, Harper & Row  (c 1967)
```

Figure 38

You will notice that the only difference between these cards is that the title or subject has been inserted above the author's name on the title or subject card. Don't be confused when the title or subject is also the name of a person. Notice that the inserted titles or subjects are typed in on the cards, but the rest of the information is printed. The subject heading is in capital letters. The subject heading and the title heading are indented, but the author's name is not.

Cards for books written by one author and cards listing that author as the first of several authors are filed before cards that list him as a second or later author. For identical words or names, the filing order is person, place, title.

>   Hudson, William Henry
>   Hudson, N. J.
>   *The Hudson and its Moods*

There are a few other practices followed by libraries in filing cards that you should know.

Filing is done word by word rather than letter by letter.

>   North America
>   North Sea
>   *Northanger Abbey*
>   Northern Ireland
>   Northern Rhodesia
>   The Northerners

Abbreviations and numbers are filed as though they were spelled out: Dr. Johnson as Doctor Johnson, St. Louis as Saint Louis, U.S. as United States, 18th century as eighteenth century.

Personal names beginning Mac, Mc and M' are all filed under Mac.

A, An, The, and their foreign equivalents are ignored when they occur initially in alphabetizing.

The foreign prefixes de, van, and von are ignored, and the card is filed as though the name were *Winkle* not *van Winkle*.

But French surnames beginning with La, Le, Dela, Du, and Des are treated as though the prefix were joined to the next word.

Saints, Popes, Kings, and common people are filed in that order by name and not by title.

Although subjects are subdivided alphabetically, history is divided chronologically.

GENERAL REFERENCE WORKS

Ayer's Directory of Newspapers and Periodicals. 1880. Current edition published in 1968.

Besterman, Theodore. *A World Bibliography of Bibliographies.* 1947–49. 2 vols. plus index.

Book Review Digest. 1906 ff. A standard source for critical reviews.

Book Review Index. 1965 ff. Monthly index to reviews appearing in more than 200 periodicals.

Cumulative Book Index. 1898 ff.

Gregory, Winifred. *American Newspapers, 1821–1936.* 1937. Lists files available in the United States and Canada.

Mudge, Isadore G. *Guide to Reference Books.* 6th ed. 1935–Sup., 1939, 1941, 1944, 1947. The standard reference to bibliographies until the 1967 publication of Winchell's work.

New Serial Titles. 1961. 2 vols. Lists all periodicals which began publication in 1950 or later; locates publications in libraries in the United States and Canada. Monthly supplements, annual cumulations.

Nineteenth Century Readers' Guide, 1890–1899. 1945.

Poole's Index to Periodical Literature, 1800–1906. 1882–1908. 7 vols.

Readers' Guide to Periodical Literature, 1900 ff. 1905 ff. The most standard magazine index. Author-title-subject index.

Ulrich's International Periodical Directory. 11th ed. 1968. A listing from over 7,500 periodicals, grouped by subject.

Winchell, Constance M. *Guide to Reference Books,* 8th ed. 1967. Annotated list of reference books classed by subject. Has replaced Mudge as the standard bibliography of bibliographies.

GENERAL DICTIONARIES

A Dictionary of American English on Historical Principles. 1938.

The Oxford English Dictionary. 1961. 12 vols. and sup. (A corrected reissue in 1933 of *A New English Dictionary on Historical Principles,* 10 vols. and sup., 1888–1928.) Excellent etymological dictionary.

The Random House Dictionary of the English Language. 1966. A standard prescriptive dictionary.

Webster's Third New International Dictionary of the English Language. 1961. A standard descriptive dictionary.

TECHNICAL DICTIONARIES

Chamber's Technical Dictionary. Revised and supplemented in 1948 by C. F. Tweney and L. E. C. Hughes. A good all-round technical dictionary.

Computer Dictionary. 1966. Identification, classification, and interpretation of terms and concepts important to electronic data processing.

Crispin's Dictionary of Technical Terms. 9th ed. 1961. Terms commonly used in aeronautics, trades, printing, and chemistry.

Dictionary of Architecture and Building. 1901. Old but still the standard dictionary in this field.

Dictionary of Electronic Terms. 1955. Helpful list of electronic terms. Now out of print.

Dictionary of Scientific and Technical Words. A convenient book with definitions of some 10,000 words. Now out of print.

A Dictionary for Accountants. 1963. Alphabetized accounting terms and definitions.

Electronics and Nucleonics Dictionary. 1967. Definitions, abbreviations, and synonyms for over 13,000 terms.

Engineering Terminology. 2nd ed. 1939. A useful guide to specialized terms in the field. Now out of print.

Hutchinson's Technical and Scientific Encyclopedia. 1935. 4 vols.

McGraw-Hill Encyclopedia of Science and Technology. 1960. 15 vols. The most current general encyclopedia in the field.

Modern Dictionary of Electronics. 1968. Analysis of words and their meanings as determined by common usage.

Scientific Terminology. 1953.

BIOGRAPHY

American Authors 1600–1900; British Authors Before 1800; British Authors of the Nineteenth Century; Junior Book of Authors; Twentieth Century Authors. 1938. A series edited by Stanley Kunitz and Howard Haycraft.

Asimov's Biographical Encyclopedia of Science and Technology. 1964. Biographic sketches of 1,000 scientists from the Greek Era to the Space Age.

Chamber's Biographical Dictionary. 1962. International listings.

Contemporary Authors. 1962. 14 vols. Guide to twentieth-century authors and their works.

Current Biography. 1968. Contemporary Americans, with photographs.

Dictionary of American Biography. 1958. A multivolume work containing biographic sketches of Americans no longer living. Frequently referred to as *DAB*.

Dictionary of American Scholars. 1963–64. 4 vols. Sketches of scholars in history, English, speech, and drama; foreign languages, linguistics, and philology; philosophy, religion, and law.

Dictionary of National Biography. 1965. British equivalent to the *DAB*. Frequently referred to as *DNB*.

National Cyclopaedia of American Biography. 1898–1946. More than 50 vols. to date, containing a broad coverage of American historical biography.

New Century Cyclopedia of Names. 1954. 3 vols. Over 100,000 proper names with short biographical sketches.

Webster's Biographical Dictionary. Brief data of famous persons.

Who's Who. An annual listing of prominent living British persons, with abbreviated biographical data. *Who Was Who* is a separate list of the biographies of persons now deceased, with date of death. Pub. 1964.

Who's Who in America. A biennial equivalent of the British work, with the companion volume *Who Was Who in America.*

BUSINESS

American Business Practice. 1933. 12 vols. Now out of print.
Black's Law Dictionary. 1957. Defines terms and phrases in legal use in America and England.
Business Information: How to Find and Use It. 1955. A valuable bibliographic guide to business.
Business Periodicals Index. 1958 ff. Guide to articles on business, trade, finance. Issued monthly, cumulated yearly.
Encyclopedia Dictionary of Business and Finance. 1960.
Encyclopedia Dictionary of Business Law. 1961. Defines legal terms in nontechnical language.
Encyclopedia of Banking and Finance. 6th ed. 1962.
How to Use the Business Library. 2nd ed. 1957. Contains a bibliography of business information classified by fields and heavily annotated. Now out of print.
Sources of Business Information. Rev. ed. 1964.

AERONAUTICAL AND MECHANICAL

Aeronautical Engineering Index. 1947 ff.
Aeronautical Reference Library. 1943. Now out of print.
Applied Mechanics Reviews. 1948 ff.
Aviation and Space Dictionary. 1961. A very good current dictionary of aviation terms.
Glenn's Auto Repair Manual. Revised annually and back-dated eleven years. A standard source for repair information.
A Guide to Information Sources in Space Science and Technology. 1963. Excellent bibliography for recent developments in the space industry.
Handbook of Astronautical Engineering. 1961. Handy reference aid.
Motor Services New Automotive Encyclopedia. A standard reference aid. Now out of print.
Recent Aeronautical Literature. 1947. Now out of print, this work provides an excellent review of developments just prior to the Space Age.

SCIENCE AND ENGINEERING

American Scientific Books. Annual list of scientific, technical, and medical books.
Applied Science and Technology Index. (Before 1958 published as *Industrial Arts Index.*) Subject index to periodicals in engineering, science, technology. Very helpful to undergraduate students. Issued monthly, cumulated annually.
Bibliography of Industrial Engineering and Management Literature. 1945. Now out of print.

Engineering Encyclopedia. 3rd ed. 1963. Condensed encyclopedia and mechanical dictionary.
Engineering Index. 1892–1919; 1920 ff.
Guide to Literature of Mathematics and Physics. 1947. Excellent source, includes related works on engineering science.
A Guide to Science Reading. 1963.
Guide to Technical Literature. 1939. Bibliography of engineering literature.
Harper Encyclopedia of Science. Important multivolume work.
Industrial Arts Index. 1913–57. Indexes more than 200 technical journals. Issued monthly, cumulated annually.
New Technical Books. 1915 ff. Ten issues per year. Excellent annotations of recent works.
Technical Book Review Index. 1914–1928; 1935 ff.
Sources of Engineering Information. 1948.

ASSIGNMENTS

I. You should be able to find the material required in the following exercises in your own school library.
   1. Locate a standard bibliography for your occupational file. Copy five of the entries that interest you most.
   2. Find what information is available about the authors you listed in the exercise above. For each author make a brief list of important biographic facts and a notation of your source.
   3. Find the etymological derivation of at least five terms that are important to your specialized area. How old are the terms? What did they mean when they first came into the English language?
   4. Assume that you are going to prepare a paper on changes in your vocational area. Make a bibliography that contains at least three very early references and three more recent ones to your field.
   5. List the journals in your school library that apply directly to your field. For each journal answer the following questions:
      a. When was the journal first published?
      b. How often is it published?
      c. Who is the present editor?
      d. How many pages are in a typical issue?
      e. What is the format? Is it largely a collection of essays about the field? Is it filled with pictures and charts? Is it written for the professional or the layman?
      f. What volumes are in your school library?

II. A good student finds that he often makes use of more than one library to find all the information he needs. The following set of exercises relates to

library facilities in your community other than those at the school where you are studying.
1. How many public libraries are in your community?
2. Where is the central library located? When is it open?
3. Where is the branch library nearest to your home? When is it open?
4. What other college libraries are close enough to be used conveniently? What are their hours?
5. Answer the following questions with specific reference to the branch library nearest your home:
   a. What standard unabridged dictionaries are available?
   b. Do they have a complete file for *Readers' Guide to Periodical Literature?*
   c. Make a list of at least five popular magazines and determine how far back their files go for each.
   d. Do they have a collection of popular records? If so, how long may you borrow these?
   e. What materials are available in their pamphlet file system? Is there anything in this material that relates directly to your field?
   f. What journals do they have that relate to your field? How far back do these files go?
   g. What are the three most recent books representing your field? Copy author, title, and date of publication for each.
   h. Find out the general operational procedures of the library. Who is eligible to check books out? Must you pay a membership or registration fee? How long may you keep books? What is the fine for returning a book late?

FOURTEEN / *Effective Reading and Note Taking*

WHY DO YOU NEED TO IMPROVE YOUR READING TECHNIQUES?

Knowing how to find the book or periodical article that contains the information you need is important, but you must also know how to locate the information within that book or article and how to read it with efficiency and understanding. Because you can't always have the book or periodical with you when you need the information and because you don't have time to reread the article and relocate the information every time you need it, you need to know how to take usable notes on what you read. To do these tasks—locate information, read with efficiency and understanding, and take usable notes—you will find certain reading and study techniques helpful.

HOW DO YOU PREVIEW A BOOK?

Before you begin to read a book, a chapter, or an article in a periodical, preview the material to save time and prepare for more effective reading. To preview a book you plan to read for information, look first at the title page of the book. Who wrote it? Is there any identifying information about the author there? Where is the book published? Does the place of publication or the name of the publisher give you a hint as to where the research behind the book was done? What is the date of publication? Does the book represent recent scholarship? Is this an older book that has proved its value in the demand for several editions? What is the exact name of the book? Does a subtitle give you a hint as to what to expect?

Now turn to the preface. Perhaps you do not usually read the preface, but here the author explains his purpose in writing the book. By reading his statement about his purpose you may find out if the book will meet your purpose. Look at the table of contents. Perhaps the title of one of the chapters will seem to indicate to you that one chapter is all you really need to read. If so, you will certainly want to read that chapter; but don't neglect to study the other chapter titles and to investigate any chapters or parts of chapters that might possibly contain relevant material.

Even though you may have selected only a part of the book to read, look through the entire book. Read the introduction or the first few pages. Notice the style and the general tone of the book. Is the author writing objectively or is he writing propaganda? Is he writing to convince or to persuade? What is probably his reason for doing so?

Finally, read the conclusion of the book. Now you should be able to see any part that you read in its relationship to the whole.

HOW DO YOU READ THE CHAPTER EFFECTIVELY?

As you read the chapter, keep in mind the question that you formed from the title and look for its answer. Turn the individual section and paragraph headings into questions for which you will also seek answers. This process may sound time-consuming and complicated, but once it becomes a habit it will take no longer than your old method, and your reading will be more rewarding.

If you are studying the material with an eye to remembering it for a later examination, stop at the end of each paragraph or section, ask yourself the question implied in the heading, then look away from the book to see if you can answer it. When you have finished the chapter, review the questions formed from the section headings to see if you know the answers; then ask yourself the question formed from the chapter title.

If the book is yours to keep, you may mark those words or phrases which form the center of each answer so that you can reread more quickly the answers that you have forgotten. Do not mark too much, however, or you will have to reread the whole thing. If your instructor lectures so that you can follow along in the book and frequently mark words and sentences which he stresses, you may want to use a different color ink in order to tell his stress from yours.

If you jot down your instructor's comments on the text in the margin beside the pertinent material, when the time comes to prepare for the examination, you can correlate the attitudes and information of the instructor and those of the author of the text.

This study method is one that has been followed successfully by many excellent students. It has been taught at numerous specialized army schools for accelerated students and at expensive speed-reading workshops. It should work for you.

HOW DO YOU READ WHEN YOU WANT TO TAKE NOTES?

If you are reading a chapter or article to gather information for some purpose, you will still preview and read as outlined here; but you won't, of course, attempt to learn any of the material in this way. Your purpose is different, and your method is different. Previewing the article allows you to find out quickly if the article contains information you need, how much of it you need, and perhaps how it will serve your purpose. You may want to read the whole article or only part of it. After you have read the article or the parts that you need, you may need to make some notes on what you have read.

WHAT KIND OF NOTES WILL YOU TAKE?

Your notes may take the form of a *synopsis*, a *direct quotation*, a *paraphrase*, or a *summary*. A synopsis is a summary of the plot of a story. In college your principal use for the synopsis is in literature courses as a study aid and as part of the content of reviews and critical papers on novels, plays, and short stories. A paraphrase is a restatement of the ideas and thoughts of the original in your own words. The paraphrase may be as long as the original because it includes all the facts, illustrations, or other material of the original. A summary is a condensation of the original. Your purpose in taking notes will determine which form your notes will take.

HOW DO YOU TAKE A NOTE THAT IS A QUOTATION?

A quotation is the easiest kind of note to take because you just copy somebody else's words. You must be very careful, however, that you copy them exactly. After you have copied a quotation, compare what you have written with the original to be certain that you have everything exactly as in the original. If you misquote the original source, you may have a piece of misinformation that will seriously affect your finished product. Sometimes you may for legitimate reasons need to make some changes as you quote material. Some types of alterations can be made, but you must notify your reader that you have made them.

Sometimes you may want to omit part of the material because it is too lengthy or because it is irrelevant for your purpose. You must be careful, however, that your omissions do not misrepresent what the author says in any way. You could leave out words and phrases here and there to make him appear to be saying anything you want him to, but you wouldn't really be quoting him and you would be dishonest to pretend you were. If you do need to delete certain portions of the quotation and you can do so without altering the writer's meaning, use three spaced dots (. . .), called an ellipsis, to take the place of one word, a phrase, or any portion of a sentence. It can be used at the beginning of a sentence, in the middle, or at the end. If it is used at the end of the sentence or at the end of material that is followed by some mark of punctuation, the ellipsis is used and then the punctuation mark. If as much as a sentence is omitted, close and reopen your quotation marks to indicate that you really have two separate quotations. Here are some examples of quotations using ellipses; the material quoted is taken from this chapter:

> "You could leave out words and phrases here and there to make him appear to be saying anything you want him to, but you wouldn't really be quoting him. . . ." (3 dots for the ellipsis, 1 dot for the period)
>
> "If you do need to delete . . . you can do so . . . ," (3 dots for the ellipsis, comma taken from the quotation)
>
> ". . . compare what you have written with the original. . . ." (3 dots for the ellipsis, 1 dot for the period)

Sometimes when you copy a quotation, a pronoun or other reference to person, place, or time is not clear because the thing referred to is named in a portion which you do not want to include. Sometimes you may want to supply a date or place name to clarify some less definite term. Here again you must be honest. You must not distort or misrepresent the writer's meaning, and you must let the reader know what you have done. To insert such information, you should use brackets. You do not change the original term; you copy it and then clarify it with whatever explanation you think will help the reader. This is the way you handle such an explanation:

> "You could leave out words and phrases here and there to make him [the writer] appear to be saying anything you want him to. . . ." (3 dots for the ellipsis, 1 dot for the period at the end of the sentence)
>
> "At the time [1892] Eldredge was still living in Boston."

Occasionally, you may want to quote a portion of a sentence which you work into a sentence of yours, not, of course, because you wish to alter the writer's meaning, but because you want to use his phrasing. Sometimes the tense of his verb does not agree with the tense you need in your sentence. You may change the tense of his verb to the appropriate one if you place brackets around the altered verb. Sometimes in material you want to quote you find a fact that you know is inaccurate or a word that you know is misspelled. You can't correct this error. You should, however, indicate that you are aware of the error. Insert the Latin word *[sic]* underlined and in brackets immediately after the term in question. Notice that brackets aren't the same as parentheses. You probably can't make them on your typewriter, but you can write them in.

If you take a note that is a quotation, be sure to put quotation marks around the quoted material and to check carefully for accuracy several times. Students have been known to include misspelled words and many strange and doubtful facts in quotations they thought they had copied accurately.

At first it might appear that you would save time if you just took all your notes as quotations. But you probably won't need many exact quotations, and you would later need to turn these quoted notes into summary or paraphrase notes. There are really only two reasons for including quotations in reports or other writing. You will use a quotation if the person who makes the statement is so important that the fact that these are his exact words will give weight to the material. You will use a quotation if the phrasing is so excellent that you would weaken the statement if you changed the words. Because long quotations must be set off by indentation and single spacing, many readers have a tendency to skip them. You should use your own words most of the time, limiting your use of direct quotations to only those instances that specifically require it.

HOW DO YOU TAKE NOTES IF YOU WANT ALL OF THE MATERIAL AND YOU DO NOT QUOTE IT?

If you find a paragraph or similarly sized section of an article or chapter that seems to serve your needs in its entirety, you should paraphrase, put the material into your own words. To paraphrase successfully, you must read the whole section, being sure that you understand it thoroughly. Then write it in your own words without looking at the text. Now compare what you have written to the original to see if you recaptured the author's intent and detail. Here again, you must not misrepresent what he says. Here is an example of a good paraphrase compared with the original material.

ORIGINAL

You should, therefore, exercise the greatest care in preparing your application. Type neatly on a good grade of white bond paper, 8½ × 11 inches. Never use company letterhead stationery, hotel stationery, lined paper of any kind, or colored, gilt-edged, or decorated personal stationery. Follow an accepted form for business letters even if the prospective employer is your father's former roommate or a figurehead in the employ of your Uncle Albert. Before you mail your letter, double-check your spelling, grammar, and punctuation and be prepared to retype your letter or even to rewrite it if it is somewhat less than perfect. Of course, you can also ask your mother, wife, or girlfriend to correct it for you; and you should certainly do so if you plan to take her to work with you to catch the little errors you make after you go on the payroll.

PARAPHRASE

The application should be prepared carefully and neatly. Plain white bond paper 8½ × 11 inches should be used. An accepted business letter form should be used in all cases. Before mailing, check spelling, grammar, and punctuation. Retype the letter if there are errors. You may even need to rewrite it. Don't depend upon anyone else to make your corrections because nobody else is going to help you hold this job.

This example of paraphrasing is shorter than the original. Sometimes the paraphrase is the same length, sometimes it is longer. In any case, it contains all the information that is in the original, but it doesn't use the words of the original.

HOW DO YOU TAKE NOTES IF YOU ONLY WANT A SUMMARY OF THE ORIGINAL?

Frequently as you read to gain information, you find that the paragraph contains more than you want to include in its entirety, even as a paraphrase. You want to give the essence of this information, but you want to give it much more briefly; in short, you want to summarize. Your procedure is similar to that which you used in preparing the paraphrase. You read carefully all of the portion you wish to summarize before you begin to write. But your emphasis is a bit different as you read. If you read to paraphrase, you have to notice detail. If you read to summarize, you pay particular attention to the whole idea. The individual facts, ideas, and illustrations are important only as they relate to the whole. Find the topic idea of each paragraph. You will see the relationship of the parts of the material if you also notice such transitional words and phrases as "on the other hand," "to illustrate," "nevertheless," "consequently," "as a result," and "however." After you understand the relationship of all the material in the paragraph, concentrate on just the sentences which are necessary to explain the topic idea and ignore the rest.

Now write the summary. Don't look at the original as you do so. Your summary should be in your own words and style, not in that of the original author. Don't string together phrases or words from the original. Doing so may distort the original meaning, and trying to blend the author's clauses and phrases with your own word choice in your own sentence construction will be more difficult and will produce a choppy style much poorer than the kind of writing that is more natural to you. It may even produce a passage that doesn't make sense. When you have finished summarizing the paragraph, reread the original and compare it with your summary. Are your individual facts accurate? Is your over-all meaning the same as that of the original? Make any necessary revisions, and then move on to the next paragraph.

In the following summary, the writer shows that he understood the meaning of the original and was able to record for his own use the major idea and the proper relationships of the minor ideas.

ORIGINAL	SUMMARY
The employer is not interested in your need for a job; so don't take his time with a discussion of your financial problems or other difficulties. He will hire you not because you need the job but because he needs a worker and you seem to be the best-qualified applicant. Starting a new employee in a job costs the employer money. Someone must take time away from other work to teach the new worker, and he will work more slowly at first and make more mistakes than one who has been on the job awhile. Therefore, the employer will feel he is taking a smaller risk in hiring you if you can sincerely assure him that you are willing to learn and that you are genuinely interested in the job.	Because training a new employee costs an employer money, he will hire the best qualified worker, not the one who most needs the job.

Even summary notes should be made in complete sentences. Taking notes that are made up of fragments rather than of whole sentences may be quicker at the time, but it may lead you into inaccuracies when you come to use the notes. The writer's meaning is clear to you when you read his words; you can summarize what he has said, and check your summary against his words for accuracy. If you took fragmentary notes and then tried to write a summary from them, you would distort the writer's meaning and you would certainly find the process more difficult than when the passage was fresh at hand. You might also find that your fragments fail so completely to convey the original meaning or any meaning that you have to return to the article. Jotting down words and phrases instead of writing whole summary sentences may also lead you to plagiarism.

WHAT IS PLAGIARISM?

Plagiarism is the practice of borrowing the words of another and passing them off as your own. Words belong to the person who publishes them. Claiming them as your own is dishonest. If your report is published, duplicated, or called to the author's attention in any way, the author may sue you. If your teacher detects your plagiarism—and teachers have an uncanny ability to detect such thefts—he will probably reward your lack of honesty with an F grade. If you want to use three or more words that the author used in the order in which he used them, you may do so provided you use quotation marks. Most student plagiarism comes from the practice of writing too closely to the source, looking at the original, almost copying it, but omitting a word here and changing one there. Here is an example of typical student plagiarism:

PLAGIARISM	If you telephone or write for permission, the person can help you better if you tell him certain things. Tell him about the job you want, why you think you will do well. Then he can focus on your qualities that will be especially important on this job. If you haven't seen him lately, bring him up to date on your educational or vocational activities. After you get the job, write and thank him.
ORIGINAL	Whether you telephone or write for such permission, the person can give a more helpful and favorable recommendation if you give him certain information. Tell him

something about the job you are trying to get, why you want that job in particular, and why you think you will do well in it. This information will allow him to focus on those qualities of yours that will be especially important in this job. If you have not seen this person in some time, you may make it easier for him to write a recommendation if you bring him up to date on your vocational or educational activities. After you have been hired, you should write a letter of appreciation to anyone who helped you get the job.

DO YOU NEED TO MAKE A NOTE OF WHERE YOU GOT THE MATERIAL?

Ideas and facts as well as words are the possession of the individual who originally recorded them; so you will have to give credit to the source from which you took them. Moreover, you will want to remember what authority is responsible for this opinion or piece of information. If you are gathering the information for use in a report or paper that someone else will need, your reader will also want to know the authority so that he can evaluate your material more intelligently. He may even want to refer to the source himself. You should, therefore, record the name of the writer, the name of the book, the publisher, the place of publication, the date, and the number of the page on which the information was found. If the material came from an article, record the name of the periodical, the date, the volume number, and the page number.

IN WHAT GENERAL FORM SHOULD YOU RECORD THE NOTES ON WHAT YOU READ?

It is possible, perhaps, that you might wish to summarize a whole article because you want the contents of the entire article for your files. If you want the whole article, you can often clip it from the periodical and file it. But many of the periodicals you will use will be from the files kept by your employer or from the library, and generally speaking, you wouldn't want to clip an article from a book, even if it's your own. In these cases you can reproduce the article on a copy machine in your office or at the local library for only a few cents. The time you save will be worth more than the cost involved.

Usually you take notes on your reading because you are gathering information to be used later in a paper or report. Perhaps only one portion of the article will pertain to your subject, or maybe the material that you need is scattered throughout the article. At any rate, you will want to use this material later in your paper in a different order from that found in the original article or in combination with material obtained from other sources. You should try to take your notes with your final purpose in mind, but of course you won't know as you take them exactly in what order this material will appear in your final paper. Consequently, if you record your notes on sheets of paper in the order that you find them, they won't be usable when you try to reassemble this information later in a different order. So you make each note on a separate 3 × 5 or 5 × 8-inch card. Cards are handier than slips of paper because, being all the same size, they are more easily handled and they don't look like scrap paper. They are neat enough and of a proper size and shape to go into your file later, and they aren't large enough to tempt you into recording more than one idea or thought on each.

This last reason is extremely important. Later you will incorporate these summaries into your paper in an order and combination which isn't completely clear to you as you take your notes. When you are ready to write your paper, you will take these note cards in the order in which you will use them in your paper. If you have two separate facts or ideas on one card, you won't be able to sort them properly. You will have to rewrite the material on two cards. You could, of course, try to move the card to the second place in the stack, or you could tear the card into two messy pieces.

On each card you should make a note of the exact source for that piece of information. Write down the author's last name and the number of the page on which the information was found. If you have information from more than one article or book by the same author, you will also need to add the title. If the title is long, perhaps you can abbreviate it in some way or use only key words.

For each source you should make one source card (sometimes called a bibliography card). On the source card write the name of the author, the book title, place of publication, publisher, and date of publication. For articles found in periodicals record the author's name, the name of the article, the periodical, the volume number, date, and page numbers. You should also include the call number of library material in case you need to use the book again. If you use more than one library, make a note of where you got this particular source.

At first, you may think that using two kinds of cards will just increase the amount of writing you have to do, but this method really

In What General Form Should You Record the Notes on What You Read? 181

saves time. You might take ten notes from one source. Recording the full bibliographic information on one card will save you the trouble of rewriting the information nine times. When you multiply that nine times by perhaps a dozen sources, you can imagine how much time you will save. Moreover, having two kinds of cards makes several operations easier when you begin to prepare your final copy of your report.

If you have some questions about how to handle books with two authors, pamphlets, newspapers, or anything else that seems to be an unusual source, consult the explanation on bibliography at the end of Chapter Seventeen.

Figure 39 is a sample note card:

```
Verry, p. 103              Reasons for Use

         Microfilm provides the most orga-
nized method of storage.  Facts are care-
fully stored and indexed until needed;
they are never lost.
```

Figure 39

Figures 40 and 41 are two sample source cards. Be certain to punctuate your source cards exactly like the models.

Call number — Z 1033.M508   *Title*
Author — DeSola, Ralph. Microfilming.
Place of publication — New York: Essential Books, — *Publisher*
1944.
Date of publication

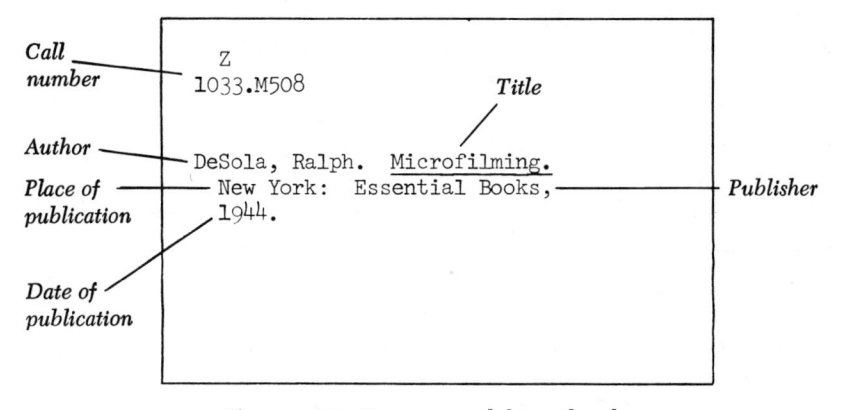

Figure 40. Source card for a book.

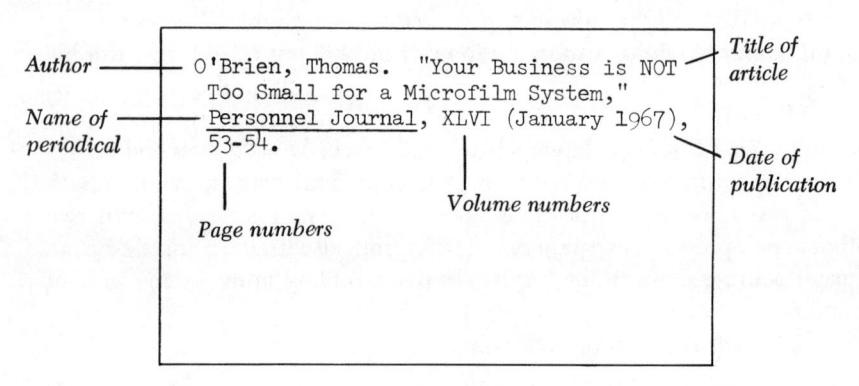

```
Author ─────── O'Brien, Thomas.   "Your Business is NOT ─── Title of
                Too Small for a Microfilm System,"          article
Name of ─────── Personnel Journal, XLVI (January 1967),
periodical      53-54.                                      Date of
                                                            publication
                                    Volume numbers
                Page numbers
```

Figure 41. Source card for a periodical article.

ASSIGNMENTS

I. By now you have probably selected some subject or problem on which you will prepare a formal report. Examine the sources in your school library that pertain to your subject. Preview the chapters or articles that you find until you locate at least five sources that will give you information that you need. Be certain the sources do not merely repeat each other. Make source cards for these five sources. You will then have completed a working bibliography. Later you will add other important sources as you discover them, but for now you will be reading and taking notes.

II. Following the instructions given in this chapter, prepare note cards from these sources. Include all of the three basic types of note cards—summary, direct quotation, and paraphrase. Take as many notes from each source as you feel necessary to cover the material properly.

FIFTEEN / Organizing

WHY IS AN OUTLINE NECESSARY?

An outline is nothing more than an organizational guide that you will use while preparing an oral or written report. Just as a football coach goes to the stadium with a detailed game plan worked out, so you as a speaker or writer need to have thought through your ideas to arrange them in their most impressive fashion.

Unfortunately, many students are frustrated by outlines because they have been drilled too hard on the techniques of the formal outline and such a formally developed outline became, in many instances, more important than the speech or theme that it was supposed to be designed to help. From such experiences, students usually learned to write the theme or speech and then to develop the outline so that it matched! This procedure is obviously backward and useless.

An outline is not useful unless it functions to help you while you do your writing. Therefore, if you spend all your time getting the headings arranged correctly, spaced correctly, and capitalized correctly, you are spending time building a tool and not using a tool.

ARE FORMAL OUTLINES ALWAYS NECESSARY?

For some short speeches and themes you will not need to develop a formal outline before you begin to work. If your presentation is short and the ideas are readily before you, a brief listing of the order in which you will present them may be sufficient outline enough. Such a listing,

```
--quotation from Senator Fishburn
--need for more x-ray training schools
--cost for establishing such schools
--possible locations
--request for positive vote next week
```

Figure 42

most often arranged in order of decreasing or increasing importance, might look as informal as the example in Figure 42.

The speaker using this brief sketch of his ideas would keep his main thoughts in the order he had determined most effective earlier. If he felt a need for more detail, he might, even without the use of elaborate subheadings, list them in a fashion similar to that shown in Figure 43.

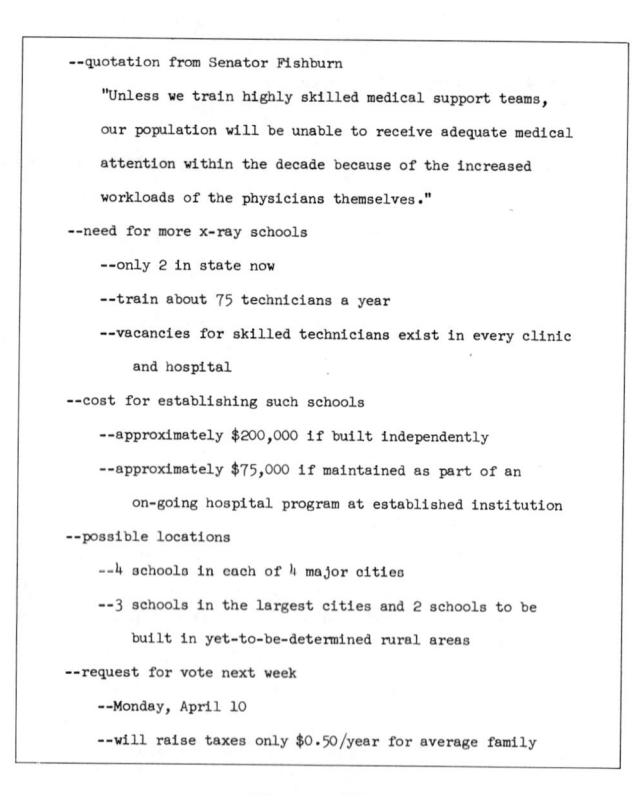

```
--quotation from Senator Fishburn
    "Unless we train highly skilled medical support teams,
    our population will be unable to receive adequate medical
    attention within the decade because of the increased
    workloads of the physicians themselves."
--need for more x-ray schools
    --only 2 in state now
    --train about 75 technicians a year
    --vacancies for skilled technicians exist in every clinic
        and hospital
--cost for establishing such schools
    --approximately $200,000 if built independently
    --approximately $75,000 if maintained as part of an
        on-going hospital program at established institution
--possible locations
    --4 schools in each of 4 major cities
    --3 schools in the largest cities and 2 schools to be
        built in yet-to-be-determined rural areas
--request for vote next week
    --Monday, April 10
    --will raise taxes only $0.50/year for average family
```

Figure 43

WHAT ORGANIZATIONAL PRINCIPLES WORK BEST?

An old but highly workable adage is that a writer (or speaker) should tell his audience what he is going to do, do it, then tell his audience what he has done. Obviously this suggestion divides itself conveniently into the more typically labeled parts: introduction, body, conclusion.

A report, oral or written, should tell your audience (listener or reader) what you are going to do. That is, it should set the idea that you propose to investigate and should state the limits of your investigation. In conventional theme writing you have confronted this concept as the *thesis sentence*. A part of the introductory statement may also be used to get your audience's attention by use of a quotation, illustration, controversial statement, etc.

The body of your report is, of course, the most important. Here you must plan your strategy carefully: What facts do you present first? How much detail is necessary?

The two most frequently used systems for ordering facts are from the most important to the least important and from the least important to the most important. Experts themselves disagree over which is indeed the most effective, but a general suggestion will prove helpful: If your report is designed to present information, begin with your most important points while your audience is still most attentive (see Figure 44). If your report is designed to stimulate action (as the report urging

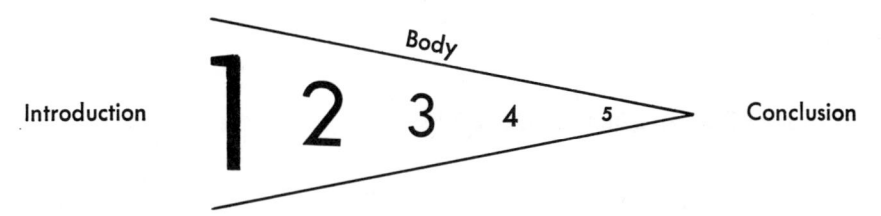

Figure 44. Most important to least important structure.

a vote for more x-ray schools), then end with your most important point so that your conclusion can call for action immediately after your most impressive fact (see Figure 45).

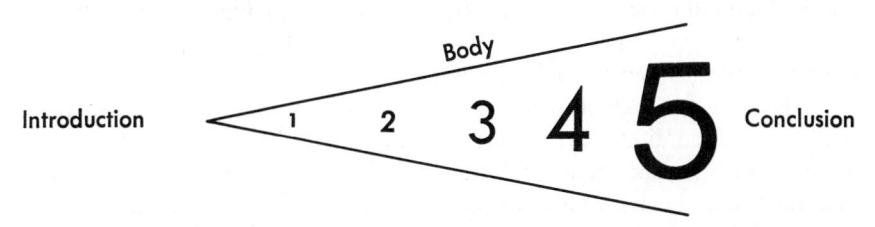

Figure 45. Least important to most important structure.

Sometimes your points are of equal importance and are organized simply by enumeration: "There are four reasons why we should change the office duplication process," or "Three new proposals for redistricting of the sales staff must be reviewed."

The conclusion of your report should be brief but direct, and it should leave your audience with a feeling that you have finished. If your report is to give information, your conclusion might briefly rephrase the two, three, or four important points and tie them back with the thesis position you established in your introduction. If your report is to stimulate action, it might rephrase the points, but its emphasis will be upon the direct call to action. The conclusion is your final chance to speak (or write) about the given subject, and the words should be yours. Most rhetoricians agree that the use of a quotation at the very end of a report tends to weaken it.

WHEN IS A FORMAL OUTLINE NECESSARY?

A formal outline is necessary if your report is very long, because the brief informal jottings in Figures 42 and 43 are not detailed enough to hold together a 20-page report or a 30-minute speech. Sometimes, too, an outline is necessary in a formal written report because it precedes that report as a kind of table of contents.

WHAT IS A FORMAL OUTLINE?

The formal outline is a structured listing of your ideas by using various levels of importance and indicating these with indentations and the use of various Roman and Arabic figures and capital and lower-case letters. Again, structuring the outline should not take more time than producing the report because the outline is a tool to aid in that production. And the outline should never be produced after the report!

One important rule needs to be remembered: the parts that are marked equally (same level of Roman or Arabic figure, for example) must be of equal importance. The informal jotting of Figure 43 might be formally outlined to look like Figure 46.

Even Figure 46 is not a purely formal outline because the parts within a given unit (II, A, for example) are not parallel with each other. Also, purists argue that the Introduction and Conclusion should not be listed the way they are here. However, this outline functions at three levels to organize the intended material, and it does this organizational task well. Remember the principle that the development of the outline should not be more involved than the subsequent development of the report itself.

```
    I. Introduction: Quotation from Senator Fishburn
   II. Body
       A. Need for more x-ray schools
          1. Only 2 in state now
          2. Train about 75 technicians a year
          3. Vacancies now exist in almost every clinic and hospital
       B. Cost for such schools
          1. Approximately $200,000 if built independently
          2. Approximately $75,000 if structured as part of a
             program at an established institution
       C. Possible locations for such schools
          1. Locate 4 schools in 4 largest cities
          2. Locate 3 schools in 3 largest cities and 2 smaller
             schools in selected rural areas
  III. Conclusion: Request for vote
       A. Monday, April 10
       B. Will raise state taxes only $0.50/year for average taxpayer
```

Figure 46

ASSIGNMENTS

I. Make an informal jotting (Figure 42) of the courses you are now taking and have taken in college. Then see if you can divide or group the courses in divisions and subdivisions so you have a two-level jotting similar to Figure 43.

II. Prepare a two-level jotting of how you spend the hours of a typical day. Think first of the broad categories into which smaller things may be fitted. Perhaps you will want your final category to be "Miscellaneous" so it can serve as a kind of catchall.

III. Develop the material from the above assignment into a formal outline with appropriate numbers and letters and correct indentation.

IV. Prepare two- or three-level outlines for one of the following topics, and be prepared to justify why you ordered material in the way that you did.
  1. Different types of employees in your vocational area.
  2. Reasons why you are attracted to your profession.
  3. Changes within your area in the last five years.
  4. Different kinds of training programs for your area.
  5. Kinds of equipment or tools that you will have to use in your particular work.

SIXTEEN / Oral Reporting

After you have gained information in one way or another, you will probably need to relay that information to someone else. Frequently you will report orally. If you're a member of a committee investigating a problem and you have been assigned to get some information, you will be expected to tell the committee what you have found. This report may contain only a few words that you can say from where you sit. It may, however, be longer and more formal. If your way has been paid to some workshop or convention, you may be asked to report on that meeting to the workers of your department or company. You may be asked to give an oral report on the success of some experiment or innovation made in your area. You may need to demonstrate the use of some machine or apparatus to a group of fellow workers. Your opportunities to stand up before a group of people and tell them what you know may be many. If you're able to express yourself clearly and forcefully when you need to, you will undoubtedly have an advantage over your fellow workers.

WHAT WILL HAPPEN TO YOU IF YOU HAVE STAGE FRIGHT?

There is no great mystery surrounding the techniques of public speaking. Most of them are a matter of common sense. If you approach the matter with confidence, you can reason your way to the basic techniques. But the truth of the matter is that most of us become a bit panicky when we think about standing in front of a room full of people who are looking at us and listening to what we have to say. Everybody feels that way at first—ministers, school teachers, politicians, magicians, nurses, policemen—everybody.

But that tight feeling in your chest and that uncontrollable jiggle of your knees as you approach the speaker's platform are out of all proportion to the danger of the situation. You should depend upon the good manners of your audience for a quiet and attentive hearing. In fact you can depend upon more than that. For one thing, your audience is probably already interested in what you have to say. For another, the members of your audience are probably not professional speakers, and they don't expect you to be one. As they watch you take your place at the front, they will probably admire you for doing what they themselves find quite difficult. You may be acutely aware of your sweaty palms and of the annoying lump in your throat, but they are not. Moreover, you know more about your subject than anyone present. Unless you call attention to yourself by a comment on your nervousness, your subject will be the first thing in the minds of your audience.

ARE THERE ANY TECHNIQUES THAT WILL HELP YOU HANDLE YOUR STAGE FRIGHT?

No doubt, these words have not removed completely your natural stage fright. But there are a few techniques that might help you just a bit. One of the things that will disturb you is the fact that your audience will be looking at you. You can relieve your mind considerably if you know you look your best. Give careful attention to your grooming. Be certain that your shoes are carefully polished, that your clothes are freshly pressed, and that your hair is neat and not too recently cut. Select an appropriate suit, shirt, and tie, or dress and accessories. You do not want your clothes to call attention to themselves and distract your audience from what you have to say. Do not wear anything that jingles and jangles or that feels uncomfortable. You do not want to be distracted by your clothes either. Give them your careful attention at home and then forget about them. A rather good thought to remember is that your audience will think about what you think about, so concentrate on your speech.

If you have to sit someplace on the platform before your turn comes to speak, sit at attention and look at the speakers preceding you and listen to them, even though you might be having trouble concentrating enough to remember your telephone number. Naturally you will not drape yourself over the back or arm of your chair, cross your legs, or read or write while you wait. You can also take this opportunity to get used to the people in front of you.

If you make a habit of following these practices when you speak and you're still nervous, don't despair. A certain amount of stage fright is a good thing. Tension stimulates the release of adrenalin into your blood stream. Adrenalin stimulates you to think and speak with greater energy than you do when you are calm and relaxed. You should try to channel that energy into productive activity rather than waste it on useless shaking and empty, nervous gestures. You can channel this extra energy productively if you redirect your anxiety to a different subject. Instead of worrying about what your audience is going to think of you, concentrate on the subject matter of your speech. How do you want your audience to react to what you have to say? If their reaction is important to you, you should naturally feel some tension concerning that reaction. But use the extra energy stimulated by your tension to find and use the best method of getting the desired response. To get that response, you will need both a knowledge of the techniques of public speaking and thorough preparation of your material.

WHAT ARE THE TECHNIQUES OF PUBLIC SPEAKING?

When it's your turn to speak, rise and go to your place at the same pace you would go to any task that interests you. When you reach the speaker's desk, place your notes where you can see them; arrange them if necessary, but not too elaborately; then look at your audience. Really look at them; look right into their eyes. Good eye contact is one of the most important techniques in public speaking. Looking into the eyes of the members of your audience will also let you know how they feel about what you are saying. You may think you do not want to know, but how else are you going to tell when your explanation is a bit fuzzy and you should explain a little more completely? Really looking at your audience will help to hold their attention in a way that looking at the tops of their heads or at a spot on the back wall will not do. And not least in importance is the fact that somewhere along the way, if you really see your audience, you will discover that you are communicating with real people, that they are communicating with you, and that all of you are having a good time.

In that moment before you begin to speak, look pleasant if possible, unless the occasion is a very sad one. You also can find a comfortable posture. If your knees are shaking, flex them slightly. Relaxed knees are not so likely to shake. Take a deep breath. That breath is important. It enables you to gain control over your whole body.

Now you begin talking. You look at your audience as much as possible. You make whatever gestures are natural and easy for you. You say what you intended to say—probably a little better than you expected to. If you forget something, you look at your notes or you stand there and think of it. Do not be embarrassed if you forget; nobody expects you to be a memory expert. Don't panic if you have to think a minute. The time seems longer to you than to anybody else, and the vision of somebody really thinking hard is an admirable sight seen all too rarely.

The most important quality for effective public speaking is enthusiasm. If you are not enthusiastic, all the techniques in the world will not help you make a good speech. If you have enough enthusiasm, you can forget most of the techniques mentioned here and still be successful. Sometimes when you are first asked to present a certain subject to a group, you may feel it's not very interesting. But after you have done some research on the matter, thought about it, and become involved in it, you will probably be so excited about it that you are eager to communicate what you know to anyone who will sit and listen. If you can bring that kind of fervor to the speaker's stand, do not become embarrassed and turn the knob of your enthusiasm fifteen degrees to the left. If you are sold on the ideas you have to present and you sincerely wish your audience to be also, deliver your speech with all the energy and vitality you would bring to any talk that really mattered to you.

One word of caution: An audience can be turned off if you seem too pushy or too determined to persuade them to think or act the way you want them to. The key to showing an enthusiasm that is catching and not repelling is the possession of the desire to share what you have learned rather than to insist on its acceptance.

When you are finished, sit down. Now that last step is the hardest of all to take. Someone has said that the secret of public speaking is to get up, to speak up, and to shut up. How often have you listened to a speech and found several places for the speaker to stop before he did? Somehow it is quite difficult to believe you have communicated what you had hoped. But if you have reached your stopping place without selling your idea or explaining your process, you aren't going to do so in a dozen tacked-on sentences. Say the words you had planned as your closing ones, gather your notes, and sit down with a positive, decisive air.

HOW DO YOU PREPARE THE BODY OF YOUR SPEECH?

All the public speaking techniques in the world will not help you give a good speech if you do not have something worthwhile to say, if you do not know your material, or if your speech is organized like a chain letter. Most of the public speeches you will give at first will probably be fixed as to content by somebody else. You will be asked to report on an investigation you have made, summarize the recommendations of a subcommittee, dedicate a drinking fountain, or introduce a speaker. But even if the subject is chosen by someone else, you will have to decide the purpose and scope of your talk yourself. Think about these things just as you do when you begin a written communication. Analyze your audience according to the knowledge and attitude they can be expected to bring to your subject. Note the place and occasion of your speech.

With all these things in mind, you should gather and organize the information and other material you will need for your speech. When you are ready to plan your speech in detail, read through what you have so that it is fresh in your mind. Then stand up and begin to talk about your subject. Do not sit down and write out a speech. You don't write the way you talk, and you will be standing when you deliver the speech. You don't want to write out a speech and read or deliver it from memory. Unless you're quite unusual, you talk much better than you read aloud. You might be more comfortable reading than speaking, but you won't communicate with your audience as well. Your purpose in speaking is to communicate. Your comfort is much less important.

Don't memorize your speech either. A speech delivered from memory is only a little less indirect than a read speech. It is not flexible enough to allow you to answer the questions on the faces of your audience. It does not allow for the spontaneity of your own personality. Moreover, if you are relying on a memorized speech, you will be more nervous than if you plan to speak extemporaneously.

An extemporaneous speech is one that is carefully planned ahead of time and given from notes. An extemporaneous speech is appropriate for all but the most formal occasions. Radio and television speeches are normally read. But, other than these few exceptions, most speeches are given extemporaneously.

As you talk to yourself about your subject, you can try various methods of organization and presentation without spending the time that would be required if you wrote out your talk two or three different ways. Do not concern yourself with your beginning or your ending at this time.

When you're satisfied that you have found the organization and manner of presentation that you want to use for the body of your speech, sit down and make an outline of your speech. If you're still satisfied with it, transfer the outline to 3 × 5-inch cards. A large notebook or sheets of paper are distracting to an audience. The pages rattle when you turn them, and they may even blow or get out of order. Cards can be carried in your pocket or your purse; and if you discover that you will have to speak without the use of a desk or table, you can hold them in one hand.

On the cards you will probably want to put more than the bare outline, but you will not want to write out your whole speech. You will need the outline so that you will know what to talk about next. You may also need some names, figures, references, and quotations which you might forget. In general, put in your notes enough to remind you of what you had planned to say and to relieve you of the anxiety that arises from having to rely completely on your memory, but not enough to tempt you into reading exactly what you have written. Don't put so much on a card that you have to study the card closely. Either type double space or print in fairly large letters. The light on the platform may not be as good as it should be, or you may not be able to read as well as usual.

If there are any difficult parts in your speech—some highly technical explanation or some paragraph that, because of the emotions involved, is difficult to word—write those portions out and memorize them. You make take a card with the exact words written on it to jog your memory if you will be more comfortable doing so, but don't allow yourself to read it to the audience. After you have completed your notes, get up and go through your speech, using your notes to see if they are understandable, usable, and complete.

WHAT SHOULD YOU SAY IN THE CONCLUSION OF YOUR SPEECH?

When you are satisfied that the body of your speech as you have planned it is the most effective way to present your material, you are ready to plan your conclusion. A good conclusion is short, forceful, and conclusive. It serves a definite purpose which depends on the purpose of the speech. If your speech is to inform, your conclusion should summarize briefly the points which you have made. If you are reporting on a workshop or convention, you may want to close by dwelling on the general tone, the key thoughts, or the overall impression of the meetings. If your purpose is to convince your audience on certain points, you can summarize your arguments in the reverse order of their importance. If you seek to persuade your audience to action, you can summarize your arguments and then add an appeal to the desire for financial gain, long life, good health, family security, personal prestige, or public betterment.

Because your conclusion is your last opportunity to clinch your argument or sell your idea, you will want to plan it very carefully. Do not be satisfied with the first wording that occurs to you. Experiment. Try several ways for closing your speech until you have found the one best way to end with the proper emphasis. When you have found it, write it out word for word exactly as you plan to say it. It is a good idea at first to memorize this conclusion, because you may not be able to phrase your ideas as well in public as you can now.

WHAT SHOULD YOU SAY IN THE INTRODUCTION TO YOUR SPEECH?

If you have noticed that you have not yet been advised to plan your opening remarks, maybe you have guessed why. The beginning of your speech should be designed to lead your listeners into the body of your speech, and you can't know the best way to lead them until you have made the trip yourself. A good introduction does two jobs: it catches the attention of the audience, and it leads the audience into the speaker's subject. It will defeat its purpose if it draws attention to itself or to the speaker rather than to his subject. Therefore, the best introductions often accomplish both of their purposes at once.

One of the most effective means of both catching attention and leading into the subject is the anecdote or illustrative narrative. Even if you have only a moderate ability as a storyteller, the ordinary listener will usually turn off his individual thoughts in order to listen to your story. If the problem to be solved in your story is concrete and close to the interests of your audience, you can build up some suspense as to the outcome. They will not only find your introduction irresistible, but they will continue to listen to you in case you should repeat the performance. A humorous anecdote can do much to get rid of tension and draw the audience to you and your subject. Because the humorous introduction is a very popular one, there are a few guides that you should observe in using humorous material:

Make the humor grow out of the situation or out of your subject.

Use a story, even a very funny one, only if it serves some definite purpose in your strategy.

Avoid using often-repeated jokes.

Keep your humor in good taste. Profanity, obscenity, and stories at the expense of minority groups or people with physical handicaps are not funny to everybody.

Be certain that you have the story straight, that the point is immediately apparent, and that you keep the story brief.

Do not label your humor either with your own laughter or with such an introduction as "That reminds me of a funny story."

If you cannot handle humor well, use something else.

Besides the anecdote there are several other effective methods of opening a speech. You can ask a few provocative questions, make a startling but factual statement or two, or point to a paradox in the problem you will discuss. The striking first statement can be an epigram, a proverb, or a poetic quotation. It can be a thought-provoking prophecy. It can, by its references to local circumstances or to national, international, or historical happenings, be a bridge between the interests of the listeners and your topic. Tracing the background of your problem or subject may create a fascinating and useful introduction. If the occasion is associated with some special date or place, a well-chosen quotation or anecdote relevant both to the occasion and to your subject may perhaps be your best bet for an opening.

One type of introduction that you should avoid is the apology. Such a negative opening prepares the audience for a second-class performance. Moreover, the audience will think about what you tell them to think about. If you remind them to notice that your voice is shaky or that you have not given enough time to the preparation of what you are going to say, they will obediently do so.

Toward the end of your introduction you probably should make some easily recognizable and well-phrased statement of your thesis or aim. Occasionally you may find it wise to avoid a definite proposition early in your speech. If you make a bold statement that you are going to convince your audience that they should use peanut oil on the valves of their hydranagers, their immediate though silent response will probably be, "I'll bet you don't," or "Not if I can help it." Even if you don't want to make an explicit statement at the beginning, you still should make some statement to indicate what you are going to talk about so that your audience can put their minds in the proper gear. Never, however, begin with such an unsubtle remark as "I thought I would talk about. . . ."

HOW LONG SHOULD THE INTRODUCTION BE?

The length of your introduction will vary. In general, the length of your introduction should be proportionate to the length of the body of your speech. Some subjects, however, need longer introductions than others. A knowledge of a rather lengthy historical background may be essential to an understanding of your subject. This particular audience may need a longer introduction to arouse their interest in your subject. You may need to take time to break down prejudice or hostility toward your subject or yourself. If, on the other hand, the audience has the information they need to approach the subject, they are already interested, and they have no strong negative feelings, you can move into the body of your speech after only a brief introduction.

Your opening remarks will set the pace for your whole speech. If you lose your audience during the first few minutes, you may not recapture them. Apply imagination, resourcefulness, and even some research about your audience; arouse their interest in your subject, and set the tone for an interesting speech. Here again you should experiment until you have chosen the right words. Then write the opening paragraph down on a card and memorize it. After you have faced that audience and taken a deep breath, you can begin with the words you have memorized. By the time you have finished them, you will have your audience's attention, you will have gained some confidence and control, and you will be moving along into the body of your speech.

HOW SHOULD YOU PRACTICE YOUR SPEECH?

Three or four short oral rehearsals at spaced intervals will give you a better preparation than one or two long ones. At your first rehearsal work on emphasis and experiment with gestures that will help to underline your words. If you are the kind of person who stands at stiff attention, hands at his side, his face an inexpressive mask even when he argues with his roommate, then it probably will be natural for you to adapt the same posture for your public speaking. Natural, but certainly not effective. If, however, you are the kind of normal individual who scowls when he is insulted, beams when he is complimented, and doubles his fists when he is threatened, you will probably loosen up and make normal and appropriate gestures when you relax and become interested in your subject.

As you practice, you may pause as you try to think how to phrase a thought, and you may fill your pauses with "and's" and "uh's." But don't worry about them now. Follow your outline and concentrate on your thought. At your next rehearsal you will have fewer such vocalized pauses. Your words and gestures will come more easily. Continue to experiment, however, as you strive for the clearest, most forceful means of communication. By the end of the second rehearsal you should have established the way you plan to deliver your speech.

At your third practice session, attempt to present your talk as you intend to before your audience. You may want to ask a colleague or friend to listen to you. If not, try to pretend that the chairs in your room are occupied and practice looking into imaginary faces as you speak. Do not practice in front of a mirror. Communication and not appearance is your first concern. You may record your speech so that you can listen critically to your phrasing. If you're not confident, if your speech is too long or too short, or if you're dissatisfied and decide to make some changes, you will need additional rehearsals. But don't rehearse so much that you have memorized your speech to the point that you can rattle it off like a robot. The emotion generated by the occasion and the friendly response of your audience may inspire you to more colorful and effective phrasing than you would now fix in your speech. Learn your speech completely enough to give yourself confidence but not so completely that your delivery is frozen and any chance of spontaneity is destroyed.

SHOULD YOU USE ANY MECHANICAL DEVICES IN YOUR SPEECH?

In many public speech situations you may want to use some visual or auditory devices. Such devices can serve three purposes: they can help you make a clearer explanation, they can help you hold the attention of your audience, and they can help you fix certain facts in the audience's minds. Communication and teaching take place through the senses; and when more than one sense is used, their effectiveness is increased. Talking pictures are more popular than silent ones; television drama is more fascinating than radio drama. Some movie producers have even experimented with adding odor to their pictures.

Such devices include charts, maps, slides, moving pictures, phonograph records, sound tapes, manikins, puppets, and any kind of instrument, apparatus, or machine that can be demonstrated. Your choice of device should depend upon your topic and audience. No matter how fascinating you may find a given mechanical device, you should not use it unless it adds to your explanation, not distracts from it. It should not have such a complicated mechanism that either you or your audience becomes carried away with its operation. Don't twist your speech so you can use some clever gadget. Remember that the device is an *aid* to your speech. Don't depend upon it to clear the fog left by a muddled explanation or to demonstrate order in your reasoning where none exists.

HOW CAN YOU USE YOUR DEVICE MOST EFFECTIVELY?

You will get the best results with your device if you observe a few basic points. All of your audience must be able to see your device. Make your charts or maps large enough to be seen by everyone and place them where everyone can see them without strain. Make the letters large enough to be read and the lines of letters and drawings dark enough and wide enough to be seen. When you're planning your speech, consider the shape, arrangement, and lighting of the room where the speech will be given. It may be that these factors will make it impossible for your device to be seen no matter how large and clear it is. Now, after you have taken these precautions, don't spoil the effect by getting in the way yourself. Stand behind it or well to one side; and, if possible, use a pointer to focus attention and to avoid obstructing the view.

Make your device easily understandable. Keep your labels short and simple and avoid unnecessary details in your drawing. Don't crowd the material in your layout. Spread it out well over the whole chart. If your chart or map is still too crowded, use more than one. Schematic drawings or charts that illustrate points progressively will emphasize the important features better than one complicated chart on which you try to show too much at once.

Because your device should direct attention to the points you are making, not distract from them, you should plan your device so that you can fit it into the talk at the moment when it supports a point. If you can, keep it hidden until you are ready for it and put it out of sight when you are through with it.

Don't devote more time to a device than it is worth. A very complicated device can take up too much time, delaying or interrupting your speech while you are getting something ready. Do any writing on the blackboard before the meeting and then hide it behind a screen until you need it. A machine should be set up, tested, and ready for operation before the meeting. If necessary, ask someone to help you so that you won't have to interrupt your talk to move furniture or adjust a screen.

When your topic involves an explanation of some complicated mechanism, you will find demonstration with the actual machine is not only helpful but absolutely essential. In making such a demonstration, explain the process first and then move into your demonstration without delay. Keep the demonstration short and as simple as possible, focusing on the specific points covered in your explanation. Practice ahead of time so that you can perform the demonstration with ease. If you are awkward, you will make the procedure seem more difficult than it really is. If you wish to show that a procedure is simple, perhaps you can take someone from your audience and teach him to do what you have just done. Such a demonstration probably will not be really effective if the audience is very large, very far away, or unable to move about and see the object from several angles.

DOES THE USE OF A DEVICE REQUIRE ANY SPECIAL REHEARSING?

If possible, you should rehearse your speech using your aid in the room in which your speech will be given. Have someone move about the room as you talk to see if your device can be seen comfortably by all the members of your audience. Your slides may be excellent, but they will not do much good in the daytime in a room without dark curtains or shades. Your chart may show the relationship between your points in a memorable manner, but there is little chance it will be remembered if you are standing in front of it while you talk. Your drawings may be well laid out and reflect the orderliness of your thinking, but they will reflect only the late afternoon sun if you fail to take into consideration the placement of the windows and the time of the meeting. If you stage an early rehearsal with a friend to serve as a roving audience, you will have a chance to catch any problems that might later arise and to be certain that your device is really an aid and not a distraction or disappointment.

HOW DID YOU DO?

After you have given a speech, you probably would like to know how you did. Better yet, you would like to plan a superior performance. The following criteria will help you do both. Because you are used to measuring your performance with letter grades, they are used here.

HOW WELL ARE YOUR NOTES PREPARED?

A. Your notes are brief, written or typed on 3 × 5-inch cards or small sheets which you can handle in one hand.
B. Your speech is written out rather completely on cards.
C. Your notes are on large sheets of paper that rattle.
D. Your notes are in a notebook which you spread out in full view.
F. Your notes are in your briefcase, and you have trouble with the lock.

HOW WELL DO YOU USE YOUR NOTES?

A. You glance at your notes at brief intervals to guide you into the different divisions of your speech or to check figures or names.
B. You interrupt your speech to consult your notes frequently.
C. You rely heavily upon your notes.
D. You read most of your speech.
F. You read all of your speech.

DO YOU HAVE EYE CONTACT WITH YOUR AUDIENCE?

A. You look into the faces of most of the people before you.
B. You look at a few people that you think you can trust.
C. You look at the tops of the heads of your audience.
D. You look out the window or at a spot on the back wall.
F. The audience looks at the top of your head.

DO YOU KEEP YOUR AUDIENCE INTERESTED?

A. You have an enthusiastic interest in your subject that is contagious.
B. Your audience listens attentively.
C. Your audience is polite but bored.
D. Some people are reading, writing, talking, or sleeping.
F. Nobody is paying attention to you.

HOW DO YOU USE YOUR VOICE?

A. You can be heard and understood as you speak in a pleasant, expressive voice.
B. You can be heard and understood.
C. You drone in a monotone without expression or variety.
D. You mumble.
F. You are struck speechless.

ARE YOUR GESTURES MEANINGFUL?

A. You move your hands, arms, and face naturally and expressively.
B. You make an unplanned, meaningful gesture.
C. You stand relaxed but motionless.
D. You play with your notes, glasses, or pen, pace the floor, or fidget nervously.
F. You stand at rigid attention.

IS YOUR WORD CHOICE GOOD?

A. Your sentences are well constructed, your word choice is good, and you make no grammatical errors.
B. Your sentence construction and word choice need some improvement, but you make few errors.
C. You have given little thought to how you say what you say and you make a number of grammatical errors.
D. You make grammatical errors, and some of your words are inappropriate for the occasion.
F. Where did you learn language like that?

DO YOU HAVE SOMETHING WORTHWHILE TO SAY?

A. You have something to say that is important to you. You have done some reading and some original thinking about it, and you cause your audience to think a new thought or look at an old thought in a new way.
B. What you have to say is important to you, but you rely almost completely on what other people have written or said on the subject.
C. You had a good idea; and if you had started to plan your speech earlier, you might have been able to develop it well.
D. Your subject is large, abstract, and overworked. It is usually discussed in vague, abstract words, and clichés. Your discussion is no exception.
F. You have nothing to say, but it took you too long to say it.

IS YOUR INTRODUCTION EFFECTIVE?

A. You catch the attention of your audience in an original way that leads easily into the body of your speech.
B. You catch the attention of your audience in an original way, but it has no apparent connection with the body of your speech.
C. Your beginning is quite ordinary, but it does introduce your speech.
D. You have no introduction at all; your audience figures out what you are talking about sometime after you begin.
F. You begin your speech by saying, "I'm going to talk about . . ."

IS THE BODY OF YOUR SPEECH WELL ORGANIZED?

A. Your organization of material is logical and clear; your subject is developed as completely as your purpose requires; and your emphasis is properly placed.
B. Your logic, clarity, completeness, or emphasis leave something to be desired but not a great deal.
C. The relationship between the parts of your speech is not completely clear.
D. You have trouble staying on the subject.
F. What on earth are you talking about?

IS YOUR CONCLUSION EFFECTIVE?

A. You draw your speech to a close with a concise summary, an effective application or brief narrative, or an emphatic call for action.
B. You try to draw your speech to a close, but the results are less concise, effective, or emphatic than they could be.
C. You just quit talking and sit down.
D. The audience found several places for you to stop before you did.
F. Only the instructor, the bell, or exhaustion (yours or the audience's) could stop you.

ASSIGNMENTS

I. Prepare and deliver a three-minute speech on one of the topics below. Prepare your notes in such a way that they may be submitted to your instructor following delivery of your speech.
   1. An appeal before your city council asking that a citywide youth council be established. Show a need for the organization of such a group.
   2. An address to your local student body informing them of new rules pertaining to the student center. Speak to them as fellow students, not as a superior.
   3. Brief comments to a local professional organization representing your area. Explain to them the positive points of your present technical training. These are professionals, so you should speak professionally.
   4. An appearance before your school's curriculum committee. Indicate to

Assignments

them one or two major weaknesses that you as a student can see in your training program. Suggest a change that might improve conditions. Don't argue; sell your ideas.
5. A brief speech before a group of graduating high school seniors. You have been sent as representative from your technical area to sell them on the opportunities that your profession can offer. Cite job openings in the area, expected openings within the next fifteen years, salaries, and fringe benefits. Make the job itself sound exciting by referring to some of the challenges it offers. They know a fraud when they see one, so be sincere.
6. A presentation of some new equipment or idea that is greatly influencing your profession. Prepare the material to be delivered to a group of students enrolled in the same program as you. As a class project you have been asked to review this important development for them. Don't be authoritative. You are merely sharing information.

II. After you have made your short speech in class, criticize yourself. What weak points did you have? Were they matters of content or delivery? What good points did you have? Write a short theme (about 500 words) in which you evaluate your own speech.

III. After you have carefully evaluated your speech, and after you have received comments on it from your instructor and other students, plan changes that will improve it. Perhaps you need more material. Probably you need to polish your delivery. Certainly you must look directly at your audience this time.

Using the same topic but adding to it and changing it where necessary, prepare and deliver a longer speech—minimum of eight minutes. Include in this presentation *at least one* visual aid.

Good speaking opens the way for further communication with the audience, and communication is a two-way process. After you have finished speaking, take about two more minutes to answer questions from your audience. Keep calm. Remember that you are the authority on your subject.

SEVENTEEN / Writing a Formal Report

WHAT IS A FORMAL REPORT?

Formal reports may be no more than two pages long. But they can also contain three hundred pages and be printed on glossy paper with multicolored ink for the charts and illustrations. But short or long, simple or elaborate, they are all based on the same format—although some parts may be combined and others omitted because of the nature and size of the report. Consequently, the first thing to decide in writing a report is who will read it and what is your purpose in writing it.

FOR WHOM SHOULD YOUR REPORT BE PREPARED?

All reports have the same purpose: to give information to someone who needs it. If you want that someone to be able to understand and use your information effectively, you must, as your first step in preparing your report, analyze the person who will receive it. In your analysis give your attention to these questions:

Who is going to read this report?
What is his background?
What will he be looking for?

You may be preparing your report for a particular person or group you know by name, or you may be trying to communicate with an official or committee known to you only by some official title. In either case try to get a clear picture in your mind of your reader. What is his job? How much does he already know about your subject? Will you need to fill him in on some background information or to define some terms for him? Why does he want this report? What will he do with it?

Probably more than one person will read your report. It may pass over many desks before it lands on the desk of the man at the top who will make a decision based upon your findings. In fact, all of your report may not reach the top man. The total report may be reviewed and approved by some lesser official and only a summary of your report may be passed on. Some official just above you may combine the important parts of several other reports to form a report which he will submit to the man above him. That man may combine several such reports to make a report which he in turn will pass on to the man above him, who will continue the process in a pyramid effect until the man at the top will receive just one report which is thus a combination of all these reports.

You should, however, write your report with the top man, his background and his needs, foremost in your mind. Consider him your primary reader. Those who read your report along the way will be secondary readers because their needs and backgrounds are not so important to you as those of the man who will make the final decision.

WHAT IS THE FORMAT OF YOUR REPORT?

The format of a report is flexible. Some of the parts may be omitted or combined. Some lengthy and very formal reports may include some parts such as an abstract or preface which will not be included here. The parts listed here, however, will meet most of your needs:

Table of contents
Introduction
Summary
Body
Conclusions
Recommendations
Appendix
Bibliography

WHAT IS INCLUDED IN THE INTRODUCTION?

The length of your introduction will depend upon the size of your report. Its purpose is to give your reader the background he needs in order to use your report. It may do one or several of the following tasks:

1. Define the scope of the report. You may tell what the report will cover. If you have made certain assumptions that affected your conclusions, you should identify these assumptions. If you failed to analyze any pertinent evidence for some reason, you should explain that omission.
2. Define the purpose of the report. You may tell what you intended to accomplish in your report.
3. Explain the method by which you gathered the information in the report. You may want to explain what procedures you used to obtain your information.
4. Justify your report. You may explain the need for your report, establish its importance, or tell who authorized it.
5. Define terms. Whether you will need to define any terms before you begin the explanation included in the body of your paper will depend upon your reader. The larger the number of people who will read your report, the greater your need to define terms.

WHAT IS INCLUDED IN THE SUMMARY?

The summary of your paper appears before the body of your paper, but you should prepare it last. It is meant for the reader who has no time to read your whole report but who needs to be able to learn the basic facts, ideas, and recommendations in a minute or two. The summary of your report may be the only part of your report that is read by some of your readers, perhaps even by your primary reader. Therefore, your summary should sum up your complete report, its information, your conclusions, and your recommendations. In a very short report you may want to combine your summary and your introduction.

Sometimes a very long or important report will also have an abstract. An abstract is a condensed summary. The abstract for a paper three thousand words long might be limited to one hundred words; for a book length report, to four hundred. The abstract is usually separated from the rest of the paper to be passed on to the various readers or filed separately. It may be prepared by the writer of the report or by someone else.

WHAT MAKES UP THE BODY OF THE REPORT?

The body of your paper will be the largest part. Here you will put the information which you have gathered. The content of the body of your report is dependent upon your subject and your audience. You will explain in detail exactly what you learned by observation, experiment, interview, questionnaire, survey, reading, or any other method you used. If any of your information was gathered by someone else and recorded by you from your reading, at an interview, or in some public meeting, you should have a footnote giving credit to the person from whom you got the information. If any of your material is detailed in such a way that presenting it in the form of a chart, graph, or table would enable your reader to understand it better, make such a table or chart to be included in your appendix and merely summarize the findings in the body of your report.

WHAT BELONGS IN THE CONCLUSION?

Your conclusions are the crux of your whole report. They may be obvious to your reader after he has read your report or you may arrive at them only after you have carefully weighed bits of conflicting evidence. Your conclusion should not introduce any new evidence but should derive from the evidence presented in the body of your paper. The reader of your report should have been given all the information that leads to your conclusion, and he should have been able to follow your logic as you weighed the information. Ideally he can now arrive at the same conclusions you do. If not, he should still be able to see how you got there. Present your conclusions clearly and support them with references to information in the body of your paper or in the appendix. You will not need to repeat this information, but you should refer to it specifically and indicate the page of your paper on which it is found. The length of the conclusion will, of course, depend upon the length of your paper. If the body of your paper was four or five pages long, you may be able to present your conclusion in a paragraph or two. A shorter paper may require only a brief paragraph for its conclusion; a longer paper, a page or more. You should try to make your conclusion brief and to the point. A short conclusion, well phrased and definitely stated, will carry more weight than a longer one that has its complete meaning hidden under a blanket of vague and wordy sentences.

WHAT DO YOU DO ABOUT RECOMMENDATIONS?

Whether you will have recommendations to make or not will depend upon the type of report you are making. If your report is the type that should contain recommendations, your recommendations should derive clearly from your conclusion. If your report contains much conflicting evidence, bear in mind that conclusions can be interpreted differently by different people. Don't let such evidence keep you from making any recommendations, but don't get carried away. If your facts lead logically to your conclusion and your conclusion logically to your recommendations, your reader will agree with you even if you state your recommendations cautiously. If he does not agree with you, your persistence will probably not persuade him.

WHAT MATERIAL BELONGS IN THE APPENDIX?

The appendix of your report, if you have one, will contain detailed data such as reference tables of statistics not immediately needed in the body of your report. The material included in your appendix should do one of two jobs:

> Give a picture. A photograph or artist's drawing can be used unless the report is to be reproduced by some inexpensive process such as mimeograph or letter duplicator. In that case, only line drawings (pictures containing no shading) can be used.
>
> Present data in an organized, easily understood form. Charts, maps, graphs, tables, or lists can be used.

Data that is too detailed to be presented easily in a paragraph should be summarized in the body of the report and reported completely in list, table, or chart form in the appendix. Preparing such a device may take extra time; but if it makes the material clearer and more usable to your reader, you should do so. If communicating your information to your reader were not important, you would not be writing a report in the first place. In some reports you may use vocabulary that is not immediately recognized by your reader or that is used in a different manner. If so, your appendix might well contain a vocabulary listing that gives key words and shows how you have used them in your report. The form you will use to tabulate detailed information will be determined by your data. You can use a table to organize data into columns and rows. A table is useful if you want to present exact quantities. To make your chart or graph, you can use bars, lines, maps, circles, squares, stick figures, or any other kind of representation that will present your data clearly and forcefully. You can give the same information on both a table and a chart if your purpose requires doing so.

WHAT IS THE BIBLIOGRAPHY?

The last part of your report is your bibliography. This is an alphabetized list of the books, pamphlets, periodical articles, and other material in which you found information. The form for the bibliography will be given later.

WHAT JOBS DO REPORTS DO?

Both formal and informal reports can be classified by the job they do.

- Informational
- Analytical
- Special Purpose

INFORMATIONAL REPORTS: Reports that give information. In informational reports you will make no data analysis or recommendations.

Progress reports: Reports of changes in conditions over a period of time. The progress report may cover a specific period of time—a week, thirty days, a year; or it may be a progress-to-date report which relates to events up to the time of presentation.
Status reports: Description of conditions at a specific moment of time.
Narrative reports: Description of an event. The narrative report can cover an event that happened at any time. It does not necessarily deal with changes in conditions or with changes at any given moment.

ANALYTICAL REPORTS: Analysis of data. In such a report you will always draw conclusions and make recommendations. Although there are three general types, in practice the three frequently overlap.

Problem solving
Proposal   Normal pattern: analyze,
Research   conclude, recommend.

SPECIAL PURPOSE REPORTS: Any reports not included in the above categories. Such reports may be informational, analytical, or both. They present a summary, give progress and status information, draw conclusions, make recommendations, and predict future conditions. The following classifications refer to the period in the life of the assignment at which a report is made.

Preliminary report: made at the beginning of an assignment, a kind of preparation.
Interim report: made at the half-way point or at a stated interval.
Final report.

WHAT IS THE FIRST THING TO DO IN PREPARING A REPORT?

The order in which you write your report will not, of course, be the same order in which the reader will examine your report or in which the report is described here. You will give your attention first to the body of your report, the gathering and presentation of information.

WHERE DO YOU GET THE INFORMATION?

The sources from which you will gather information are limited only by your subject and your resourcefulness. In the report involving the problem of the employee cafeteria, for instance, you might visit the kitchen when it is empty in order to analyze the layout, then again at various times of the day to observe the different phases of meal preparation, serving, and cleanup. You might also visit cafeterias in similar companies and commercially operated cafeterias. You can interview several individuals in the department to ask what they thought was the problem—the dietitian, the baker, the cooks, the servers, the dishwashers, the tray boys. The more people you talk to, the more suggestions you will hear and the less you will be influenced by a self-satisfied cook or server or an intolerant baker or dishwasher. Interviews with people involved in the training or directing of personnel in successfully operated cafeterias may yield ideas. You may need to call in several experts to advise you concerning the equipment and facilities of the kitchen. You may send for a relevant government bulletin. You might examine pamphlets put out by the utilities companies and brochures issued by appliance companies. Various professional periodicals published for business or industry managers or hotel and restaurant managers might contain helpful articles. Books at the local library may contribute general and background information. Your company may send you to a professional meeting or convention where you can attend workshops, listen to informative talks, and visit product exhibits.

HOW DO YOU MAKE NOTES ON THIS INFORMATION?

From all these sources you gather information on which you make careful notes. Whether you are recording information gathered from observation, interview, or reading, you will record it accurately only if you make your notes on the spot. Do not trust your memory for anything. Except for statistical information, specifications, or lists, use whole sentences. Clauses, phrases, isolated words may seem meaningful to you while you are gathering information; but later, when your notes are cold and all you have seen, heard, or read must be warmed over, the bits and pieces that you have jotted down may not convey much information. Faced with such uncommunicating fragments, you will have several choices: you can go back and reread, reobserve, reinterview, and renote; you can forget the whole thing and change jobs; or you can string the clauses, phrases, and words together in what appear to be sentences and paragraphs, hoping your reader will know what was meant in the original sources although you do not. He will not either. Your work will go more easily at each step and your finished report will be more usable if you take down your information in whole sentences you and your reader can understand. You will find little need to quote directly in report writing. If you do have such a need, check and recheck for accuracy. Nobody likes to be misquoted, and misquotations lead to misconceptions along the way and to errors in your conclusions.

Make your notes on 3 × 5 or 5 × 8 cards according to the form given in an earlier chapter. You should be especially careful to take only one piece of information on a card. As you read and take notes, you will often find together in one paragraph or sentence several facts which the writer saw as closely related to each other in a certain way. Later you may want to relate those facts to each other in a different way and to other facts in other ways. If you have blindly lumped several pieces of information together on one card, you may fail to see these new relationships. You will find it difficult to use your notes without violating the unity of your paragraphs, distorting the organization of your report, or tearing your notes into scraps of "subnotes." If for some reason you had to take some notes on a larger piece of paper or if you discover later that what you have on one notecard is more than one piece of information, copy your notes over with one fact to a card.

You will handle your information more quickly and easily if you make two kinds of cards: a *source card* containing the complete information about the book, periodical article, interview, or meeting, and a *note card* containing the piece of information, the last name of the writer or speaker who reported the information, and the page number. If you put all the bibliographic data on each note card, you will just do a lot of unnecessary and repetitious writing. Don't, however, rely upon some code of symbols or letters which you plan to cross-match with some master list. Rely upon this simple method:

Long, p. 82.
Abbott, pp. 69, 70.

Figure 47 illustrates how a source card might look. Notice that it contains the same parts as a formal bibliographic entry.

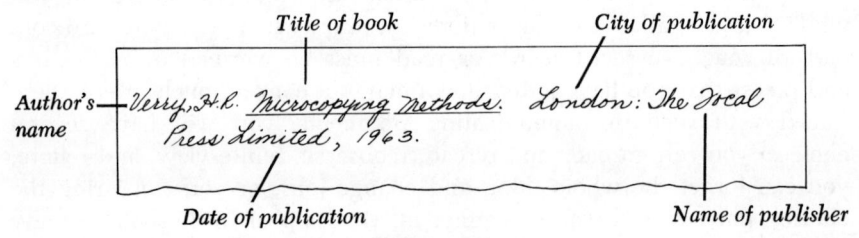

Title of book — *City of publication*

Author's name — Verry, H.R. *Microcopying methods.* London: The Focal Press Limited, 1963.

Date of publication — *Name of publisher*

Figure 47

Figure 48 shows how a note card taken from Verry's book might look.

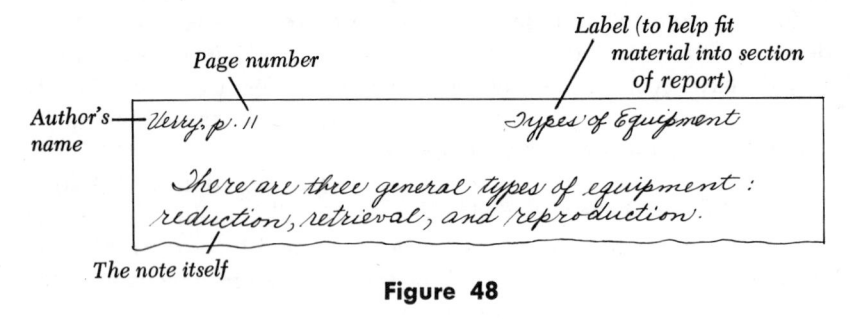

Page number — *Label (to help fit material into section of report)*

Author's name — Verry, p. 11   Types of Equipment

There are three general types of equipment: reduction, retrieval, and reproduction.

The note itself

Figure 48

When you are satisfied that your outline provides the best organization of your material, finish arranging your notes. If you stack your cards exactly in the order in which you will use them, you can follow your outline, working each note into your report as you come to it. Writing your report will then be easy. You will just use the data you have gathered to put meat on the bare bones of your outline. Often by adding a transitional word or phrase or by shifting a clause, you can use many of the sentences you wrote on your note cards.

HOW DO YOU WRITE THE CONCLUSION AND RECOMMENDATIONS?

When you have finished writing the body of your paper, you should be ready to state the conclusions which you have reached as the result of your research. The reader who has followed you carefully should be able to reach the same conclusions. In your conclusions you should summarize the information and the steps in your reasoning that lead to your conclusion. Refer by page number to the places in your report, but do not repeat the details. You need not try to sell your ideas. If you have handled your information well, your reader will agree with you.

Your recommendations, if the type of report you are writing calls for them, should follow your conclusions as logically as the conclusions follow the body of your paper. In a very short report the two may go together.

HOW DO YOU WRITE THE INTRODUCTION?

Some people write the introduction first and some write it last. If you thought through your report completely as you outlined it, you might have been able to write the introduction first. More than likely, however, you did not realize all the implications involved in your material until you actually shaped the sentences and paragraphs of your report. You can't write an introduction until you know what you are going to introduce; and the more completely you know what you are going to introduce, the better the introduction will be. Now that you have written the body, conclusions, and recommendations, you can decide what you need to include in your introduction. Ask yourself what your reader will need to know before he can properly understand and evaluate your report. Go back and examine the kinds of information that are usually included in a report and decide what is the purpose of your introduction. You can write a paragraph or two telling why your study was made and explaining the problem you are trying to solve. That explanation may involve explaining some aspect of the history or background of the problem. Then you may need to write a paragraph or several paragraphs defining some of the terms you have used, describing the way you gathered your information, or explaining what your report will cover. Remember your reader as you plan your introduction and be sure to tell him the things he needs to know.

HOW DO YOU WRITE THE SUMMARY?

Now you are ready to write the summary of your report. Without going into details, your summary should pull together the basic ideas of the body of your report and give your conclusions and recommendations. Whoever reads your summary should be able to learn there what you found. If he wants the details, he can read the rest of the report. If not, he should be able to act on the basis of what he learned in your summary.

In some ways your summary is the most important part of your report. Some of your readers, perhaps your most important and influential readers, will read only your summary. Mr. Busy Executive will read your summary to answer one of two questions:

- Is this a report I should take time to read?
- What basic information, conclusions, and recommendations are contained in this report?

If you keep these questions in mind as you write your summary, your reader will be able to use it to serve his purpose:

- To tell him if he needs to read the report.
- To orient him quickly to the report if he does decide to read it.
- To substitute for the whole report if he does not have time to read it.

You should be able to prepare an effective summary if you take the following steps:

1. Read your entire report through carefully and thoughtfully.
2. List the points you want to cover in your summary. Arrange them in the best order. Note which ones deserve the most emphasis. Omit any that are of minor importance.
3. Put your information into effective sentences following the same overall organization as your original report.
4. Check your summary to see if it conveys your basic information.
5. Read your summary, preferably aloud. Check your logic. Rewrite any sentences that do not present your information in a clear, usable way.

WHAT IS A LETTER OF TRANSMITTAL?

With your report should also go a *letter of transmittal*. It can be quite brief, saying only "Here is the information you asked for." Or it can be like Figure 49.

You can also use the letter of transmittal to express your personal ideas and opinions to emphasize what you feel is most important. If you write your letter carefully, your reader will be able to learn from it the scope and direction of your report. A typical letter of transmittal should not be more than one page long and would include these things:

1. An opening section naming the source and date of the authorization for the report and a statement that the report is attached or included.
2. A central section making necessary acknowledgments, offering your opinions, calling attention to those items which you think should be stressed, defining the scope of the report, or indicating special problems.
3. A concluding section suggesting possibilities for additional investigation, offering to provide further information, or making some recommendation.

Figure 50 is a good letter of transmittal.

March 13, 1974

Mr. Alfred Pierway
General Office Manager
AB Products
1320 Ocean Drive
Waterview, California 99998

Dear Mr. Pierway:

In answer to the request made in your letter of December 3, I have investigated the advisability of installing an intercom system between the reception room and the inner offices. My report is submitted herewith.

Sincerely,

J. M. Norse

I. M. Norse
Technical Advisor

Figure 49

HOW DO YOU BIND YOUR REPORT?

Some companies have special binders for their reports. Others use a regular file folder. In either case the title of your report will appear on the cover. The title you give your report is very important. Most of the life of your report will be spent in a filing cabinet from which it can emerge to receive attention only if you have titled it so it can be recognized. Clever titles that catch the eye or ear, arouse curiosity, or provoke imagination may sell books and stories, draw long lines at the box office, or please a high school English teacher, but they are not appropriate or helpful on a report. You can choose a satisfactory title for your report by selecting and arranging the best words to give a preliminary description of your report. Here are some examples:

The Effect of Welding Thermal Cycles on the Microstructure of T-1 Steel

SOUND INSURANCE, INCORPORATED
1018 Hillside, Fort Worth, Texas 76112
(817) 924-8753

May 16, 1974

Mr. Ted Arbuckle, Business Manager
Zemkex Products United
1171 Pedestrial Way
Fort Worth, Texas 76116

Dear Mr. Arbuckle:

    On April 5, 1974, you authorized me to prepare a formal proposal for a group insurance program for your employees. My report is attached.

    You requested that we structure a program to cover a maximum of 150 employees. I have followed your instructions, but I have also shown figures for a program to include 250 employees. You may want to consider the latter program quite seriously. Your business is growing, and I believe you will have no trouble enrolling 250 employees. The savings to the individual employee is quite significant in the latter plan.

    You will notice, too, that throughout the report I have referred to Plan A and Plan B. Plan A is designed to cover direct medical expenses: doctor, drugs, hospital. Plan B covers these expenses but also makes provision to pay an employee 60 percent of his weekly salary while he is ill up to a period of one year, payment to become effective after the second full week of illness. The additional cost of Plan B is quite small for the coverage included, and you will want to call it to the attention of your employees. They may, however, sign for either of the two plans.

    Please contact me at my office within the next two weeks and we can discuss the details for initiating this program in your business. As I indicated to you earlier, we will be happy to send a team of three agents to your location for a one-week enrollment period. We can work out the exact details of the plan after you have studied the enclosed materials more closely.

                                Sincerely yours,

                                Ronald Clark

                              Ronald Clark, Commercial Sales

Figure 50

A Comparison of Three Intercommunication Systems for Installation in the Outpatient Department

An Evaluation of Two Duplicating Machines

A Report on the Present State of Race Relations in Arlington, Texas

The material in your report should be placed in the file folder or report binder in the following order:

Title page
Letter of transmittal
Table of contents
Summary
Introduction
Body of report
Conclusions
Recommendations
Appendix
Bibliography

HOW SHOULD FOOTNOTE AND BIBLIOGRAPHY ENTRIES BE MADE?

Examples of the type of reference material that you will most frequently use are given below. Any of several good research manuals can help you with forms not included. Keep in mind that research forms vary from manual to manual and sometimes from teacher to teacher. The forms given here are quite standard and will be correct for this course, but another instructor may wish you to use a slightly modified form.

1. Book with One Author

F.N.
(footnote)
1. Ralph DeSola, <u>Microfilming</u> (New York, 1944), p. 419.

The author's name is not reversed in the footnote, and commas separate the parts of the notation. Notice, though, that there is no comma between the title and the material in parentheses. Remember to put a period after p. and at the end of the footnote.

Bib.
(bibliography)
DeSola, Ralph. <u>Microfilming.</u> New York: Essential Books, 1944.

Notice that the book entry has three parts—author, title, and publishing information—each separated by a period. No page numbers are given. The entry ends with a period.

2. Book with Two Authors

F.N.   1. Henry Ewbank and J. Jeffery Auer, <u>Discussion and Debate</u> (New York, 1951), p. 118.

Bib.   Ewbank, Henry Lee and J. Jeffery Auer. <u>Discussion and Debate</u>. New York: Appleton-Century-Crofts, Inc., 1951.

When you have two or more authors, you reverse the name of only the first one in the bibliography.

3. Book with Three or More Authors

F.N.   1. J. N. Arnold, <u>et al.</u>, <u>Introductory Graphics</u> (New York, 1958), pp. 17-18.

Use the abbreviation pp. when you refer to more than one page of material.

Bib.   Arnold, J. N., <u>et al.</u> <u>Introductory Graphics</u>. New York: McGraw-Hill Book Co., Inc., 1958.

Et al. is a common bibliographic abbreviation meaning and others. It saves your having to list all of the authors for a work.

Notice that you write the name of the publisher exactly as it appears on the title page of the book, abbreviating only items that are abbreviated there.

4. Book with Author's Name Followed by a Title

F.N.   1. Joseph L. Kish, Jr., and James Morris, <u>Microfilm in Business</u> (New York, 1966), p. 12.

Observe that Jr. is a title and is set off from a person's name by a comma.

Bib.   Kish, Joseph L., Jr. and James Morris. <u>Microfilm in Business</u>. New York: The Ronald Press Company, 1966.

5. An Anthology with One Editor

F.N.   1. L. V. Ryan, ed., <u>A Science Reader</u> (New York, 1959), pp. 5-7, 9.

List consecutive pages by connecting them with a hyphen; indicate nonconsecutive pages by using a comma.

Bib.   Ryan, L. V., ed. A Science Reader. New York: Holt, Rinehart & Winston, Inc., 1959.

6. An Anthology with Two Editors

F.N.   1. F. R. Moulton and J. J. Schifferes, eds., The Autobiography of Science (New York, 1950), p. 12.

Bib.   Moulton, F. R., and J. J. Schiffers, eds. The Autobiography of Science. Garden City, N. Y.: Doubleday & Company, Inc., 1950.

7. An Article in a Magazine

F.N.   1. C. T. Graver, "Power Supply for Nuclear Research Laboratory," EE, (March 1953), 72:214.

If the magazine is one generally known to the audience who will read your paper, you may abbreviate its title in the footnote but not in the bibliography. Again notice that no abbreviations come before the volume and page numbers. Note that the volume number and the page number follow the date and are separated from it by a comma and from each other by a colon.

Bib.   Graver, C. T. "Power Supply for Nuclear Research Laboratory," Electrical Engineering (March, 1953), 72:212-216.

Put the title of the article in quotation marks and underline the title of the magazine.

8. An Essay in an Anthology

F.N.   1. Thomas Henry Huxley, "The Method of Scientific Investigation," Subject and Structure, ed. John M. Wasson (Boston, 1963), p. 217.

Bib.   Huxley, Thomas Henry. "The Method of scientific Investigation," Subject and Structure, ed. John M. Wasson. Boston: Little Brown and Company, 1963, pp. 214-219.

List the title of your essay. Indicate the editor of the collection immediately after the title by using the abbreviation ed. Note that no period separates the editor's name from the city of publication in the footnote.

9. An Article without an Author

F.N.   1. "Coming Next: Push Button Banking," <u>U. S. News and World Reports</u>, (February 14, 1966), 60:110.

Bib.   "Coming Next: Push Button Banking," <u>U. S. News and World Reports</u>, (February 14, 1966), 60:108-110.

Alphabetize your entry by the first major word in the title.

10. An Article in a Newspaper

F.N.   1. "New Data Processing Procedures Employed by Local Firms," <u>The Big City Register</u> (July 8, 1968), Sec. A, p. 2.

Bib.   "New Data Processing Procedures Employed by Local Firms," <u>The Big City Register</u> July 8, 1968, Sec. A, p. 2.

If the name of the reporter is given, that name will go first in your entry.

11. Pamphlet

F.N.   1. "Communications Services Anytown," Promotional pamphlet published by Bell Telephone System, n.d.

Bib.   "Communications Services Anytown," Promotional pamphlet published by Bell Telephone System, n.d.

Alphabetize by title. If the pamphlet has page numbers, indicate page cited in footnote. Use the abbreviation n.d. (no date) when there is no publication date given.

12. Interview

F.N.   1. Fred Alexander, Personal Interview by the author, Austin, Texas, January 10, 1968.

Omit the professional position of the person interviewed in the footnote entry.

Bib.   Alexander, Fred, Office Manager, Zimmerman Corporation.
        Personal Interview by the author, Austin, Texas, January 10, 1968.

The complete author listing should include the professional position of the person so that the reader can know why an interview with him is important. Include location of the interview and date.

13. Correspondence

F.N.   1. Elizabeth Freeman, Letter to the author, May 15, 1967.

Bib.   Freeman, Elizabeth, Director of Nurses, James Hospital (Dallas). Letter to the author, May 15, 1967.

Include professional position of the writer in the bibliography, but omit it in the footnote.

14. Encyclopedia

F.N.   1. "Data Processing," The Modern Encyclopedia, 5th ed. (1966), 2:179.

Bib.   "Data Processing," The Modern Encyclopedia, 5th ed. (1966), 2:179.

Be certain to include the edition and the date of the encyclopedia. Indicate volume and page as you would in a magazine entry. If the article is signed, enter by the author's name as you would in a magazine entry.

HOW SHOULD SUBSEQUENT FOOTNOTE ENTRIES BE MADE?

You need to enter a footnote in complete form only the first time you cite a work in your paper. Your subsequent references to the same work may be abbreviated. There are two basic ways you may do this.

1) You may use the author's name and the page number alone. For example:

    1
      Ralph DeSola, <u>Microfilming</u> (New York, 1944), p. 419.
    2 DeSola, p. 555.

If, however, you cite more than one work by the same author, you should enter along with his name and the page number, the title or a shortened form of the title

    6
      DeSola, <u>Microfilming</u>, p. 29.

2) You may prefer the long standing practice of using the Latin words, ibidem (Ibid.), opere citato (Op. Cit.), and loco citato (Loc. Cit.) for subsequent footnote reference.

  a) Ibid. means "to the same place." You use it to refer to the footnote immediately preceding. For example

    10
      C.T. Graver, "Power Supply for Nuclear Research Laboratory," <u>EE</u>, (March 1953), 72:214.
    11
      Ibid.
    12
      Ibid., p. 208.

  b) Op. Cit. means "in the work cited." You use it together with the author's name and the page number to refer to a work already cited but not immediately preceding. For example:

    1
      Ralph DeSola, <u>Microfilming</u> (New York, 1944), p. 419.
    2
      L.V. Ryan, ed., <u>A Science Reader</u> (New York, 1959), p. 9.
    3
      DeSola, <u>Op. Cit.</u>, p. 66.
    4
      Ryan, <u>Op. Cit.</u>, p. 30.

  c) Loc. Cit. means "in the place cited." You use it with the author's name but no page number to refer to an exact passage already cited but not immediately preceding it. For example:

    9
      Elizabeth Freeman, Letter to the author, May 15, 1967.
    10
      "Data Processing." The Modern Encyclopedia, 5th ed. (1966), 2:179.
    11
      Freeman, <u>Loc. Cit.</u>
    12
      "Data Processing." <u>Loc. Cit.</u>

WHAT DOES THE COMPLETE REPORT LOOK LIKE?

Following is a complete report for your examination. Notice how the various parts fit together.

ALCOHOLISM: COMMUNITY HEALTH PROBLEM

A Report

Presented to

Health Occupations Division

Western Wisconsin Technical Institute

In Partial Fulfillment

Of the Requirements of Health and Health Worker

Course #5-10-300

---

by

Carol Erickson

March 20, 1974

La Crosse, Wisconsin
March 20, 1974

Mrs. LaVerne E. Ness
Health Occupations Division
Western Wisconsin Technical Institute
La Crosse, Wisconsin 54601

Dear Mrs. Ness:

Attached is one copy of my report "Alcoholism: Community Health Problem" submitted in partial requirement of Health and Health Worker #5-10-300.

Sincerely yours,

Carol Erickson

Carol Erickson

TABLE OF CONTENTS

	PAGE
LETTER OF TRANSMITTAL.	
TABLE OF CONTENTS.	
SUMMARY.	1
INTRODUCTION	
COMMON SENSE ABOUT ALCOHOLISM	2
WHO IS THIS SOMEONE.	3
CAUSES OF ALCOHOLISM	5
WORN-OUT ATTITUDES	7
THE ALCOHOLIC PROFILE.	9
TOWARD RECOVERY.	12
TREATMENT.	15
CONCLUSION	
ALCOHOLISM - AN INCREASING PROBLEM.	16
RECOMMENDATIONS	
LET'S GO.	18
VOCABULARY LIST	19
BIBLIOGRAPHY	20

SUMMARY

The problem of alcoholism in our society, while perhaps as grave as it ever was, is being viewed and approached in a more realistic and hopeful light. First of all, it is no longer viewed in medieval contexts of evil and depravity. Rather, it is being realistically and scientifically approached as a type of drug problem which can induce, and frequently exists in conjunction with emotional and physiological disorders. Success in combatting this society-wide problem seems most attainable through abandonment of traditional and unscientific attitudes, and adoption of a realistic approach based on the medical and psychological nature of the problem.

Introduction: Common Sense About Alcoholism

Alcoholism is a disease. It is an illness unlike most others in at least one important respect: the affected person will not, in most cases, voluntarily seek assistance, or treatment! Any rehabilitation program must, therefore, give full recognition to this fact, and be so designed and administered as to convince the problem drinker at an early stage that alcohol is the primary cause of his difficulties, that he needs assistance, and that such help is available to him.

Perhaps as many as five million Americans are victims of Alcoholism.[1] Alcohol is a hard drug. Therefore, the victim is an addicted person. For some people, the problem is a matter of health. In some cases, it is a matter of life and death.

---

[1] "How Teens Set the Stage for Alcoholism," Pamphlet published by AMA, (1965), p. 2.

Who Is This Someone?

An alcoholic is a person who cannot control his drinking, whose drinking gets him into problems. It means anyone who has any kind of a problem with drinking; anybody whose drinking interferes with his life in any way.

Mrs. Marty Mann, author of New Primer on Alcoholism writes, "The victims of alcoholism only rarely sets out to get drunk. Usually they wish simply to enjoy a few drinks, like other people. This they find to their horror and dismay, does not seem possible for them; almost every time they drink they end up drunk, entirely against their will and intention. At a later stage of their progressive illness, they find matters even worse, for by then they frequently determine not to drink at all, only to find themselves drinking once more to drunkeness in total contradiction to their expressed will in the matter."[2]

Huge numbers of alcoholics are hidden from public notice, until their diseases become all too apparent. Lots of them are women in their homes, who may even drink for years, and be well along the road to alcoholism before their husbands and friends are really conscious of what is happening.

Not everyone who drinks is a problem drinker. Consumption of alcohol is not a sure sign of the disease. For the approximately one out of fifteen drinkers who has difficulty with alcohol, the problem is

---

[2]Marty Mann, *New Primer on Alcoholism* (New York, 1958), p. 9.

one of control.[3] He finds it extremely difficult, if not impossible, to control his behavior. Problem drinkers belong to no particular group, nor can they be characterized in terms of income, education, work experience, or sex. As a disease, alcoholism reaches into every segment of American society.

---

[3] "Alcohol - Its Place in the Total Drug Problem," Pamphlet published by the Wisconsin Department of Public Instruction, (April, 1971), p. 19.

Causes of Alcoholism

Obviously, there is no germ or bug that causes alcoholism. There is no cause of compulsive drinking.

Not long ago, the public, and the doctors too, had a simple explanation. Alcoholics were merely weak people with no stern will. They really could stop drinking if they wished. Or, the answer was that alcohol was responsible. If no alcoholic drinks were available, there wouldn't be any problem. That was true enough so far as symptoms are concerned. But it was a superficial explanation.

For alcoholics, alcohol is a terrific poison. They know it. Still, they are driven to take it to excess. It only makes things worse. They know that, too. The outward expression of their sickness is that, knowing all this, they still can't stop.

The real reason for their sickness is whatever is driving them to indulge in uncontrolled use of alcohol.[4]

While intensive research into the disease of alcoholism continues, it is impossible to pinpoint any single cause.

Recognized as a disease by the American Medical Association, it is believed that alcoholism is the result of many causes; in most cases a combination of causes.[5]

---

[4] "Alcoholism - A Sickness That Can Be Beaten," Public Affairs Pamphlet No. 118A, Published by Public Affairs Committee, Inc. (Sept., 1968), p. 6.

[5] "Common Sense About Alcoholism," Pamphlet No. PR 172, Published by United Steelworkers of America, (n.d.), p. 4.

What is generally accepted about the disease is that it is progressive, chronic, and cuts across all social and economic lines.

Medical authorities believe that a combination of three major factors can result in alcoholism: Physical, psychological and emotional, and social.[6]

A person's biological or constitutional make-up appears to be involved in alcoholism. Current scientific research is focusing on such factors as body deficiencies and a disturbed metabolism.[7]

While it is not possible to speak with any certainty about an alcoholic personality, there is wide belief that a certain emotional immaturity and dependency are prevalent in many cases of alcoholism. It is true, of course, that no individual is immune from anxiety, depression, and insecurity. However, many alcoholic personalities may rely on the use of alcoholic beverages to take the edge off such feelings as inferiority, anxiety, and to manage tension producing situations.

Attitudes toward alcoholism vary from nation to nation, and in many instances from region to region. In some cultures, alcohol is literally forbidden, while in others it is recognized as a very useful product. Such social attitudes and traditions influence the use of alcoholic beverages. The Italians of both sexes have customarily used wine with family meals. Jews traditionally drink wine during family religious observances.

Another social factor that may loom large is the extent of tension and pressures generated by social standards and practices. It is felt problem drinkers tend to be more vulnerable to the stresses and strains induced by complicated community life.

---

[6]Ibid., p. 4.

[7]Ibid., p. 5.

Worn-Out Attitudes

There are many misconceptions about the nature of alcoholism which keep the person with a drinking problem from recognizing or admitting that he has difficulty. "I can't be an alcoholic because I am not a skid row bum." This is the most common delusion found among alcoholics and the general public. The idea that the only person who could possibly be an alcoholic is the falling down drunk on skid row is, unfortunately, a misconception.[8] Most of them still have good jobs, are maintaining their families and are getting along, although often having a difficult time of it because of drinking.

Some people have the mistaken idea that no one is an alcoholic unless he has to have a drink in the morning. It is not when one drinks, but whether he can control the amount he drinks that determines whether he has a drinking problem.[9]

It is true that the need for a morning drink is one of the symptoms of the crucial or chronic stages of alcoholism. But simply because one does not crave a drink in the morning does not mean that he is free from the disease of alcoholism.[10]

Many people mistakenly believe that the low alcoholic content of beer reduces the danger of intoxication or addiction, and that beer is less intoxicating or addicting than gin, whiskey, vodka, or wine. However, it is

---

[8]"I Can't Be An Alcoholic Because," Pamphlet Published by Michigan Alcohol Education Foundation, (1969), p. 1.

[9]Ibid., p. 3.

[10]Ibid.

232

the chemical, ethyl alcohol, to which the alcoholic is allergic, and this chemical is found in all alcoholic beverages. There is about as much ethyl alcohol in the average can of beer as there is in a 4-ounce glass of wine or a one-ounce shot of whiskey.[11]

Many people believe that the only person who is an alcoholic is one who drinks great quantities every day, or is drunk all the time. But many alcoholics can go a long time without taking a single drink. Some alcoholics can stay dry for weeks, even months or years.

A man may drink only on week-ends, but if he often gets drunk on week-ends, he certainly has a drinking problem. If his drinking causes him continuing difficulty in any area of his life; job, family, health, or is costing more money than he can afford, he needs help.

A common fallacy about excessive drinking is that the only person who becomes an alcoholic is the man in his fifties or sixties.[12] Age has very little to do with alcoholism. The young person who repeatedly gets drunk intentionally or unintentionally is already in trouble, and may be hooked.

When did he last go on the wagon and why? It was undoubtedly because his drinking was giving him trouble. A drinker who is not an alcoholic does not need to go on the wagon, for he is always able to control his drinking. The alcoholic goes on the wagon to try to prove to himself and others that he can go without it. Usually he discovers that he can't do it. For the person who has lost control in drinking there is no compromise with abstinence; he will never be able to drink safely again.[13]

---

[11] Ibid., p. 4.
[12] Ibid., p. 5.
[13] Ibid., p. 6.

The Alcoholic Profile

Contrary to popular beliefs, the problem drinker is not the pitiful derelict sleeping in the doorway of an abandoned store on skid row. A few may terminate their lives amid such surroundings, but for the most part, many victims of alcoholism live and work in quite average and normal settings. It is here, in so-called standard home and job situations that drinking eventually gets out of control, becoming an increasing emotional and health problem to the alcoholic and a source of growing anguish to his family and friends.[14]

While it is difficult to make a hard and fast list of symptoms and results of problem drinking, certain broad guidelines can be enumerated. A major symptom to keep in mind is loss of control.[15] This shows itself in two specific ways: The growing inability to refuse a drink under most situations, but especially under circumstances that may arouse tension. Thus, under conditions that the alcoholic sees as personally painful, he turns to alcohol, almost compulsively. A second form of lack of control is evidenced by the inability to stop drinking once the first drink is taken.

In the vast number of cases, the problem drinker increases his tolerance to alcoholic beverages. This increase in consumption is often accompanied by such behavior as morning drinking to shake off hangovers, gulping drinks and a growing dependence on alcohol.

---

[14] Pam. PR172, op. cit., p. 11
[15] Ibid., p. 6.

There are increasing episodes involving memory blackouts. Here, the alcoholic, upon gaining a state of sobriety, cannot recall his drinking or what happened while he was intoxicated.[16] As to be expected, reactions to blackouts is often a deep sense of remorse and frequent worry about one's behavior.

Specific forms of erratic behavior among those suffering from alcoholism vary greatly. More prevalent actions include the verbal abuse of others, easy provocation, a certain chip-on-the-shoulder attitude that leads to hostility and general pugnacity.

Among the more prominent inner feelings experienced by the problem drinker are such painful moods as an overwhelming sense of guilt, a tendency toward excessive personal blame, and a general feeling of worthlessness and remorse.

The more evident physical signs of alcoholism, especially in its latter stages, include such symptoms as tremors, increased nervousness, lack of sleep, absenteeism from work, steady drinking and what might be called general personal disorganization.

Only rarely do alcoholics become insane. But many or most eventually show personality changes from their excessive drinking. This is sometimes called simple alcoholic deterioration.[17] The alcoholic may become unstable, suspicious, irritable, over emotional, quick to take offense, even callous or brutal toward the people he loves.

Some develop mental disease, while others started becoming alcoholics because they already had some psychosis or mental illness in the first place. Their treatment must be directed at the basic mental illness as

---

[16] Ibid., p. 7
[17] PA Pam. 118A, op. cit., p. 11.

well as at their drinking.

D.T.'s or delirium tremens accounts for about thirty-seven percent of all cases of alcoholic psychosis.[18] The victim sees things, usually animals, and shakes uncontrollably. Usually he recovers from this seige within a week. The condition is found among excessive drinkers; often it follows an injury or some infectious disease.

Another mental effect can be an impairment of memory, called Korsakoff's psychosis.[19]

In its terminal phases, alcoholism impairs such vital organs as the brain, liver, and gastrointestinal system.[20] It shortens life.

Regarding this last point, it is believed that some excessive drinkers demonstrate a strong unconscious tendency toward self-destruction. One of this country's foremost psychiatrists has said that some chronic alcoholics should really be called "chronic suicides."[21]

---

[18] Ibid., p. 11.
[19] Ibid., p. 11.
[20] Pam. PR 172, op. cit., p. 7.
[21] Ibid., p. 7.

Toward Recovery

Once alcoholism was an almost hopeless sickness - hopeless because the only treatments were scorn, shame, vilification, and jails.

Now it is a sickness that can be overcome in many cases. Thousands of alcoholics have won their fight against it, have been restored to health and happiness and freedom from the condition that was ruining their lives. It can't be cured in the sense that many other diseases are cured. The recovered alcoholic can't again drink the alcohol that had become a poison to him.[22] But he can learn that he doesn't need it. He can come not to want it.

There is no magic cure, no simple easy way, no pills in coffee, no simple vow to quit with no effort needed. These are basic truths, and to sugar-coat them would be dangerous. Alcoholism can be controlled, can be beaten, can even be prevented, only by knowing the complete facts about this ruinous, insidious disease and how to overcome it.

In the opinion of practically all medical specialists, recovery, while possible, calls for total abstinence.[23]

The decisive factor is the desire, the determination of the person himself.[24] This determination is indicated by a willingness to face frankly and to personally admit the uncontrollable nature of his drinking. The next step is to stop drinking.

---

[22] PA Pam. 118A, op. cit., p. 1.
[23] Pam. PR 172, op. cit., p. 8.
[24] Ibid., p. 8.

How can his family and friends help in this process? First, by recognizing and understanding that alcoholism is a disease and the problem drinker is a sick person. Such an awareness can call forth a patience, encouragement, and moral support that comes through understanding. Frequently, the victim of alcoholism needs the assurance from his friends that his situation is not hopeless. However, in the endeavor to assist a problem drinker, the temptation to explain away the situation by minimizing either its seriousness or belittling the personal effort required for recovery should be avoided. Second, in addition to personal support, friends can encourage and if necessary, assist him to seek professional help.

The family doctor should be among the first contacts for those afflicted with alcoholism. The physician can treat the acute phase as well as diagnose and prescribe for any resulting disabilities.

According to a recent publication, a majority of the Nation's 245 state mental hospitals admit alcoholics, while some fourteen percent of them have separate treatment programs for alcoholism.[25] Hopefully, one day all state hospitals will provide specialized facilities and services.

There are forty states with alcoholism programs.[26] Again, the nature and effectiveness of these programs vary. Some sponsor education programs only, while others operate both small inpatient services and provide financial support to community-based outpatient clinics.

A major source of general information on alcoholism is the Alcoholism Information Center.[27] While actual agency names may change somewhat from community to community, such centers generally provide advice and assistance in referring individuals to proper sources of help in the community.

---

[25] Ibid., p. 8.
[26] Ibid.
[27] Ibid., p. 9.

More and more general or community hospitals are admitting those suffering from alcoholism. Hospital treatment is essential for emergency care, especially in instances of unconsciousness, alcoholic convulsion, delirium tremors, etc.

A growing number of communities now maintain clinics that provide from several days to a week of intensive care and treatment. Usually supported by private contributions, United Fund allocations, fees, and some municipal tax money, these voluntary clinics offer a range of services from detoxification or drying-out, to counselling and group therapy. Some clinics may be a part of a general hospital.

Relatively new on the scene is the halfway house.[28] A place of short-term residency that serves as a bridge for the recovered patient; it is a connection between the hospital and the community.

A pioneering and perhaps the best known of all sources of help for the problem drinker is AA.[29] Practically every community has one or more AA local groups. Those AA members who fully recognize that they are alcoholics, willingly give mutual support to each other through sharing their experiences.

---

[28]Ibid., p. 9.
[29]Ibid., p. 10.

Treatment

Two new medicines are helping some alcoholics stick to their determination to stop drinking and break their drinking cycles. The most important one is Antabuse (trade name), known chemically as Disulfiram.[30] Though harmless in itself, this medication renders the body so sensitive to alcohol that even one ounce of whisky or one glass of beer will cause the patient to feel quite ill within twenty to thirty minutes. A second drug is called Temposil (trade name), known chemically as Calcium Carbimide.[31] Though the same reaction will follow, the effect of Temposil lasts only eighteen hours. Therefore, it is not as efficacious as Antabuse with its four-day action.

During the acute withdrawal phase, some form of tranquilizer is essential. It may even be preventive of delirium tremens and convulsions. The new tranquilizers produce refreshing and much-needed sleep and cut down tension state. They also help the patient to begin eating promptly.

Tranquilizers and sedatives should be used extremely sparingly, if ever, with an alcoholic after he has attained sobriety. Help should be given him to relax and sleep well without the use of artificial measures. Having an addictive personality means that the alcoholic could readily become dependent upon the tranquilizer or sedative. In some few cases where there are deeply neurotic problems underlying the alcoholism, a doctor may suggest the use of a tranquilizer. Each patient should be warned that this is a temporary measure and be helped to learn to live a life without artificial props.

---

[30] PA Pam. 118A, op. cit., p. 19.
[31] Ibid.

Conclusion: Alcoholism - An Increasing Problem

The overwhelming majority of adult Americans drink. The figure is placed at more than eighty million.[32] For the most part, they drink for social reasons, as a form of relaxation, and in the entertainment of family and friends. For the majority, the use of alcohol is no problem.

For others the story is quite different - in some instances, tragic. These are problem drinkers. There are an estimated five million alcoholics in the United States.[33] It is also estimated that of these about six percent or one out of every fifteen teenagers are likely to become alcoholics.[34] Some believe this to be a low figure. The percentage of women who drink are approaching that of men, but women are still much less likely to become heavy drinkers.

Persons with serious drinking problems are found in every American community. There is no group, neither rich nor poor, which does not have its share. Only seven percent of all alcoholics are on Skid Row; the other ninety-three percent are members of a conventional community - your community.[35]

Alcoholism is ranked as the fourth major health problem in the United States.[36] Outranked only by heart disease, cancer and mental disease. Alcoholism costs business and industry more than two billion dollars annually, five hundred million dollars in wages are lost, accidents, care of dependents, hospital and institutional care accounts for another three hundred million dollars.[37] No attempt is made to estimate the value of wasted lives,

---

[32] Pam. PR 172, op. cit., p. 3.
[33] Ibid.
[34] AMA Pam. on Teen Alcoholism, op. cit., p. 2.
[35] "Alcoholism and Drug Abuse", Pamphlet published by State of Wisconsin Department of Health and Social Services, (n.d.)
[36] "Alcoholism", Published by Dane County Alcoholism Information & Referral Center, (n.d.)
[37] Wis. Soc. Svcs. Pam., op. cit.

broken homes and neglected children.

There are approximately one hundred twenty-nine thousand alcoholics in the State of Wisconsin.[38] It is estimated by the National Council on Alcoholism that each alcoholic affects the lives of four other people. Six hundred forty-seven thousand people are affected either directly or indirectly by alcoholism.[39] It is conservatively estimated that there are between one thousand to fifteen hundred deaths occurring in Wisconsin each year in which alcoholism is an underlying or contributing cause.[40] Ten percent or less of all alcoholics in Wisconsin are seen for treatment.[41] Chronic alcoholics die on the average of seventeen years before non-alcoholics.[42] Vernon, Monroe, and La Crosse Counties have the highest rate of alcoholism in the State of Wisconsin.[43] But Vernon County leads all the other counties in bandy consumption per capita.[44]

---

[38]"Facts About Alcoholism in Wisconsin", Pamphlet published by Alcoholism Services, (n.d.), p. 1.

[39]Wis. Social Services Pam., op. cit.

[40]Ibid.

[41]Goeffrey Banta, Personal Interview by author, Viroqua, Wis., Sept. 27, 1972.

[42]Ibid.

[43]Neil Snyder, Personal Interview by author, Viroqua, Wis., Sept. 23, 1972.

[44]Dr. J. E. Day, Personal interview by author, Sept. 30, 1972.

Recommendations: Let's Go!!

Everything indicates that the problem of alcoholism is going to be tackled.[45] Prevention of this sickness is not too much to hope for, even on the basis of present knowledge of this chronic ailment. It needn't wait even upon discovery of the absolute reasons why some people turn or are driven to uncontrolled use of alcohol. Much can be done now. It can be done without total prohibition.

Giving people the facts about alcoholism will go far toward preventing the sickness. Treating it as a sickness, as a public health responsibility, and providing enlightening care and centers, will restore hundreds of thousands more alcoholics to useful lives.

If I as a health worker should happen to come in personal contact with an alcoholic, I feel that it would be my responsibility to show a real concern and empathy. I could also help him by being ready to suggest resources such as AA, the local Committee on Alcoholism or a well informed doctor, but only at the right moment. That moment comes when he is really desperate about his drinking, when he admits he cannot control it and that he needs help.

In all of this we can help. "Many hands make light work" is particularly true in alcoholism.[46] Your hands are needed, and your heads, and your hearts. Let's go!

---

[45]Mann, op. cit., p. 233.

[46]Ibid., p. 235.

VOCABULARY LIST

AA (Alcoholics Anonymous): An organization of former drinkers to help alcoholics.

Alcoholic Convulsion: An involuntary muscular contraction, and relaxation that is caused by the action of a poisonous substance on the nervous system. It is often referred to as a withdrawal symptom.

Alcoholic Deterioration: An impairment of mental or physical functions.

Antabuse: A drug given to alcoholics to create an aversion to alcohol.

Blackouts: A temporary loss of consciousness.

Chronic Alcoholism: The state of habitual use of harmful amounts of alcohol which cause toxic reactions.... impairment of body functions.

Delirium Tremens: A mental disorder involving hallucinations, that affect vision, hearing and other senses.

Detoxification: The process of removing alcohol from the system. It is also referred to as the drying-out period.

Korsakoff's Psychosis: The lack of ability to remember recent events, and disorientation in time and place.

Tremor: Continuous quivering, of a convulsive nature.

BIBLIOGRAPHY

Books

Chafetz, M.D., Morris E. and Harold W. Demone Jr., *Alcoholism and Society*. New York: Oxford University Press, 1962.

Mann, Marty. *New Primer on Alcoholism*. New York: Rinehart and Co., 1950.

Roueche, Berton. *The Neutral Spirit*. Boston: Little, Brown and Co., 1960.

Wilkinson, Rupert. *The Prevention of Drinking Problems*. New York: Oxford University Press, 1970.

Periodicals

Craig, Sara "Help for Women Alcoholics," *Opportunity* (June 1972) 2:18-23

Williams, Elizabeth "Ethel Alcohol and Its Effects on the Body," *The Union Signal* (February 24, 1968) 94:9-11

Miller, Lois Mattox "What the Doctor Can Do About Alcoholism," *Harper's Magazine* (March, 1953) p. 73-77

Pamphlets

"Alcoholism," Pamphlet published by Dane County Alcoholism Information and Referral Center, n.d.

"Alcoholism and Drug Abuse," Pamphlet published by State of Wisconsin Department of Health and Social Services, n.d.

"Alcoholism - A Sickness That Can Be Beaten," Public Affairs Pamphlet No. 118A published by Public Affairs Committee, Inc., September 1968.

"Alcohol Facts," Pamphlet published by Wisconsin Temperance Movement, n.d.

"Alcohol - Its Place in the Total Drug Problem," Pamphlet published by the Wisconsin Department of Public Instruction, April 1971.

"Common Sense About Alcoholism," Pamphlet No. PR-172 published by
United Steelworkers of America, n.d.

"Facts About Alcoholism in Wisconsin," Pamphlet published by Alcoholism
Services, n.d.

"How Teens Set the Stage for Alcoholism," Pamphlet published by
American Medical Association, June, 1962.

"I Can't Be An Alcoholic Because," Pamphlet published by the Michigan
Alcohol Education Foundation, n.d.

"Pertinent Paragraphs," Pamphlet published by Temperance Education, Inc.
May 1960.

Interviews

Day, Dr. J. E., Case Finder for Viroqua AA
Personal Interview by the author,
Viroqua, Wisconsin, September 30, 1972

Douglas, Mrs. Aashild, Director of Vernon County Mental Health Assn.
Personal Interview by the author,
Westby, Wisconsin, October 5, 1972

Snyder, Mr. Neil, Counselor for Community Action Program
Vernon County
Personal Interview by the author
Viroqua, Wisconsin, September 23, 1972

Banta, Mr. Geoffrey, Sheriff of Vernon County
Personal Interview by the author
Viroqua, Wisconsin, September 27, 1972

Hubbard, Mr. Lowell, Juvenile Court Officer Vernon County
Personal Interview by the author
Viroqua, Wisconsin, September 27, 1972

English Handbook

INTRODUCTORY STATEMENT

SENTENCES

    What Is a Sentence? What Is a Fragment? What Is a Clause? What Is a Run-on Sentence?

SUBJECT AND VERB AGREEMENT

    What Is Subject and Verb Agreement? What Is the True Subject? What Are Some Other Problems with Agreement?

PRONOUNS

    What Is a Pronoun? What Is the Nominative Case? What Is the Objective Case? What Is the Possessive Case? What Are the Indefinite Pronouns? What Are the Demonstrative Pronouns? What Are the Relative Pronouns? What Are the Three Types of Pronoun Agreement? How Are the -self Pronouns Used?

VERBS

    What Is the Function of a Verb? What Are the Two Major Problems in Using Verbs? What Are the Principal Parts of Verb Tenses? What Are the Tenses Most Often Used? What Are the Progressive Tenses? What Are the Correct Tense Forms? What Are Some Problems in Consistency?

STYLE

    What Is Style and Why Is It Important? What Is Specific Diction? What Is Connotative Meaning? Are There Some Word Clusters to Avoid? How Is Brevity Achieved? When Is a Sentence Confused?

What Words Are Often Confused? What Is Parallel Structure? What Is a Dangling Modifier? When Is a Modifier Misplaced?

ABBREVIATIONS

What Are the Important Guides for Technical Abbreviations? Rules for Technical Abbreviations

FIGURES

What Are the General Guides for Using Figures in Technical Writing?

INTRODUCTORY STATEMENT

Suggestions contained in the following pages are designed to assist you in your writing. Not every possible problem is confronted, obviously, but you will find presented in this *Handbook* the information you will need to avoid the major trouble spots as they have been defined by other students.

Language is fascinating, and though language study is interesting, it is not necessarily easy. You do not speak the way your parents or your grandparents do, and you definitely detect marked differences in the way you use the language and the way Shakespeare or Chaucer used it. But your grandparents, Shakespeare, and Chaucer all used English. The lesson is obvious: the English language is not fixed, but it changes constantly to meet the growing demands of its ever-changing audience. New words and methods of putting them together replace the old. Usage patterns acceptable fifty years ago may appear quite dated today.

From a purely technical point of view there are no *rules* for using the English language. Rather, there is a listing of the *conventions of usage* that have been found workable in given situations by a majority of people. For example, no English instructor sat up late at night figuring out that a comma was needed after an introductory adverb clause; it was simply observed that most writers whose work was clear and precise used commas in that position.

Although this *Handbook* will detail many conventions of usage, you can readily name times when you do not follow them and when you see them violated in newspapers and magazines of national repute. What are cataloged here for you are the conventions most acceptable to the business and professional communities. That is, most successful persons in these areas use these patterns when they communicate. Even though you may deviate from these conventions when you write a note to a friend or talk over a cup of coffee, you would do well to follow them in your more formal on-the-job communication tasks.

SENTENCES

What Is a Sentence?

Although definitions vary according to theory and situation, an English sentence is generally considered to meet the following two considerations:

- It should be a two-member structure, having both a *subject member* and a *predicate member*.
- It should express a feeling of completeness.

In its simplest form, then, such a standard sentence may be composed of only two words:

Secretaries   type.

Secretaries is the subject member, and *type* is the predicate member. The subject member is the part of the sentence which performs the action or is in a condition limited by the predicate member, and the predicate member defines the action or limits the condition of the subject member. In the example, *secretaries* names the performers, and *type* defines the action.

These two essential members form the *sentence kernel*, which may then be expanded to add further meaning:

The three new secretaries   type.
The three new secretaries in the office pool   type.
The three new secretaries in the office pool   type detailed reports.
The three new secretaries in the office pool   type detailed reports for the department supervisor.

You would obviously not have a sentence if you wrote the complete part of one member from the above examples but failed to include the other:

The three secretaries in the office pool
    OR
type detailed reports for the department supervisor.

What Is a Fragment?

A fragment is an incomplete sentence part. It may be incomplete because it is only one member of the construction, or it may be incomplete because it does not make complete sense. The following examples are fragments because they do not have both the subject and the predicate members:

SUBJECT MEMBERS ONLY The work on the corner of my desk
The ringing telephone
PREDICATE MEMBERS ONLY received the order yesterday morning
set an appointment for Thursday afternoon

The above fragments could easily be corrected by supplying the missing member to the construction:

The work on the corner of my desk had been there for over a week.
The ringing telephone upset his train of thought.
Our order department received the order yesterday morning.
The receptionist set an appointment for Thursday afternoon.

The missing member is rather easily detected and the fragment completed, but often a more difficult task is spotting the fragment that results from a feeling of incompleteness. Read the following examples aloud:

After work, I always enjoy
The retyped report still looked
Because I got to work late today

If you stop to think as you read such statements, your mind immediately begins to ask questions: What do you enjoy? How did the retyped report look? What happened because you got to work late? The examples above contain subjects and predicates, but they are not complete because they leave you in need of additional information to complete the communication process.

Correcting such problems is much easier than spotting the problems might be. Simply supply an answer to the questions that come when you first read the fragments:

After work, I always enjoy a quick game of tennis.
The retyped report still looked too messy to submit.
I am not going to be able to take my afternoon coffee break because I got to work late today.

What Is a Clause?

A *clause* contains a subject member and a predicate member. If the clause makes complete sense, it is an *independent clause* and stands

Sentences

as a sentence. Many clauses, however, are used merely as modifiers and do not make complete sense by themselves. These *dependent clauses* should be recognized and their function understood so they will not lead you into writing unnecessary fragments.

The greatest problem caused by dependent clauses and resulting in fragments comes from the use of adverb clauses at the beginning of sentences. Look carefully at these examples:

> When I finish processing this set of x rays
> Although you are very tired
> After she had completed her file work
> Until you get the replacement part

Each of the above examples has a subject member and a predicate member, but each also needs more information to avoid a feeling of incompleteness:

> When I finish processing this set of x rays, I must meet with the consulting physician.
> Although you are very tired, I need your help with one more chore.
> After she had completed her file work, she resumed posting bills.
> Until you get the replacement part, you should work on another motor.

Some dependent clause structures are used as adjectives within the sentence, and these, too, can often lead to fragments. Observe these examples:

> that you duplicated yesterday
> who is usually conscientious
> that I left on the counter

Again, each example has the two-member construction, but there is no communication because there is no feeling of completeness. The completed sentences might look something like these:

> Mr. Robertson needs to see the report that you duplicated yesterday.
> My assistant, who is usually conscientious, did not report for work today.
> Has anyone seen the wrench that I left on the counter?

What Is a Compound Sentence?

A *compound sentence* is composed of two or more independent clauses, each of which might stand alone and be a complete sentence. Mature writers use compound sentences to put together closely related ideas and to avoid a series of short, choppy sentences.

The independent parts of a compound sentence are joined by *coordinating conjunctions* or by *conjunctive adverbs* or *correlatives*. The coordinating conjunctions are the simplest but you must be careful to use the correct one to indicate the desired meaning. Study the following list:

AND	shows simple addition of another idea
BUT	shows contrast with another idea
YET	shows contrast with another idea
NOR	shows an alternative or gives a contrast
OR	shows an alternative, gives a contrast, or indicates a condition
FOR	indicates a cause or result
SO	adds an idea or shows a cause or result

To further separate the parts of the compound sentence, the coordinating conjunction is usually preceded by a comma:

He sold his quota yesterday, *but* he is still eager for more.
She asked for her vacation, *and* the request was granted.
The supervisor does not want any more of those machines, *nor* do I.

Sometimes in very brief sentences where the subject of both parts is the same, the comma is not necessary, but it is never incorrect:

I want to finish this work *and* I want to go home.
OR
I want to finish this work, *and* I want to go home.

When the subject of the second clause is not stated but is understood to be the same subject as that in the first clause, the comma is omitted:

I want to finish this work and need to do so quickly.
Larry talked for an hour on the telephone but claimed he did not neglect his customers.

The conjunctive adverbs used in compound sentences include *therefore, however, otherwise, furthermore, then, moreover, consequently, nevertheless, accordingly,* and *afterward*. A semicolon is necessary before the conjunctive adverb:

He did not meet the appointment; *however* he was charged the fee.
Ms. Alison will be in San Francisco in June; *therefore* she can personally check on the report.
You should complete the request form; *then* you should take it to the purchase counter.

Sentences

The correlatives used in compounding sentences are *not only . . . but also, either . . . or,* and *neither . . . nor.* Correlatives are used in patterns similar to the following:

Not only was he the best salesman of the year, *but* he *also* was winner of the President's Award.

Either you must improve the quality of your work, *or* the supervisor will dismiss you.

For your convenience, the most used connectives are arranged in Figure 51 according to their usage.

CONNECTIVES

To Add an Idea	To Show an Alternative	To Show Cause or Result
and so furthermore then moreover not only . . . but also	nor or either . . . or neither . . . nor	for so therefore consequently accordingly
To Show Contrast	To Show Condition	To Show Time
but yet nor or therefore however otherwise nevertheless not only . . . but also	or otherwise	then afterward

Figure 51

What Is a Run-on Sentence?

The label *run-on sentence* is often used interchangeably with the labels *comma splice* and *sentence fusion.* Although there are technical differences, the problem is the same in each instance: two or more main clauses have been joined without using proper coordination or punctuation.

The following sentences are run on because they do not have coordinating connectives between the two independent parts:

> I hope that Ralph will finish the task you can learn from him.
> You should report to the supervisor he can give you additional directions.

These sentences may be corrected by supplying connectives with appropriate punctuation:

> I hope that Ralph will finish the task; *then* you can learn from him.
> You should report to the supervisor; *afterward* he can give you additional directions.

A run-on sentence may also result when you use a comma instead of a semicolon before a conjunctive adverb:

> She did an outstanding job, *therefore* she was rapidly promoted.
> Benjamin should finish the assignment, *otherwise* you must help him.

The correction is simple. Place a semicolon before the connector:

> She did an outstanding job; *therefore* she was rapidly promoted.
> Benjamin should finish the assignment; *otherwise* you must help him.

SUBJECT AND VERB AGREEMENT

What Is Subject and Verb Agreement?

One of the basic conventions of good writing is that subjects and verbs agree in number. A singular subject always requires a singular verb, and a plural subject always requires a plural verb:

> The *mechanic is* ready to begin work on your car.
> The *mechanics are* ready to begin work on your car.
> The *secretary* always *answers* the telephone promptly.
> The *secretaries* always *answer* the telephones promptly.

The problem with such basic sentences as these is to locate the true subject and true verb and then to know the correct forms for singular and plural patterns. Although these forms are generally familiar

Subject and Verb Agreement   255

to you, a good dictionary is a handy reference tool to verify your thinking.

What Is the True Subject?

You may sometimes have a problem with agreement if you fail to locate the true subject of your sentence. Do not become confused with intervening words, especially other nouns, that appear to be the subject of your sentence. Look at these examples:

> The *problem* with those reports *is* that they were filed too late.
> Long forgotten in the corner of the desk drawer *were* the data *cards*.

The subject of the first sentence is *problem*, not *reports*, and the subject of the last sentence is *cards* even though it appears at the end of the sentence.

Another problem with locating the true subject sometimes occurs when you have a singular subject followed by phrases such as these: *in addition to, as well as, with, together with, except,* and *no less than.* In these situations, the verb always agrees with the primary subject:

> The *president*, as well as the board members, *was* excited by the report.
> My retirement *income*, together with my social security, *provides* me sufficient money to live comfortably.
> The *nurse*, together with the laboratory technician, *gives* the required medical attention.

What Are Some Other Problems with Agreement?

A major portion of your agreement troubles will be solved when you identify correctly the true subject and make it agree in number with the verb. However, there are some instances that require special consideration, and these are detailed for you below.

- A compound subject (two or more parts) always requires a plural verb even if its parts are singular:
  > The *letter* and the *call do* impress me with your sincerity.
  > Dr. *Haggar* and his *nurse are* out of the office this afternoon.
- With subjects joined by *neither-nor, either-or,* and *not only–but also* the verb agrees with the subject nearer to it:
  > Either the *supervisor* or his *employees were* at fault.
  > Either the *employees* or their *supervisor was* at fault.

Not only the architect's frontal *sketch* but also all other *plans* for the home *were burned* during the big fire.

- The pronoun *you* always requires a plural verb:
You are the most capable person for the job.
You talk as though *you have* authority.

- These pronouns always require singular verbs: *anybody, anyone, anything, another, each, either, everybody, everyone, everything, nobody, no one, one, somebody, someone.*
Is anyone going to work overtime today?
Nobody wants to be the one to ask for a raise.
Either works just fine.

- A subject that is plural in form but suggests a singular unit always requires a singular verb:
Economics is a very difficult subject for him.
Seventeen *dollars was spent* for the office reception.
Two-thirds is a good majority.

- If the subject is *the number,* you should use a singular verb; but if the subject is *a number,* you need a plural verb:
The number of absences during the month *was* very high.
A number of workers *were* sick with some unknown infection.

- The relative pronouns *who, which,* and *that* require a verb that agrees in number with the antecedent of the pronoun (the word it modifies):

The students *who were* absent came to class today.

The student *who was* absent came to class today.

- The words *more, some, part, most,* and fractions and percents are sometimes followed by an *of* phrase. In such instances the verb must agree with the object of the *of* phrase:
Some of the money *is* missing.
Most of the students *were* present for the guest lecture.
One-fifth of the overtime *was* unnecessary.
One-fifth of the workers *were* absent from the meeting.

- A collective noun requires a singular verb if it is regarded as a unit and a plural verb if it is regarded individually:
The *crew was working* hard to prevent further flooding. (The crew is functioning as a single unit.)
The *crew were carrying* their tools with them. (Members of the crew are carrying individual tools.)
The *crew was carrying* its tools with it. (Members of the crew are carrying tools as a singular activity.)

PRONOUNS

What Is a Pronoun?

A *pronoun* is a word or word group that fills the same sentence position as a noun. Thus a pronoun may be used as a sentence subject, as a direct object, object of preposition, complement, or at any other sentence position where a noun might occur. Pronouns are most frequently discussed in terms of *case:* nominative, objective, and possessive.

What Is the Nominative Case?

The *nominative case* pronoun is found as sentence subject, subjective complement, or appositive:

SENTENCE SUBJECT	*He* was late for the morning meeting.
SUBJECTIVE COMPLEMENT	It was *he* who was late for the meeting.
APPOSITIVE	Two of us, *he* and *I*, were late for the meeting.

Here are the nominative case forms:

	Singular	Plural
FIRST PERSON	I	we
SECOND PERSON	you	you
THIRD PERSON	he, she, it, who, whoever	they, who, whoever

What Is the Objective Case?

The objective case pronoun is used as a direct object, object of verbal, indirect object, object of preposition, object of infinitive, and subject of infinitive:

DIRECT OBJECT	The racing auto hit *him*.
OBJECT OF VERBAL	The telephone rang all day, making *him* very nervous.
INDIRECT OBJECT	The board gave *him* the raise.
OBJECT OF PREPOSITION	Give the finished report to *him*.
OBJECT OF INFINITIVE	I want to give *him* the finished report.
SUBJECT OF INFINITIVE	I want *him* to give you the finished report.

Here are the objective case forms:

	Singular	Plural
FIRST PERSON	me	us
SECOND PERSON	you	you
THIRD PERSON	her, him, it, whom, whomever	them, whom, whomever

What Is the Possessive Case?

The *possessive case* pronouns are used to show possession and also to modify certain gerund structures:

OWNERSHIP	The board members left *their* reports on the table.
GERUND MODIFIER	The board members were pleased by *your* reporting on the new developmental process.

Here are the possessive case forms:

	Singular	Plural
FIRST PERSON	my, mine	our, ours
SECOND PERSON	your, yours	your, yours
THIRD PERSON	his, her, hers, its, whose, whosoever	their, theirs, whose, whosoever

What Are the Indefinite Pronouns?

The *indefinite pronouns* are so named because they refer to an indefinite person or thing. The list includes such words as *each, every, either, neither,* and the *-body,* and *-one* combinations: *somebody, anybody, someone, anyone, no one,* etc. The important things to remember about indefinite pronouns is that they are *always singular* and always require singular verbs:

Everyone is entitled to *his* sick pay.
Each wanted *her* just recognition for the task.

What Are the Demonstrative Pronouns?

The *demonstrative pronouns* are those that demonstrate or point out. *This, that, these,* and *those* are demonstrative pronouns.

What Are the Relative Pronouns?

The *relative pronouns* always introduce a relative (or related) clause that modifies the noun preceding the pronoun: Here is the book *that* you asked me to bring for your report. *Who, whom, whose, that,* and *which* are often used as relative pronouns.

Always use *who* or *that* to refer to people, and always use *that* or *which* to refer to animals and inanimate objects:

>He is the employee *who* scored the highest on the exam.
>>OR
>
>He is the employee *that* scored the highest on the exam.
>
>Here is the report *that* you requested.
>>OR
>
>Here is the report *which* you requested.

What Are the Three Types of Pronoun Agreement?

Problems in pronoun usage occur when the pronoun fails to agree with its *antecedent* (the word it refers back to) in number, gender, and person.

>1. Problems with *agreement in number* often occur when you do not carefully identify the noun to which your pronoun refers.
>
>   The causes of unrest are so intense that *they* must be studied. (Antecedent of *they* is causes, plural)

Two subjects joined by *and* always require a plural pronoun:

>The secretary and her assistant took *their* coffee break later than usual.

Two singular subjects joined by *or* or *nor* require a singular pronoun:

>The supervisor or his assistant left *his* watch on the work bench.

Several specific problems with determining whether a pronoun is singular or plural are identical with determining whether a subject of a sentence is singular or plural. You might wish to refer back to that section of the Handbook for further review.

>2. Problems with *agreement in gender* (masculine, feminine, or neuter sexual references) can be solved if you remember two basic guides.

Pronouns referring to masculine or feminine antecedents are always of similar genders:

> Mr. Walker left *his* briefcase on the train.
>
> Ms. Alison gave *her* comments to the board meeting.

Pronouns referring to neuter antecedents are always neuter:

> Roger picked up the file but dropped *it* to the floor.
>
> He brought the part *which* you ordered yesterday.

3. Problems with *agreement in person* can be avoided if you make certain your pronoun agrees with its antecedent in person and if you avoid shifting person when you make the same pronoun reference in a later sentence. Perhaps the most frequent problem with person occurs when you make an unnecessary shift from either the first or third person to the second:

SHIFT	A new worker in the department should be able to do some work on *your* first day.
CONSISTENT	A new worker in the department should be able to do some work on *his* first day.
SHIFT	Even though we were new workers, the supervisor expected *you* to be familiar with the working area.
CONSISTENT	Even though we were new workers, the supervisor expected us to be familiar with the working area.

How Are the -self Pronouns Used?

Certain pronouns may be combined with *-self* and used in either a reflexive or intensive pattern:

REFLEXIVE	The board chairman gave *himself* credit for the new profit showings.
INTENSIVE	The doctor *himself* ordered the changed prescription.

Never use *myself* instead of *I* or *me*, but you may use *myself* to give emphasis:

INCORRECT	*Myself* went to the library to research the report.
	John and *myself* went to the library to research the report.

Verbs

CORRECT   I *myself* went to the library to research the report.
          OR
          I went to the library to research the report *myself*.

VERBS

What Is the Function of a Verb?

As you discovered in the first section of this *Handbook*, every formal sentence must have a verb member that is composed of the simple verb and its related modifiers. A *verb* may perform one of two possible functions in the sentence: it may show an action or it may describe a condition. The first example below describes an action, and the second example indicates a condition of ownership:

The decorator *framed* the picture in a dark wood.
The decorator *has* a picture similar to that in his own home.

What Are the Two Major Problems in Using Verbs?

You use verbs constantly in your talking and your writing, and generally you use them without any difficulty. When you do encounter problems, those problems are usually one of two types: failure to use the correct tense or failure to use the correct form for the tense even though you may understand the tense correctly.

What Are the Principal Parts of Verb Tenses?

Before you can familiarize yourself with the common tenses of verbs, you need to recognize the principal parts from which those tenses are derived. A good dictionary is an extremely valuable tool for helping you determine these principal parts of any given verb: *infinitive, present, present participle, past,* and *past participle*. Here are some sample verbs and their principal parts:

Infinitive	*Present*	*Present Participle*	*Past*	*Past Participle*
to type	type(s)	typing	typed	(have) typed
to listen	listen(s)	listening	listened	(have) listened
to have	have (has)	having	had	(have) had

What Are the Tenses Most Often Used?

Although there are actually twelve tenses for most modern verbs, six of those are *progressive tenses* whose specialized use will be discussed separately. For practical purposes, you need to understand the tense ordering of only six tenses:

1. *Present tense* indicates action taking place *now:*
   I *listen* attentively to the conversation.
2. *Past tense* indicates action that took place before now:
   I *listened* attentively to the conversation yesterday.
3. *Future tense* indicates action that will take place in the future:
   I *will listen* to the conversation tomorrow.
4. *Present perfect tense* uses *have* or *has* plus the past participial form of the main verb to indicate action just completed or continuing into the present:
   I *have listened* to conversations all my life.
5. *Past perfect tense* uses *had* plus the past participial form of the main verb to indicate action that was completed at a definite past time:
   I *had listened* to the conversation until he began to bore me.
6. *Future perfect tense* uses *shall* or *will* along with *have* and the past participial form of the main verb to indicate an action that will be completed by a certain future time:
   I *will have listened* to his conversation for three hours by the time the plane gets to Atlanta.

What Are the Progressive Tenses?

Each of the six tense forms discussed above has a progressive tense pattern also. This progressive pattern is used to show an action taking place (progressing) at the described time (past, present, future):

PRESENT PROGRESSIVE	I *am listening* to the conversation.
PAST PROGRESSIVE	I *was listening* to the conversation.
FUTURE PROGRESSIVE	I *will be listening* to the conversation tomorrow.
PRESENT PERFECT PROGRESSIVE	I *have been listening* to the conversation for an hour.
PAST PERFECT PROGRESSIVE	I *had been listening* to the conversation for an hour.
FUTURE PERFECT PROGRESSIVE	I *will have been listening* to the conversation for an hour by the time we get to Atlanta.

Style

What Are the Correct Tense Forms?

Most modern English verbs form their tenses by adding *-d* or *-ed*. Other verbs such as *swim, hang, lie, lay,* and many others are irregular and have their independent verb patterns. You have seen lists of such irregular verbs in the past. However, such lists are not helpful unless you memorize them entirely. Learn to use your dictionary to verify tense patterns for the irregular verbs. Also, do not fail in your writing to add the *-ed* or *-d* endings when they are needed by the regular verbs. Sometimes, as with such past forms as *talked* and *walked,* the ending does not receive emphasis in oral pronunciation patterns, and it becomes easy to omit it in written patterns.

What Are Some Problems in Consistency?

If you are not careful, you will sometimes shift verb tenses within the same sentence or in a sequence of sentences that all belong to the same tense structure. The following examples show you tense shifts and then how they should have been written to be correct:

INCONSISTENT	After he *went* to the office, he *answers* his letters.
	When she *answered* the telephone and *took* the call, she *made* an immediate appointment with the doctor because the patient *is* obviously quite sick.
CONSISTENT	After he *went* to the office, he *answered* his letters.
OR	After he *goes* to the office, he *answers* his letters.
	When she *answered* the telephone and *took* the call, she *made* an immediate appointment with the doctor because the patient *was* obviously quite sick.

STYLE

What Is Style and Why Is It Important?

Style is the *how* of written communication, and *content* is the *what.* The same ideas may be communicated differently by two different persons, and the results may be quite different. When you are completing an order form or certain other types of formulaic writing, style may not be so important. But in your business letters and your detailed written reports, you may find the *how* to be almost as important as the *what*.

There are many aspects of style, and it is not the purpose of this *Handbook* to review all of them for you. Any of several excellent style manuals are probably available in your library or bookstore. The following broad suggestions are made to cover those areas of style most often abused in business and technical writing.

What Is Specific Diction?

Specific diction is that word choice that explains exactly and to the fullest extent your intended meaning. Too often business writing is clouded by general catchall words and phrases. The more concrete your descriptions, the sounder your writing will be because your reader will know exactly what you intend to communicate.

Following is a listing of some general words and phrases and then a listing of the same ideas as they have been specifically detailed.

General	Specific
window	third window from the left
desk drawer	second desk drawer from the top
tool	thin-nosed pliers
check	check for Invoice #23-78A
secretary	secretary for Mr. Rollins
walked into the room	strutted into the room

After you have finished a piece of writing, you should go back through that writing to check your nouns and verbs. Will your reader know exactly what you mean by your nouns or do you need to add some details? Would more specific verbs add a dimension of meaning to your message?

What Is Connotative Meaning?

Connotative meaning is the emotional meaning that a word carries with it. *Denotative meaning* is the dictionary meaning. If your goal in business and technical writing is clear, direct prose, then you should usually avoid heavily connotative words because they cloud your message with emotional overtones.

Some words have a connotative meaning only to certain audiences who identify the word with a particular experience or concept; other words have more universally identifiable connotative meanings. Each of the following words has a literal denotative (dictionary) meaning, but each also communicates either highly positive or highly negative emotional feelings:

left wing	honor	love
church	rightist	fat
bitch	muddy	home
security	religious	mongrel

Are There Some Word Clusters to Avoid?

Some writers attempt to impress their readers by their ability to use long or impressive words or by their ability to use a large number of words. Both attempts to impress merely result in weaker style for the entire message.

Sometimes writers put together word clusters that really say the same thing in two or more different ways. Here is only a partial listing of such phrases:

consensus of opinion	new innovation
final result	exactly identical
end result	free gratis
return again	completely finished
large in size	cooperate together
round in shape	quite unique
few in number	over again

Sometimes writers use pompous words or lengthy phrases that ultimately detract from their message:

POMPOUSLY WORDY

We *are cognizant* that you are *experiencing difficulty* during *this period of reorganization* of your central office.

Under ordinary circumstances we do not *in every instance find it necessary to make this request.*

STRAIGHTFORWARD

We *know* that you are *having difficulty* during *the reorganization* of your central office.

Ordinarily we do not *need to ask this.*

How Is Brevity Achieved?

No one likes to listen to a long-winded conversation, and no one has time to read unnecessary words to get at the meaning of the message. You can make your communication brief by cutting out unnecessary phrases that add nothing to the meaning.

WORDY	BRIEF
I have been wondering if it might be possible and convenient to make the necessary arrangements that might be in order for us to get together for a short conference to talk things over sometime near the beginning of next week, perhaps on Monday or Tuesday.	Could we have a short conference Monday or Tuesday?

Another way to make your writing brief is to pay close attention to sentence patterns. Wordy writing is often the result of attempting to pack too much meaning into one sentence, resulting in a structure that is itself wordy or unnecessarily cumbersome.

SENTENCES THAT TRY TO COVER TOO MUCH AT ONE TIME	SENTENCES THAT COVER ONE ITEM AT A TIME
Mr. Medwell tells me that several dealers in the area which you cover are disturbed because their orders are not always filled promptly and they are not notified when these items are out of stock and they don't know when new items are replacing older models which they wish to be notified of when such items will soon be released for sale.	Mr. Medwell reports that dealers in your area are dissatisfied for several reasons: (1) Their orders are not always filled promptly. (2) They are not notified when items are no longer in stock. (3) They do not know when new models can be expected to replace older ones. They would like notification of the date when new models will be released.

When Is a Sentence Confused?

Confused sentences are usually the result of confused or unclear thinking. If you write ideas in the order they pop into your mind, you will probably leave your reader confused because there will be little connection between the various ideas. Always arrange your sentences so you

Style

omit the irrelevant material and put that which is important in a clear and coherent order.

HERE IS A CONFUSED EXPLANATION

We are writing to let you know that we have located the problem that was responsible for the shipment which you have not received. When the manager talked to Mr. Holdsome, the shipping clerk, he was certain that the merchandise could be obtained at once because he had inspected the factory's new machinery that has occupied the same premises for fifteen years and has never failed to produce the desired results which means it was natural to expect that it would now. The difficulty has been remedied and your order will be filled at once, but we thought you would appreciate understanding exactly what happened.

HERE IS A CLEAR EXPLANATION

We are writing to explain the delay in your shipment. There was a breakdown in one of the machines necessary to supply the product which you had ordered. The machine has now been repaired, and your order can be filled at once. We had not had such a machine failure in the fifteen years that our plant has occupied these premises, and we trust that we shall not be so forced to disappoint you again. Thank you for your patience.

If you simply write ideas as you think of them, your writing may show no connection between the facts that you wish communicated. Study your sentence patterns carefully to be certain they show proper relationships between facts.

SENTENCES THAT SHOW NO RELATIONSHIP BETWEEN THE FACTS

There is a strike at the steel mill. We have not received any parts from the factory for two weeks. We have been unable to make the repairs on your machine.

We recommend the Type 182 amplifier. You can use it in your maintenance shop. It can be used for instrumentation and test purposes.

The first large-scale computers were used during World War II. They were used for ballistic calculations. They were introduced in the early 1950s as commercial machines.

SENTENCES THAT SHOW THE RELATIONSHIP BETWEEN THE FACTS

Because the steel mill strike has delayed our shipment of parts from the factory for two weeks, we have been unable to make the repairs on your machine.

We recommend the Type 182 amplifier for instrumentation and test purposes in your maintenance shop.

Although the first large-scale computers were used during World War II for ballistic calculations, they were not introduced as commercial machines until the early 1950s.

What Words Are Often Confused?

Some words are often confused with others that sound or look alike or that have similar meanings. Clear writing requires that you use the exact word to give your intended meaning. The list of possible problems in this area of diction is large, but here are those words that cause the greatest problems.

ability, capacity *ability* is the power to do; *capacity* is the power to receive.

accept, except *accept* is a verb meaning "to take"; *except* is most often a preposition meaning "but," and it is also used as a verb meaning "to exclude."

adapt, adopt *adapt* means to change to make suitable; *adopt* means to take charge of or to put into effect.

advice, advise *advice* is a noun; *advise* is the verb.

affect, effect *affect* is a verb meaning to change or modify; *effect* is usually a noun meaning the result of change and it is sometimes a verb meaning "to put to use."

among, between *among* refers to more than two possibilities; *between* is used when there are only two possibilities.

anxious, eager *anxious* means looking forward to something with fear or apprehension; *eager* suggests looking forward with desire.

can, may *can* signifies ability to do something; *may* suggests permission.

complement, compliment *complement* is a verb meaning "to complete" or is a noun naming that which completes; *compliment* is a verb meaning "to praise" or is a noun referring to the praise.

continual, continuous *continual* refers to an action that takes place at repeated intervals; *continuous* refers to an action that never stops.

decided, decisive *decided* suggests being free from uncertainty; *decisive* suggests having the power to decide.

desirable, desirous *desirable* refers to something that is worth wanting; *desirous* describes the person who wants something.

deteriorate, degenerate both mean to worsen, but *deteriorate* usually refers to things and *degenerate* to people or morals.

exceptional, exceptionable *exceptional* refers to something uncommon or rare; *exceptionable* refers to something likely to cause objections.

explicit, implicit *explicit* refers to something plainly stated or clear; *implicit* suggests something understood although not actually stated.

few, less *few* is used with units that can be counted; *less* is used with quantities not counted.

infer, imply *infer* means to draw an unstated opinion from something that is said; *imply* means to suggest something without actually stating it.

Style

ingenious, ingenuous *ingenious* suggests something or someone clever or shrewd; *ingenuous* suggests frankness or candidness.

kind of, sort of both are very colloquial expressions better replaced by *rather, somewhat, a little,* etc.

last, latest *last* suggests the final members of a series; *latest* suggests the most recent member and implies that there may be more.

percent, percentage *percent* is most often used with a number reference (30 percent of the people); *percentage* is most often used when there is no number reference (a small percentage of the people).

practical, practicable *practical* refers to something that can be done without much effort or money and that is sensible; *practicable* means "capable of being put into practice."

principal, principle *principal* is a noun meaning head of school, amount of money owed on a loan, or an adjective meaning "main" or "major"; *principle* is a law or rule.

universally, generally *universally* means everywhere at all times; *generally* means most of the time or most everywhere.

What Is Parallel Structure?

Ideas that are written in a structural series or that have closely related meanings are often best cast in parallel form. The parallelism may be in the form of words, phrases, clauses, or even sentences. By placing related ideas in such a structure you not only improve style but you also show the relationship of the items that are paralleled.

In each of these examples notice how much more effective the parallel structure is to the mixed structure.

MIXED	Laverne worked in an office that was too crowded and smelled musty.
PARALLEL	Laverne worked in an office that was too crowded and that was musty smelling.
MIXED	Seeing what needs to be done, knowing how to do it, then to do it are the traits of a qualified worker.
PARALLEL	Seeing what needs to be done, knowing how to do it, then doing it are the traits of a qualified worker.
MIXED	This outdoor work will help you in building muscles and to make money at the same time.
PARALLEL	This outdoor work will help you to build muscles and to make money at the same time.

What Is a Dangling Modifier?

A *dangling modifier* is a word, phrase, or clause that dangles or does not connect because the word to which it should be connected is either missing from the sentence or is hidden internally.

Here are two examples of dangling modifiers that have resulted because their connected words were omitted in each instance. Observe how simply they may be corrected:

DANGLING	Filing the reports, the error was quickly discovered.
CORRECTED	Filing the reports, she quickly discovered the error.
DANGLING	Seriously wanting a raise, his work improved.
CORRECTED	Seriously wanting a raise, he did improve his work.

Sometimes a modifier dangles because the word or phrase that it should be connected to (should modify) is hidden in the sentence. Most often in such situations, the word that should be connected to the dangling modifier is used in a prepositional structure:

DANGLING	Speaking very loudly, the telephone was answered by the receptionist.
CORRECTED	Speaking very loudly, the receptionist answered the telephone.

When Is a Modifier Misplaced?

A *misplaced modifier* occurs when the modifying element is placed at a spot in the sentence where a reader cannot tell clearly what word or phrase it is intended to modify. The most common problem is with the *squinting modifier*. In this structure the writer places a modifying element in a position where it might possibly modify two different words or phrases; thus the reader has to "squint" at them both for meaning.

SQUINTING	The salesmen were told *by noon* that they were over their quota.
CORRECTED	*By noon* the salesmen were told that they were over their quota.
	OR
CORRECTED	The salesmen were told that they were over their quota *by noon*.

Abbreviations

Not all problems with modifiers occur in squinting structures, but most of the other problems can readily be detected by slowly reading for the logical structure in sentences. Notice the illogical structure of these two sentences:

MISPLACED	The new plant was for sale with all of its fixtures.
CORRECTED	The new plant with all of its fixtures was for sale.
MISPLACED	The secretary in our office with the large diamond ring was recently engaged.
CORRECTED	The secretary with the large diamond ring in our office was recently engaged.

The words *only, almost,* and *nearly* require special consideration because they can completely change sentence meaning if not positioned carefully:

The accountant was nearly always correct in his report.
The accountant was always nearly correct in his report.
I only want you to handle my account.
I want only you to handle my account.

ABBREVIATIONS

What Are the Important Guides for Technical Abbreviations?

Writers have always made use of abbreviations to aid them in their task, and perhaps nowhere has the use of abbreviations been so great as in business and technical writing. Almost every profession has its own abbreviation code that covers the terminology within its own specialty. The following guides will review for you the basic considerations of general abbreviation practices in business and technical writing.

Rules for Technical Abbreviations

1. Unless it is extremely short, a term used for a unit of measurement is abbreviated when it follows a figure.
   92 ft.   200 hp.   50 cc.
   A unit of measure is not abbreviated when it does not follow a figure.
   The amount is given in cubic centimeters.
   The molasses is sold by the gallon.

2. Some extremely short terms of measurement are not abbreviated.
   day   mile   acre
3. The abbreviation for a unit of measurement is always singular.
   5 lb. (not 5 lbs.)   10 gal. (not 10 gals.)
4. Some professional terms used with extreme frequency are abbreviated when it is reasonable to suppose they will be readily understood.
   F. Fahrenheit   C. Centigrade
   a-c alternating current (only when used as an adjective)
5. Whatever practice you adopt for abbreviations, you should be consistent.
6. Some signs and symbols are considered standard.
   $ dollar sign   ° degrees   ¢ cent (use with discretion)
   Do not use symbols when words or abbreviations are usually used.
   8 in., not 8"   12 by 15 ft., not 12' × 15'   percent, not %
7. In some professions the period is omitted after many abbreviations. Follow the practice of books and periodicals from your own field. Always use a period if its omission would cause misreading, as with the abbreviation *in* for *inch*. Use periods with these abbreviations:
   A.M.   P.M.   c.o.d.   B.C.   A.D.   Fig.   ibid.
   op. cit.   Vol.   p.   ff.
8. Capitalization is not affected by abbreviation. Abbreviations are not usually capitalized unless the terms they stand for are capitalized.

For the answer to particular problems not covered here, consult the pages of abbreviations in any collegiate dictionary.

FIGURES

What Are the General Guides for Using Figures in Technical Writing?

The various charts and statistics necessary to much business and technical writing often demand more use of figures or numbers than is required in other types of writing. Although specific requirements vary from one type of writing to another, the following suggestions are most often used.

1. Use figures for 10 and all numbers above 10:
   10 sales   122 sales   four sales
2. Use figures for numbers below 10 when they precede a measurement unit:
   3 inches   5 feet   6 days

Figures

3. Use figures to express sums of money:

   $5.95 $10 (or 10 dollars) $0.75 (or 75 cents)

4. Use figures to express decimal fractions. Place a zero before the decimal if the value is less than a whole:

   1.33   17.56   0.89

5. Use figures for any section of writing where numbers are very frequent:

   The 7 board members met for 35 minutes to discuss the 9 proposals submitted by the 2 standing committees.

6. When one number appears immediately after another as part of some phrase, one of the numbers, usually the shorter one, is spelled out:

   8 six-inch boards   two 5-man teams

7. Use words and not figures to indicate common fractions:

   one-third   two and three-eighths

8. Use figures to indicate definite percentages:

   80 percent   3.2 percent   10 percent

9. Use figures to precede the words *million* and *billion* when stating a quantity:

   3 billion dollars   2.7 million people

10. Use words for numbers that are approximations:

    The company was started nearly fifty years ago.

    The building should stand for another fifteen years.

11. Use figures to indicate latitude, longitude, and temperature:

    45° South   98.6° F.

12. Use figures to indicate time of day when followed by *a.m.* or *p.m.* but not when followed by *o'clock:*

    3:00 P.M.   3:00 A.M.   three o'clock

13. Use figures for references to dates:

    July 13, 1973   13 July 1973

14. Never use figures to begin a sentence; spell out the quantity:

    Three billion dollars will be spent in marketing this year.

    Sixty-two percent is too low a figure to justify the increased cost.

Index

Abbreviations, 109, 271
Adjourn, motion to, 122
Adjustment letters, 44–53
Adverbs, conjunctive, 252
Agenda, for committee, 114
Amending motions, 119–20
Analogy, reasoning by, 132–34
Appendix, formal report, 208
Application form, job, 63–64
Application letters, job, 63–73
Audience analysis, 192, 204
Author card, 164

Bandwagon fallacy, 142
Bibliography, formal report, 208
Bibliography, sample, 217–21
Bibliography, useful books, 165–69
Bibliography card, 180–81, 211–12
Body, formal reports, 206–7
Brackets, use of, 174
Brainstorming session, 116
Brevity, 107–8, 266
Business letters (see Letters)

Call number, 163
Card stacking fallacy, 143
Causal relationships, 131, 134–35
Chairman, committee, 114, 118
Charts, use of in speech, 198
Claim letters, 44–53
Clauses, defined and used, 250–51
Close debate, motion to, 121–22
Collection letters, 54–61
Comma, in compound sentences, 252
Comma splice, 253–54
Committee activity, 113–24
Committee chairman, 114, 118

Committee, parliamentary procedure, 119–24
Committee reports, 188
Committees, various types, 113–14
Communication, defined, 1
Communication etiquette, 10
Communication, listening, 3–4
Communication, non-verbal, 2
Complimentary close, 31
Compound sentence, 251–52
Conclusion, content of, 186
Conclusion, formal report, 207
Conclusion, speech, 193
Conjunction, coordinating, 252
Conjunctive adverbs, 252
Connotation, 103–4, 264–65
Conventions, attending, 153–54
Coordinating conjunctions, 252
Correlatives, 252

Dangling modifiers, 269–70
Data gathering, 147–58
Deductive reasoning, 129
Demonstrative pronouns, 258–59
Denotation, 264–65
Dewey Decimal System, 161
Diction, 20–22, 45–46, 103–4, 264–65, 268
Dossier, 65
Dress, for job interview, 95

Education training, in Vita, 68
Ellipsis, use of, 174
Envelope, business letters, 73
Et al., use of, 218
Evaluation of information, 128–29
Extemporaneous speech, 192

275

Fallacies, 137–45
　Bandwagon, 142
　Card stacking, 143
　Glittering Generalities, 140
　Hasty Generalization, 138
　Name Calling, 138
　Plain Folks, 141–42
　Poisoning the Well, 143
　Red Herring, 143–44
　Testimonial, 144–45
　Transfer, 144
Figures, in outlines, 187
Figures, use of in writing, 109, 272–73
File, keeping, 6, 151
Footnote form, samples, 217–21
Fragment, sentence, 250
Fused sentences, 253–54

Generalization, reasoning by, 131–32
Glittering Generalities, 140

Handbook for grammar, 247–73
Handshake, 94
Hasty Generalization, 138
Humor, use of in speaking, 194–95

Indefinite pronouns, 258
Inductive reasoning, 131
Inferences, in reasoning, 129
Information gathering, 147–58, 210
Instructions, writing, 108–9
Intensive pronouns, 260–61
Interview, for information, 9, 148–50
Interview, job, 89–97
Introducing others, 15–18
Introducing yourself, 19
Introduction, formal report, 205–6
Introduction, speech, 194

Job application, forms, 63–64
Job application, letters, 63–73
Job application, other letters, 73–81
Job interviews, 89–97

Language, 248
Letter, importance of in business, 25
Letter, outline for planning, 27
Letter, parts, 28–32
Letter, planning, 25
Letters, types of:
　adjustment, 44–53
　application, 63–73
　collection, 54–61
　transmittal, 214
Library, using, 160–69
Library of Congress System, 161–63
Listening, 3–4, 155–56
Logic, fallacies in, 137–45, 155

Mechanical devices, use of in speech, 197
Memorandum, 99–100
Misplaced modifiers, 270
Modifiers:
　dangling, 269–70
　misplaced, 270
　squinting, 270
Motions, primary, 119
Motions, secondary, 119
Motions, types of:
　motion to adjourn, 122
　motion to amend, 119–20
　motion to close debate, 121–22
　motion to object, 121
　motion on point of order, 122
　motion to postpone, 120–21
　motion to recall, 120–21
　motion to reconsider, 120–21
　motion to refer, 120
　motion to suspend Rules, 122
　motion to table, 121
　motion to withdraw Motion, 121

Name Calling, 138
Nominations, 122
Nominative pronouns, 257
Note cards, 211
Note taking, 117–18, 126–27, 148, 150–51, 155–57, 173–82, 211–12
Note taking, types of:
　direct quotation, 173–74
　paraphrase, 175
　summary, 176–77
　synopsis, 173
Numbers, use of (see Figures)

Objective pronouns, 257–58
Objectivity in writing, 115, 127, 147
Oral reports (see Speech)
Organizing, 183–87
Outlines, 183–87

Parallelism, 269
Paraphrase, 175
Parliamentary procedure, 119–24
Passive voice, 106
Pictures, use of in applications, 70–71
Plagiarism, 178
Plain Folks fallacy, 141–42
Poisoning the Well fallacy, 143
Possessive pronouns, 258
Postpone, motion to, 120–21
Problem solving, 115–16, 126–35
Pronoun agreement, 259–60
Pronouns, use in reports, 106
Pronoun types:
　demonstrative, 258–59
　indefinite, 258

Index

Pronoun types (*cont.*)
  intensive, 260–61
  nominative, 257
  objective, 257–58
  possessive, 258
  reflexive, 260–61
  relative, 259
Proofreading, 37
Propaganda, 137–45, 155

Questionnaire, use of, 37
Quotation marks, use of, 175
Quotations in notes, 173–74

Reading effectively, 171–73
Reasoning, types:
  analogy, 132–33
  causal relationships, 134–35
  deductive, 129
  generalization, 131–32
  inductive, 131
  syllogisms, 130
Recall, motion to, 120–21
Recommendations, formal report, 207–8
Reconsider, motion to, 120–21
Red Herring fallacy, 143–44
References, job application, 67–70, 79–80
Reflexive pronouns, 260–61
Relative pronouns, 259
Report, formal:
  binding, 215
  parts, 205 ff
    appendix, 208
    bibliography, 208, 217–21
    body, 206–7
    conclusion, 207
    footnotes, 217–21
    introduction, 205–6
    recommendations, 207–8
    summary, 206
    title, 215–16
  purposes, 209
  sample, 221–46
Reports, informal, 101
Reports, research (*see* Reports, formal)
Report writing:
  abbreviations, 109
  brevity, 107–8
  figures, 109
  style, 102–8
Research writing (*see* Reports, formal)
Run-on sentences, 253–54

Salary expectations, 93
Salutation in letters, 28
Semicolon in compound sentences, 252
Sentences:
  compound, 251–52
  confused, 266–67

Sentences (*cont.*)
  defined, 249
  fragment, 249
  run-on, 253–54
  style, 105–6
Shaking hands, 18
Shelf list, 163
Sic, use of, 175
Signatures, in letters, 31–32
Sincerity, 19–20
Source cards, 179, 181, 211–12
Speech:
  delivery, 192
  evaluation, 199–202
  extemporaneous, 192
  parts:
    body, 191–92
    conclusion, 193
    introduction, 194
  practicing, 196
  stage fright, 188–90
  techniques, 190
  use of aids, 197–98
Stage fright, 188–90
Stationery for business letters, 73
Style, 105–6, 263–64
Subject cards, 164
Subjects, sentences, 255
Subject-verb agreement, 254–56
Subsidiary motions, 120
Summary, formal report, 206
Summary notes, 176–77
Suspend Rules, motion to, 122
Syllogism, 130
Synopsis, 173

Table, motion to, 121
Telephone, using, 11–14
Tenses, verbs, 262–63
Testimonial fallacy, 144–45
Thesis sentence, 185
Title cards, 164
Tone, 32–34
Transfer fallacy, 144
Transmittal letter, 214

Verbal skills, importance of, 2
Verbs:
  functions of, 261
  principal parts, 261
  tenses, 262–63
Visual aids, use of, 197–98
Vita sheet, 65–70

Withdraw, motion to, 121
Word choice (*see* Diction)
Words, confused pairs, 268–69
Work experience, 69
Writing instructions, 108–9